The Salisbury & Dorset Junction Railway

Nigel Bray

©Kestrel Railway Books and Nigel Bray 2010

Kestrel Railway Books
PO Box 269
SOUTHAMPTON
SO30 4XR

www.kestrelrailwaybooks.co.uk

All rights reserved.

No part of this publication may be reproduced, stored in a retrieval system, transmitted in any form or by any means, electronic, mechanical, or photocopied, recorded or otherwise, without the consent of the publisher in writing.

Printed by The Amadeus Press

ISBN 978-1-905505-19-7

Front cover: *Standard class 4 2-6-0 No 76061 enters Fordingbridge station with a Bournemouth West to Cardiff train in July 1962. (GH Hunt/Colour-Rail.com/BRS1287)*

Back cover, top: *Sister engine No 76063 is seen passing the crossing keeper's cottage at West Moors in July 1959 with a 9.13 New Milton to Swansea service. (GH Hunt/Colour-Rail.com/BRS1288)*

Back cover, bottom: *Standard class 4MT 4-6-0 No 75003 runs into Downton station with a 9.23 Salisbury to Bournemouth West train in November 1963. (PA Fry/Colour-Rail.com/BRS1424)*

Contents

Introduction v

Chapter 1. A Route from Salisbury to the Sea 1

Chapter 2. Frustration and Tragedy 9

Chapter 3. The South Western Makes Amends 21

Chapter 4. The Southern Railway Era 29

Chapter 5. An Uncompetitive Service 39

Chapter 6. A New Lease of Life as a Gateway to the Seaside 45

Chapter 7. The Dark Forces Gather 55

Chapter 8. Going Down Fighting 61

Chapter 9. The Line Described 75

Appendix A. Extract from Southern Railway Census of Staff, 1st November 1926 (PRO Ref RAIL 648/131) 113

Appendix B. List of Signal Boxes and Opening Times from the LSWR Appendix to Service Timetables, 1892 114

Appendix C: Extracts from the Western Appendix to the SR Working Time Tables, March 1934 114

Appendix D: Extract from the BR/SR Western Section Appendix, 1960 117

Appendix E: BR Southern Region Engine Workings, Summer 1954 117

Appendix F: Calling Points of Long Distance Expresses Routed via Fordingbridge, Summer Saturdays, 1960 121

Bibliography

DL Bradley, *LSWR Locomotives – The Drummond Classes*, Wild Swan
HC Casserley and SW Johnson, *Locomotives at the Grouping, Southern Railway*, Ian Allan, revised 1974
RA Cooke, *Track Layout Diagrams of the SR and BR (SR)*
J Coulthard, *Verwood Village to Town*, J & JC Publications, 2007
J Draper and P Copland Griffiths, *Around Verwood*, Tempus Publishing, 1999
BL Jackson, *Castleman's Corkscrew, Vols 1 and 2*, Oakwood Press, 2007, 2008
A Light and G Ponting, *The History of Fordingbridge*, Charlewood Press, 2001
JH Lucking, *Railways of Dorset*, Railway Correspondence & Travel Society, 1968
AT Morley Hewitt, *The Story of Fordingbridge in Fact and Fancy*, 1965
NH Pattenden, *Special Traffic Arrangements*, South Western Circle, 2007

B Perren, *Resorts for Railfans: Bournemouth*, article in *Trains Illustrated*, April 1960
GA Pryer, *Signal box diagrams of the GWR and SR, Vol 2, SR Lines in East Dorset*
South Western Circle Portfolio 5b, *Salisbury–West Moors*
C Stone, article in *Steam Days*, March 2000
DR Steggles, *The Downton Accident 1884*, article in *South Western Circular*, April 1980
P Street, *Portrait of Wiltshire*, Robert Hale, revised 1980
DW Winkworth, *Southern Special Traffic*, Irwell Press, 2000
T Woods, *The Branch that Served Three Counties*, article in *Railway Bylines*, September 2005
D Wragg, *Wartime on the Railways*, Sutton Publishing, 2006

Ministry of Transport file on Salisbury–Fordingbridge–Bournemouth line closure, PRO ref MT 124/777

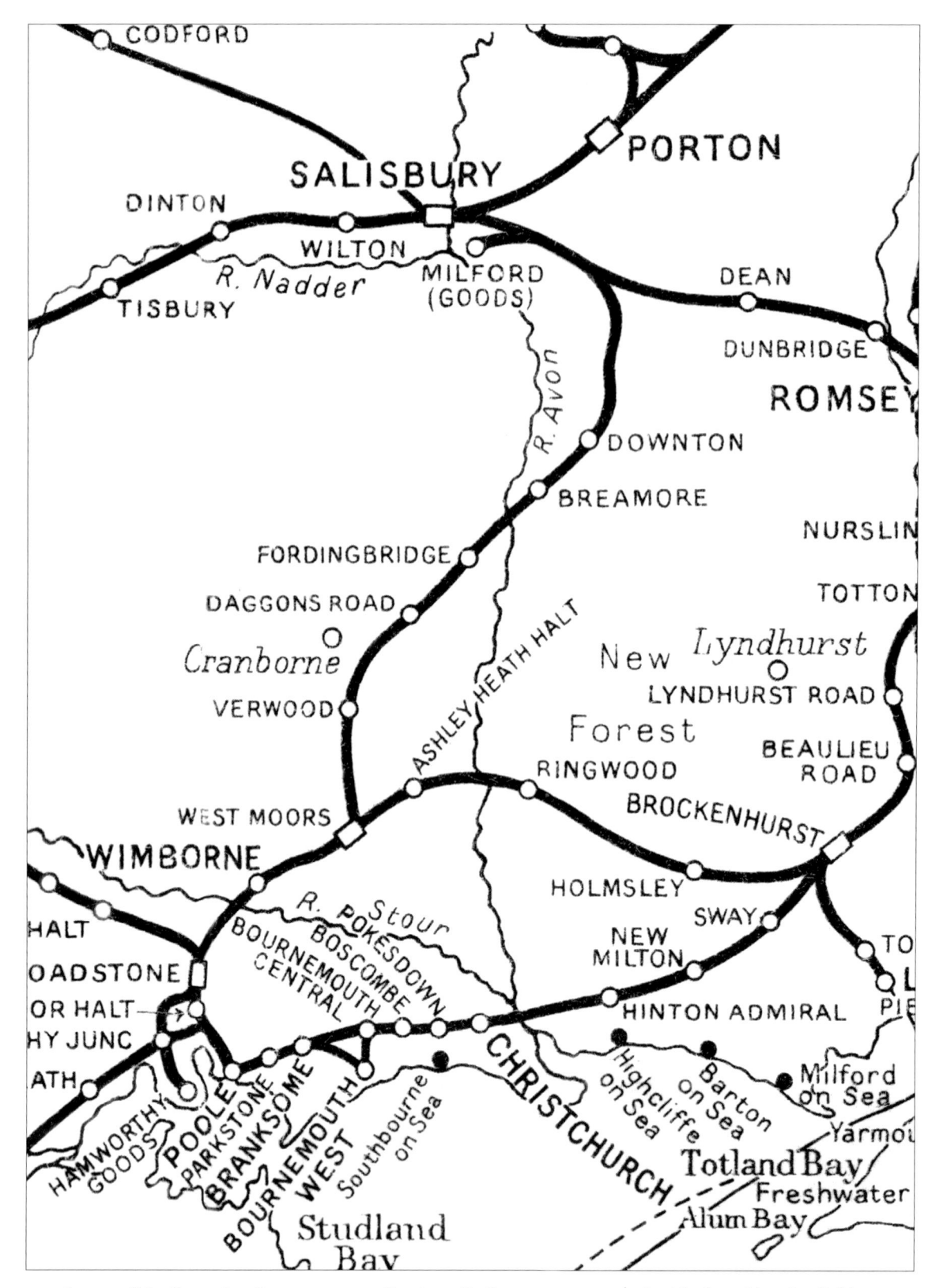

A map of the line taken from a pre-war Southern Railway system map. Its ideal position for linking Salisbury with the coast at Bournemouth is perfectly illustrated. Note that the cartographer has mistakenly drawn the River Avon to the west of Breamore, thus putting that station in Wiltshire! The river (which forms the county boundary) actually runs between Breamore and Downton.

Introduction

The Salisbury & Dorset Junction Railway was built to consolidate the London & South Western Railway's domination of Hampshire and South Dorset, partly with a view to keeping the Great Western away from Bournemouth. It also met the aspirations of Salisbury businessmen for a more direct route to Poole and Weymouth. Almost half of the 18½-mile route between Alderbury Junction and West Moors was in Dorset, with less than five miles apiece in Wiltshire and Hampshire. Passing through three counties it traversed contrasting landscapes, and served a wide if thinly populated agricultural area.

The different types of terrain were reflected in the variety of local freight traffic. The water meadows between Downton and Fordingbridge produced cattle, milk and watercress. South west of Fordingbridge the clay soil had given rise to brick and tile manufacture centuries before the coming of the railway, which enabled these industries to expand and distributed their wares over a much wider area. The heathland around Verwood was of little use for agriculture, but a few miles away, watercress grown in the Crane Valley provided business for the station. Unusual freight at Fordingbridge included grapes from the Quertier vineyard and fibreglass boats, the latter being a regular cargo in the final years.

A respected historian of railways in the region has described the line's passenger traffic as "always exiguous". This did the line less than justice, as five- and seven- coach trains were normal in summer during the 1950s. I came across one report of passengers being left behind at Fordingbridge on 9th June 1919, when 100 people were waiting to join a train to Bournemouth, which arrived almost full. "Some were accommodated in the guard's van", commented the *Salisbury & Winchester Journal*, "but the majority had to return home, many with families having come from a distance." Indeed the line became a major gateway for travel to Bournemouth and neighbouring resorts after the Southern Railway agreed to accommodate through trains from the Great Western, notably from South Wales. Another source of long distance traffic from the 1880s onwards was Fordingbridge Regatta, which led to the town being referred to as the Hampshire Henley.

It would, however, be fair to say that all year round passenger traffic on the line was at best erratic. The passenger service was never generous, partly because more lucrative freight trains tended to occupy much of the route's limited capacity in terms of signalling sections. Another weakness of the railway was that some stations, Fordingbridge in particular, were not well sited and these two factors led to much of the local travel into Salisbury being lost to the bus services that developed rapidly in the 1920s. Trains cut out during the Second World War, or in response to the coal shortage of 1951, were not restored and, despite a resurgence of holiday and excursion traffic from the mid 1950s, commuter traffic remained light. The line's other strong point was its usefulness as a diversionary route but this and the holiday business were regarded as liabilities, not assets, by the Beeching philosophy which knew the cost of everything and the value of nothing.

In the circumstances, it is not surprising that the line became a victim of the Beeching axe in 1964. Since then the population of the towns it served has grown considerably, especially at Verwood, which is estimated by Jo Draper, author of several books about the area, to have risen from 3,300 in 1966 to 11,000 in 1996. Naturally there has been a great increase in road traffic, and it goes without saying that the railway would be very useful, particularly for travel to Salisbury and the Bournemouth/Poole conurbation, if it had remained open.

In my research I am grateful for the help received from Richard Benstead, Colin Chivers, Larry Crosier, Peter Cupper, David Evans, Tim Hale, Rod Hoyle, Brian Jackson, Roger Merry-Price, John Nicholas, Roy Patterson, Nick Pomfret, Kevin Robertson, Geoff Smith, Howard and Clare Sprenger, David Vidler, Andrew Waller (for information on Hants & Dorset and Wilts & Dorset bus services), Charles Whetmath, David Wigley, Edwin Wilmshurst and Glen Woods.

Thanks are due to Mrs Penny Lyndon, Special Collections Librarian at Brunel University; the Dorset History Centre, Dorchester; Hampshire Archives, Winchester; Wiltshire & Swindon History Centre, Chippenham; Salisbury Reference Library; Fordingbridge Library and the National Archives, Kew.

Nigel Bray
February 2010

In addition, Kestrel Railway Books would like to thank Mrs Zena Pryer for permission to use the signal box diagrams drawn and previously published by her late husband, George Pryer.

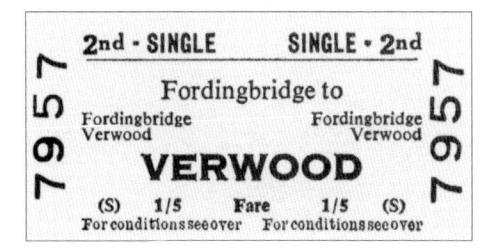

Early views of West Moors (top) and Fordingbridge (bottom). The train entering Fordingbridge station is running from Dorchester to Salisbury, the headcode discs being in the 12 and 3 o'clock positions, used between 1905 and 1921 for such trains. (Both, Lens of Sutton Collection)

Chapter 1

A Route from Salisbury to the Sea

The Wiltshire River Avon links Salisbury with Christchurch on the coast of what is now part of Dorset, by way of Downton, Fordingbridge and Ringwood, which have been market towns for centuries. By the 16th century Fordingbridge was specialising in the manufacture of calico, rope and sailcloth. Its proximity to abundant reserves of clay resulted in brick and tile making being well established by the 19th century, when it was also a centre for flour milling and the location of an iron foundry.

Attempts to create a canal from Salisbury to Southampton ended in failure with the works being abandoned in 1808. Within a few decades most towns in Britain were clamouring for railways. Soon after the London & Southampton Railway opened in 1840 and changed its name to the London & South Western, it set its sights on expanding its system to Poole, Dorchester and Salisbury.

The Southampton & Dorchester Railway, worked from the outset by the LSWR, had opened on 1st June 1847, and took a devious route through the New Forest in order to connect established towns such as Ringwood and Wimborne. The line was nicknamed Castleman's Corkscrew or Snake, after Charles Castleman, the Wimborne solicitor who was its prime mover. The promoters were keen to provide a branch to Poole from what is now Hamworthy Junction.

Poole was also a major objective in schemes for north–south lines linking it and the Dorset coast with the Midlands via Salisbury. The other major generators of long distance traffic on such a railway were anticipated to be Dorchester, the county town of Dorset and a well-established market town, and Weymouth, the port for the Channel Islands and also rapidly developing as a health resort.

Salisbury's first railway linked it with Southampton by means of a branch from the LSWR main line at Bishopstoke (later known as Eastleigh). This opened on 20th January 1847, but schemes had already been mooted to place the city on routes from the Midlands to Poole and Weymouth.

Despite its commercial importance arising from its position as a route centre, Salisbury was then a relatively small town and anxious not to lose influence to neighbouring market towns, particularly those such as Romsey and Ringwood, which were either already (or very soon to be) rail connected. From another direction the broad gauge Wilts, Somerset & Weymouth Railway, authorised in 1845, would soon connect Salisbury via Warminster and Westbury with the Great Western main line at Thingley Junction, near Chippenham, or so it had anticipated.

Unfortunately the WSWR, which had opened its first section from Thingley to Westbury in 1848, was already meeting difficulty with raising capital to complete its system. Railway companies throughout Britain were now facing a climate of refused loans from bankers or defaulted subscriptions from shareholders. A crisis of confidence in rail schemes had arisen because the financial returns from completed lines had often been disappointingly low. The result was that schemes advanced in the mid 1840s for long-distance routes through areas with little population or industry tended to fade away by the end of the decade. Among these were the Salisbury, Dorchester and Weymouth scheme of 1844, which had featured a branch from near Wimborne to Poole, and the Salisbury, Wimborne & Poole Railway proposed in 1845.

Both of these projected lines would have connected Salisbury with Wimborne via Downton and Fordingbridge. Neither came to fruition, and it was to be more than a decade before an alternative proposal for a railway in that corridor was put forward with a realistic hope of success.

By 1860 the outlook seemed brighter. The Southampton & Dorchester line, which had been absorbed by the LSWR in 1848, had now been open for 13 years, and the length of new railway required to create a route from Salisbury to the Dorset coast was considerably less than would have been the case in 1845. Through running by the LSWR between Southampton and Weymouth had been possible since 20th January 1857 because the Board of Trade had insisted on the final five miles of the WSWR between Weymouth and Dorchester Junction being built to mixed gauge [1]. Salisbury had now been on a direct route to London since 3rd July 1854, when the South Western had opened its branch to Basingstoke. To its west, the Salisbury & Yeovil Railway was under construction, reaching Yeovil on 1st June 1860. A further extension from Yeovil Junction to Exeter was also at an advanced stage, being completed on 19th July of the same year. Against this background of a rapidly-expanding LSWR network, new proposals for a line between Salisbury and Wimborne were regarded more favourably by potential shareholders, who were now being asked to connect two

> **SALISBURY AND DORSETSHIRE RAILWAY.** Plans and Prospectuses of the above undertaking, with the names of an influential Provisional Committee, will be ready for delivery in the course of a few days.
>
> This line will commence near Salisbury, 83 miles (by railway) from London — will pass near Fordingbridge, through Wimbourn and Bere to Dorchester and Weymouth with a branch from Wimbourn to Poole. It will be at least 12 miles shorter between London and Dorchester than the Southampton and Dorsetshire line, and 2 miles shorter between Dorchester and the Towns situate on the eastern coast line of railway. This advantage will apply to Poole and other towns on the line.
>
> The London and South Western Railway Company will guarantee to the subscribers 4 per cent. on their subscriptions with an equal division of surplus profits.
>
> In the mean time further particulars may be obtained on application to the following Solicitors:—Messrs. Bircham and Dalrymple, Bedford-row, London; Messrs. Hodding, Hodding, and Townsend, Salisbury; J. T. King, Esq. Blandford; Messrs. Coombs and Son, Dorchester; and George Arden, Esq. Weymouth.
>
> GEO. WM. HORN, Secretary pro tem.
> Offices, 5, John-street, Adelphi, London,
> October 24, 1844.

Early notice of a proposed line in "The Railway Times" of 26th October 1844.

1

more-or-less complete main lines instead of risking investment in what would have been some 50 miles of new railway across virgin territory.

In 1856, the LSWR Directors had decided, after much deliberation, to extend to Exeter via Yeovil instead of from Dorchester. Had the latter course been adopted, it might well have hastened the coming of a Salisbury–Wimborne line, and would have placed Fordingbridge on a more direct route to Somerset, Devon and Cornwall. Nevertheless, the South Western anticipated sufficient traffic between Salisbury and the two major Dorset ports, Poole and Weymouth, to sustain a new branch railway.

The 1860 scheme was for a line from Alderbury, south east of Salisbury on the existing Bishopstoke line, to West Moors, in the parish of West Parley, east of Wimborne on the Southampton & Dorchester. A branch to Poole was also included, and this would have been nearer to the town centre than was the LSWR terminus, which was actually at Hamworthy on the west side of Poole Harbour. From Fordingbridge, the main route would head in a south-westerly direction to join the Corkscrew at West Moors. From a traffic perspective it might have been better to have routed it directly south to an east facing junction at Ringwood instead. Ringwood was not only considerably larger than Fordingbridge but more main roads converged on it.

Nevertheless, the proposals did include a west to south spur linking West Moors with the Ringwood, Christchurch and Bournemouth Railway, which had been authorised on 8th August 1859 with construction starting by the spring of 1860. Bournemouth had been bypassed by the Southampton & Dorchester Railway because of its insignificance in the 1840s, but was now fast developing as a resort. The junction at Ringwood faced Southampton, but the spur would have enabled passengers from the Salisbury direction to reach Christchurch and Bournemouth with one change (or a reversal) at West Moors.

A meeting at Salisbury on 20th October 1860 to discuss the Salisbury, Poole & Dorset Junction scheme was chaired by the Earl of Shaftesbury, who lived at Cranborne, about three miles from the proposed route at Verwood. He, Anthony Cooper, was the Seventh Earl, who had succeeded to the title in 1851, and would achieve lasting honour for his work on behalf of factory children and the mentally ill. He founded the Ragged School movement to educate the poorest children decades before schooling was made compulsory by the 1870 Education Act, which incidentally was introduced by another Dorset man, W.E. Forster.

The Earl told those present that the line would be of great public benefit, because there was abundant potential traffic scattered along its intended course. He added that other major landowners along the route supported the project, reading letters from William Fryer of Verwood Manor; the Right Honourable Sidney Herbert; Earl Nelson of Trafalgar House, Downton; and a Mr Shafto, who was descended from the Bobby Shafto of the famous song and lived at Barford. The meeting unanimously carried a motion, proposed by Lord Shaftesbury and seconded by Matthew Marsh, MP for Salisbury, "that in the opinion of this meeting it is desirable that a railway should be constructed to connect Salisbury with Wimborne, Poole and the northern parts of Dorset, and that the line now submitted, traversing the valley of the Avon, near Downton and Fordingbridge, and uniting with the

This page and opposite: Two views of Breamore station looking north around the turn of the century. (Both, Lens of Sutton Collection)

South Western on the east side of Wimborne, is satisfactory for the above purpose."

Matthew Marsh, born locally at Winterslow in 1810, was the son of an Anglican canon. He was educated at Westminster School and Christ Church College, Oxford, and then became a barrister on the Western Circuit. Despite his privileged background he married the daughter of an Army sergeant, a move which might be an indication of his subsequent unconventional career. In 1840 he went to Australia where he took up sheep farming on an extensive scale. After returning to Britain, he became Liberal MP for his home city in 1857, standing down in 1868.

Hamilton Fulton, Engineer for the proposed line, advised the meeting that the probable cost of construction would be £180,000. He estimated revenue conservatively at £14 per mile per week and after deducting operating expenses at half of this amount, predicted a net dividend of 5¼ per cent. Thomas Pain moved that committees be appointed at Salisbury, Downton, Fordingbridge, Cranborne, Poole and Wimborne to assist in raising capital. This resolution, seconded by Mr Coventry of Burgate, near Fordingbridge, was also carried unanimously [2].

The Salisbury, Poole & Dorset Junction Railway Bill met with little local opposition and received the Royal Assent on 16th July 1861, although not before the intended branch to Poole and the link from West Moors to the RCBR been struck out at the Committee stage. The LSWR already served Poole by means of its branch from Poole Junction (later known as Hamworthy Junction). The more modest aspirations of the company were reflected in the title of the Act: Salisbury & Dorset Junction Railway. Soon afterwards, the *Salisbury Journal* expressed the hope that people who had declined to risk money on the venture because they had not expected it to win Parliamentary approval, would now become shareholders in it. The newspaper claimed that Salisbury itself had the most to gain from the line, because "it will open up a large and important agricultural district, the inhabitants of which will naturally resort to Salisbury as their market town". It expressed the hope that the line would be completed rapidly, especially if Salisbury businessmen invested in the project [3].

Construction of the Line

In the event, it was over two and a half years before construction started. The first three half-yearly General Meetings of the company, on 21st July 1862, 28th February and 31st August 1863 had to be abandoned for lack of a quorum. At last on 27th February 1864 there were sufficient attendees for business to be transacted. All these and subsequent General Meetings were held at the company's offices at 1 Poets Corner, Westminster. Possibly the remoteness of London from the proposed line's territory discouraged attendance and subscription by local people.

This first productive General Meeting, chaired by Matthew Marsh, heard that work had begun on 3rd February in a field close to Trafalgar House, the home of the Earl and Countess Nelson, about two miles north of Downton. Although the meeting was told that construction had begun under "auspicious circumstances", the *Hampshire Chronicle* suggested otherwise by pointing out that the Earl and Countess arrived about 1.00pm in "very unfavourable weather". Lady Nelson had cut the first sod with an inscribed silver spade presented to her by Mr Jackson, one of the engineers, and had then wheeled it a short distance in a mahogany barrow, unloading it to loud cheers of the assembled shareholders and local inhabitants. The shareholders and Directors had then adjourned to a tent for lunch, at which Mr Marsh presided [4].

The Directors reported to the General Meeting that the contract for construction had been let "on very favourable terms", and the contractor now had possession of the required land between Alderbury Junction and Downton. If no unforeseen difficulties arose, the line was expected to open by the summer of 1865, provided more shares were taken up. Mr Fulton added that fencing work had begun on the Alderbury–Downton section, which would involve the heaviest earthworks of the route. Completion of that section would give the measure of the time required to finish the whole line. Work was imminent on the southern section from West Moors to Alderholt, which included the easiest earthworks, with a view to opening it within six months for the transport of materials from Poole Harbour to the more northerly sections.

The meeting re-elected the existing Directors, Matthew Marsh, Thomas Pain and CW Squarey. The two remaining places on the Board were filled by Samuel Frankish and Walter Fry.

The next General Meeting on 31st August learned that the company had acquired two-thirds of the required land, although it was still trying to reach a settlement with Sir Edward Hulse of Breamore House, Major Brice and one or two other landowners. Construction of the Alderbury Junction–Downton formation had begun at the end of March. Bridges, culverts and earthworks were progressing on the West Moors–Alderholt section. About 75,000 cubic yards of earthwork and 2,200 cubic yards of brickwork had been completed, and 250 tons of rail had been delivered. Despite this achievement, Mr Fulton sounded a note of caution by adding that, "the progress of the works have been somewhat interrupted by the harvest and other causes". A number of labourers had left for harvest work but the contractor, a Mr Garrett, was said to be negotiating an (unspecified) arrangement to allow him to "proceed with renewed vigour" and thereby complete the line within the period required by the Act. The Salisbury & Dorset was not the only railway company to lose navvies to seasonal farm work, and the contractor was probably doing his utmost to entice them back with the promise of more favourable pay and conditions.

So far, the expenditure on construction had been modest. The authorised capital of the scheme was £213,000, but by 30th June 1864 only £20,281 11s 5d had been drawn from the capital account. £13,210 of this was for land and works, and £4,848 had been spent on preliminary and Parliamentary expenses. It seems difficult to believe the Directors' repeated claim that the line was expected to open by the summer of 1865 when less than 10 per cent of the budget had been consumed in the first five months of work. In all probability, they were talking up the project to give potential shareholders an impression of a quick return. Privately, they may have had few illusions about the likelihood of more subscriptions, as the General Meeting authorised the company to borrow up to £53,300 on mortgage.

Matters came to a head in September when work on the line stopped. Mr Garrett's previous assurances had not been fulfilled, and the Directors dismissed him. The contract was re-let to Henry Jackson (possibly the same Jackson who had assisted Lady Nelson at the sod cutting ceremony?) The next General Meeting on 14th February 1865 was told that work had resumed between Alderbury Junction and Downton, "on most of the heaviest sections of the line". The large cutting near Trafalgar House would proceed more rapidly when new plant arrived. Mr Fulton said Mr Jackson had assured him the line would be ready by the end of September 1865, yet expenditure up to the end of 1864 had amounted to only £29,039, of which £22,605 was for Land and Works. Messrs Fry and Squarey had ceased to be Directors, being replaced by William Blackmore and Octavius Ommaney.

A shareholder referred to the hardship caused to workmen whose wages had not been paid when the company had dispensed with Mr Garrett. Mr Marsh replied that some of the Directors had, at their own expense, assisted the workmen to some extent, but added that shareholders' money could not be used to pay the former contractor's liabilities [5].

Within a week Garrett was telling the national press that he was seeking £25,000 from the company for work he had carried out. He claimed to have completed nearly half of the line, having spent £8,000 on materials and preliminaries. He added that the workmen would have been paid if the company had paid him monthly, but he had received nothing for two months' recent work involving 700 men and some 80 horses. He still had possession of the route, on which his plant remained, and was confident he could complete the railway by the end of July. His lawsuit was still pending in June 1866 when the line was almost ready for opening [6].

The General Meeting of 24th August 1865 heard that construction had advanced significantly, with some 350,000 cubic yards of earthworks and 6,000 cubic yards of brickwork made. Mr Fulton advised that about one quarter of the earthworks and half the brickwork remained to be done, subject to revision if it should prove necessary to substitute a short tunnel for the cutting near Trafalgar Park. About 5½ miles of track had now been laid, and most of the permanent way materials had been delivered, except for about half of the sleepers and some chairs. Sounding a somewhat more cautious note than the Directors, he said, "There is reason to hope that the line will be completed by the latter end of October next."

Over half of the authorised capital had now been spent. Expenditure to 31st July was £121,312 of which £119,951 was for land, works, Parliamentary expenses and administration. The income had been raised from share capital (£85,212), debentures (£34,500) and a temporary loan (£1,600).

The Directors went on to paint a rosy picture of the line's prospects because three proposed new routes, "unexpected at the time of the (Salisbury & Dorset Junction) Act" had been authorised by Parliament. One was for a line from the Midland Railway to Salisbury, another was the South Wales and Great Western Railway, while the third scheme was for a Wilts and Gloucester Railway. None of these lines materialised, although direct routes between the

Midland and the LSWR systems would later become available at Wimborne, after completion of the Somerset & Dorset Joint Railway's Bath extension, and at Andover Junction via the Midland & South Western Junction Railway.

Nevertheless, hopes of an 1865 opening were to be dashed by adverse weather and protracted negotiations for the remaining portions of land. The next half-yearly meeting, on 28th February 1866, was told that prolonged wet weather had considerably slowed construction and that two or three landowners, who in the Directors' view would benefit from the railway, had made what the company considered to be excessive demands for compensation. No doubt they were driving hard bargains in the belief that, with the line largely complete, the company would settle on their terms rather than seek Parliamentary powers for deviations. 16 miles of track had now been laid, of which about 12 had been partially ballasted. 400,000 cubic yards of earthworks had been made, together with 8,000 cubic yards of brickwork, leaving three public road bridges, some occupation road bridges and some culverts outstanding. North of Downton a tunnel had been built instead of the original plan for a cutting and this required only the completion of its brick portals. Buildings were said to be nearly finished "at four of the five stations" (the fifth station took much longer to materialise, as we shall see), while signals at Alderbury Junction and Downton had been "partly erected".

Six months later the Directors expressed their disappointment that the line, "for some time completed", had not opened, blaming this delay on the "constantly increasing requirements of the Board of Trade", a reference to criticisms made by the BoT's Inspecting Officer, Captain Tyler, who had insisted on certain improvements to track, signalling and to passenger accommodation at Breamore, before he was prepared to pass the line for public traffic.

Expenditure up to the end of June 1866 had risen to £193,535 but only around £10,000 had been subscribed locally, the Directors' report commenting that "the want of local support has added considerably to the difficulties in raising funds for construction." It stressed that additional funds were urgently required to meet the unsettled claims of several landowners and to rectify deficiencies highlighted by Captain Tyler in his recent Inspector's report.

In the circumstances, it is hardly surprising that the Salisbury & Dorset gave in to pressure from the South Western to withdraw its application for powers, announced at the February meeting, to construct two connecting lines. One was intended to run from Downton to Totton, a distance of 13¼ miles with an estimated cost of £158,000. The other was to have been a spur of almost four miles from north of West Moors, to Hurn on the Ringwood, Christchurch & Bournemouth Railway, which had been estimated at £52,000. The latter connection would have enabled through running from Salisbury to Bournemouth without reversal at West Moors station. Both projects had been justified on the grounds that they would develop traffic and meet the wishes of major landowners. In return for dropping them the company secured an agreement by which the LSWR would work its line but give 55 per cent of gross receipts to the Salisbury & Dorset.

Noting that gross receipts over the Salisbury & Yeovil

Daggons Road, in the early 1900s with LSWR 4-4-0 No 467 approaching from the Bournemouth direction. (Lens of Sutton Collection)

THE SALISBURY & DORSET JUNCTION RAILWAY

Downton station photographed early in its life. (Both, Lens of Sutton Collection)

and the Somerset & Dorset Railways were averaging £35 and £20 per mile per week respectively, the Salisbury & Dorset company now estimated that even on the lower of these figures, its working agreement would yield net revenue (after deducting working expenses) of £10,668 per year, which it claimed would pay the debenture interest and a 5 per cent dividend on the share capital. This bright forecast was followed by an appeal for more subscriptions!

Captain Tyler had found much wanting with the permanent way, fencing and signalling. His report of 6th August declined to allow the line to be opened. He made a further inspection in October and noted that many defects remained. It was not until 20th December 1866 that the company was finally able to open its line, at a few days' notice to the public. Financial stringency was probably the main reason for the difficulty in completion and opening of the railway. Although the company's next half-yearly meeting on 28th February 1867 claimed, in the absence of official working results from the LSWR that, "residents had reported a most satisfactory level of traffic", the Directors again lamented the reluctance of local people to take up shares in the railway. After 11 days of operation, and nearly three years after construction had begun, expenditure up to 31st December 1866 had been £197,845 16s 2d, including £174,980 for expenses and administration and £20,276 for land & compensation. At least it was comfortably within the budget for the scheme.

A disappointment for local residents was the location of Fordingbridge station. Once the route for the line had been decided, it became clear that its nearest point would be at least half a mile from the town centre, and there had been much argument locally as to whether the station should be built at Ashford or Sweatford. The company chose the former, despite its greater distance from the town, but the choice may well have been motivated by the opportunity to reuse a large drift of gravel, which had to be excavated to create the station site, for ballasting the line. One positive result of the station being ¾ mile from the town centre was that Ashford grew into a suburb supporting industries reliant on the railway for bringing in raw materials or for distribution of finished goods.

Among these was JR Neave, producer of farinaceous (cereal based) food. Josiah Neave is recorded as attending the company's first successful meeting in London in 1864, and he established a corn mill next to the goods yard so that crates of his products were despatched by train. In the 20th century, these were orientated towards the needs of babies, invalids and the elderly. Another entrepreneur was coal merchant Alfred Hood, who opened the Railway Hotel about a fortnight before trains began running. He dealt not only in coal and coke, but also hay and straw from premises in the station yard. His family ran the coal business at the station until the line closed, although by 1915, the proprietor of the Railway Hotel was Henry Hockey. A third industry which developed next to the eastern perimeter of the yard in the late 19th century was the Quertier vineyard.

Early Days of the Salisbury & Dorset Junction

The first train on opening day, Thursday 20th December 1866, left Wimborne at 6.50am, being met at Fordingbridge by the town's brass band which then joined the train to Salisbury. The *Hampshire Chronicle* commented that the railway had been well and economically constructed [7]. The earliest timetable consisted of four trains each way, weekdays only. The first pair of trains were mixed (there being no separate goods services) and crossed at Downton. The up train started from Dorchester at 5.45am, reaching Salisbury at 8.15. The down train, 7.15am Salisbury, terminated at Wimborne. The next working was a round trip from Salisbury to Poole, starting at 10.12am and returning at 2.30pm. The South Western's Poole station at this time was at Hamworthy, on the opposite side of Poole Harbour from the town centre and present day station. The final down service, leaving Salisbury at 6.40pm, ran through to Weymouth. This latter train was worked from Dorchester "by the Weymouth goods engine", although only two minutes was allowed for the engine change and station work. This arrangement seems not to have worked well, because the train terminated at Dorchester from February 1867.

From the same date the direct Poole train was diverted to Weymouth, although connections were provided at Poole Junction in both directions. The through working now returned from Weymouth at 1.40pm, less than an hour after arrival, but it was possible to spend about four hours at the seaside by returning on the 4.50, changing at Wimborne.

Whilst the first up train offered a five minute connection at Salisbury into a semi-fast train reaching Waterloo at 11.8am, the latest return service from the capital was at 3.50pm. Southampton West [8] could be reached at 11.20am via Wimborne, but the final train back was at 1.34pm. In terms of journey opportunities, the Salisbury & Dorset seemed to be getting a poor deal from the South Western, which had no illusions about the traffic on offer from a thinly populated rural area. The service appears to have been resourced by just two sets of rolling stock, one beginning and ending at Salisbury to provide two round trips to Wimborne, and the other starting from Salisbury with the Weymouth working, then from Salisbury to Dorchester with the evening down train, returning the next morning as the up mixed train.

The next major event was the opening of West Moors station, the "Dorset Junction" promised in the 1861 Act, on 1st August 1867. This was about 1½ miles west of St Leonard's Siding on the Ringwood line, which had existed at least since April 1860, when gravel for William Fryer's estate was unloaded for repairs to a road. West Moors itself was then just a hamlet, although it grew substantially in the 1920s and again from the 1970s as a suburb of Bournemouth.

Another station, which should have opened with the line, remained unbuilt. This was at Alderholt, nearly two miles south west of Fordingbridge. It had been the subject of a contract in 1864 between the company and George Onslow Churchill, as the condition on which he agreed to sell land for £400 to enable the line to be built. The Churchill family had owned Alderholt Park, an early 19th century mansion, since 1854 and remained there until 1920. The other main landowner in the village was Lord Salisbury, who was lord of the manor. He also was keen for the station to open, but both gentlemen were to be kept waiting.

The Minutes of the Board meeting on 17th March 1865 refer to difficulties with the station site. Very little appears in the Minutes on this subject until 4th January 1867, a fortnight after the line opened, when a letter from Lord Salisbury and Mr Churchill was referred to the company's Solicitor. The Minutes for 26th February 1868 mention that an injunction had been granted pending an enquiry into the merits of the case. This rather suggests that the company, finding that its line was no gold mine, was not in a hurry to incur the expense of constructing a further station. In any case it was not until March 1869 that Mr Churchill's lawsuit was heard at the Court of Chancery.

After due deliberation, Vice-Chancellor James decreed that Churchill must convey the land to the Salisbury & Dorset company with a covenant requiring it to provide and maintain the proposed station for as long as the line remained open for traffic. The covenant was signed in June, but work did not proceed. Matters became complicated as a result of Acts of 1867 and 1873 by which the LSWR had been empowered to take a lease of the line for 1,000 years and work it on the Salisbury & Dorset's behalf. In May 1873, Churchill filed another suit seeking to compel both railway companies to build the station and serve it with passenger and goods trains.

When the case was heard again in March 1874, Vice-Chancellor Bacon ruled that the South Western was subject to all the liabilities and obligations which the Salisbury & Dorset had entered into for working the line, including Churchill's requirement for trains to call at Alderholt. He therefore granted an injunction, restraining the LSWR from working the line without a station at Alderholt, the injunction being suspended for three months to give the Salisbury & Dorset, which did not deny its obligation, time to build it.

On 29th May the Salisbury & Dorset's Engineer agreed to arrange to commence works as soon as a cheque for £500 had been received by the company's solicitors. The South Western regarded this sum as well short of what was required, for on 20th November, Archibald Scott, its General Manager, advised that the estimated cost of the station was £1,300 exclusive of land. The March 1875 Board meeting learned that the LSWR was prepared to carry out the work if the Salisbury & Dorset would forward that amount. This was agreed in May.

In the meantime the South Western had appealed against Vice-Chancellor Bacon's decree, by which it was restrained from working the line unless the station were opened within three months. Lord Justice James heard the appeal in Chancery on 28th June and ruled that whilst the LSWR was under no obligation to provide a station on Mr Churchill's land, it was obliged to stop its trains there once the station had been built. He confirmed that Vice-Chancellor Bacon's decree had to be carried out, but noted that the Salisbury & Dorset had paid the necessary funds to the LSWR upon the latter's undertaking to construct the station within six months. He therefore ordered Churchill to pay the costs of the South Western's appeal, but have them transferred to the Salisbury & Dorset [9, 10].

So the Salisbury & Dorset was saddled with the £295 costs of Churchill's lawsuit. This was confirmed as paid by the February 1876 Board meeting, by which time the new station was already in use. Under threat of further litigation from Churchill, both companies also complied with his condition that all passenger and goods trains on the line would stop at Alderholt [11].

One has to admire Churchill's tenacity in fighting for a station to serve his corner of Dorset, although he continued to push his luck even further. In July he wrote to Thomas Pain complaining that the road approach to the station was narrow and inconvenient. Unimpressed, the Salisbury & Dorset replied that it would make the improvements if he and the other major landowners in the area would take up shares to the value of the work required!

Alderholt station opened four weeks late on 1st January 1876, but its name created confusion with Aldershot, giving rise to stories of soldiers arriving unintentionally in rural Dorset, so by 1st May, the name had changed to Daggens Road (sic), after a village to the west. The Board Minutes for 29th September refer to "Daggens Road (Alderholt) station". The spelling changed to Daggons Road in 1903.

18 months after the station opened, the South Western sent the Salisbury & Dorset a bill for £2,111, less £1,300 already paid, for construction of the station. The Salisbury & Dorset declined to pay the balance, pointing out that the station had been built under an order of Chancery that had required it to pay the sum of £1,300 [12]. Whatever the reason for the overspend, the facilities provided at Daggons Road were not lavish. Whilst the station house was a double-gabled brick building, staff and passengers had to be content with wooden outbuildings for the offices and waiting rooms.

References
1. The 1845 Wilts, Somerset & Weymouth Railway Act provided for mixed gauge south of Dorchester Junction, but this became mandatory in the subsequent 1854 Act that gave the GWR additional time to complete the WSWR, which it had absorbed in 1850.
2. *Railway Times*, 27.10.1860.
3. ibid, 10.8.1861.
4. *Hampshire Chronicle*, 6.2.1864.
5. *The Times*, 15.2.1865.
6. ibid, 21.2.1865 and 8.6.1866.
7. *Hampshire Chronicle*, 22.12.1866.
8. The station appears in the Service Timetable as "Southampton West End", which is misleading as West End is a suburb to the north east of the present city.
9. *The Times*, 29.6.1875.
10. Salisbury & Dorset Junction Railway Board Minutes, PRO ref RAIL 594/2.
11. ibid, 28.1.1876.
12. ibid, 31.7.1877.

Chapter 2

Frustration and Tragedy

Ten years after its line opened, the Salisbury & Dorset company had reason to feel disappointed with its lot. In contrast to the railway development close to the southern end of the line, very little enhancement, beyond the opening of Daggens Road station, had taken place on the line itself. The Salisbury & Dorset remained a rural backwater, despite providing a potential route via West Moors to the South Western's new line to Poole and Bournemouth West. The rapid growth of Bournemouth had created the impetus for new routes serving the resort, although another factor had been demands from Poole for a more central and better appointed station than the original one at Hamworthy. A source of increasing frustration for the Salisbury & Dorset's Directors, shareholders and customers was the indifference of the LSWR to the Fordingbridge line as a link in its own expanding system.

The line's opening in 1866 had shortened the distance between Salisbury and stations west of Wimborne by about 30 miles. It also offered connections at Wimborne for the Somerset & Dorset line and at West Moors for journeys to and from the Ringwood and Southampton direction, although these were limited by the sparse passenger service of four trains each way via Fordingbridge. It irked the Salisbury & Dorset that the South Western's commercial policy appeared to treat its line as of little value for other than local journeys.

The weekday train service had expanded slightly by 1875 to five trains each way, of which three up and two down were mixed. The mixed trains included a round trip from Salisbury to Fordingbridge, starting at 4.35pm and returning at 5.40. One down and two up trains ran through between Salisbury and Weymouth, although there were still no Sunday services. The same timetable offered passengers a connection at Alderbury Junction, where platforms had been provided for the use of local staff, from the first up train (5.40am Dorchester) into the South Western's 7.55 Salisbury–Southampton, subject to punctual running of the Salisbury & Dorset service.

Many allegations were brought to the notice of the Salisbury & Dorset Board of LSWR officials refusing to issue tickets via Fordingbridge for through journeys, even where this seemed a perfectly logical route. There were also cases where the South Western was charging higher fares for travel via West Moors and Salisbury than via Southampton despite the former being the shorter route. In August 1876, Elias Squarey urged his fellow Directors of the Salisbury & Dorset to challenge the LSWR after learning that a relative

An early 1900s view of Daggons Road with a train approaching from Salisbury. (Lens of Sutton Collection)

had been refused a ticket from Salisbury to Christchurch via Fordingbridge.

Christchurch was at that time served by a branch line from Ringwood, which had opened in November 1862 as the first stage of the Ringwood, Christchurch & Bournemouth Railway. This line was extended to Bournemouth East on 14th March 1870, and became the first railway to serve the resort. It has to be said that the rail journey from Salisbury, involving changes both of train and direction of travel at West Moors and Ringwood, was far from direct. The RCBR had been planned to feed the Southampton & Dorchester Railway, with a view to attracting business from the London and Southampton directions, so the junction at Ringwood faced west. By contrast, the junction at West Moors faced east. Matters would have been easier if either the 1861 or 1866 proposals for a spur from West Moors to the RCBR had materialised, but without them a train journey from Salisbury or Fordingbridge to Bournemouth East was a test of endurance. The railway was also at a disadvantage for travel between Fordingbridge and Ringwood, which were only six miles apart by road (the present A338) but about 14 miles by rail via West Moors.

Not surprisingly, Archibald Scott replied that there were, "no connections between trains on the Christchurch branch and those on the Salisbury & Dorset line", so through tickets would therefore not be issued. The Salisbury company realised it had more to gain by pressing the LSWR to run through services over the branch from New Poole Junction (later known as Broadstone) which had opened to a new, more central, station in Poole on 2nd December 1872, and extended to Bournemouth West on 15th June 1874. This new line offered a more direct route between Salisbury and Bournemouth than did the RCBR. From New Poole Junction into Poole this was over South Western metals, having been authorised in 1866, but from Poole to Bournemouth it followed the route of the independent Poole & Bournemouth Railway, which had received the Royal Assent on 26th May 1865.

In January 1877, Elias Squarey renewed his campaign on ticket routeing. This time he had discovered that a passenger holding a season ticket between Wimborne and London was not allowed to travel via Salisbury without payment of excess. When he raised the matter at the Salisbury & Dorset Board meeting, he was asked to gather evidence for a meeting with the LSWR to seek improved Salisbury to Weymouth services, a better supply of wagons, and a fairer share of through traffic where there was the option of routeing it via Fordingbridge or the Corkscrew.

At first, the South Western appears to have taken a conciliatory line. At the Board meeting of 25th April, JW Batten, a Director, reported on "a very satisfactory meeting" with Archibald Scott, who had promised that a list of timetable enhancements proposed by Squarey would be carefully considered. Three months later the Salisbury & Dorset was deeply disillusioned with Scott's reply that only two of Squarey's suggestions, involving later timings for the first down and last up trains, could be accommodated. The Board concluded that all negotiations with the LSWR had failed, and therefore resolved to take its case to the Railway Commissioners, with a view to securing "a proper train service, reasonable booking arrangements, a fair division of traffic from Christchurch and stations west of Ringwood to stations east of Salisbury, and equal facilities for tourist and excursion tickets by the (Salisbury & Dorset) line as are now afforded by the Southampton route."

The two companies seem to have tried to settle their differences by dialogue because the Salisbury & Dorset Board meeting for November referred to a meeting on 31st October at which these grievances were aired. Evidence of some progress is provided by the company's half yearly shareholders' meeting of 1st March 1878, which unanimously supported a resolution thanking the company for having obtained a more convenient service between Salisbury and Wimborne. However, the motion also called, "in view of the vast amount of building at Bournemouth West", for through carriages from that station via Wimborne and Salisbury to London, as well as for a better standard of rolling stock on the line.

More comfortable coaching stock for the Salisbury & Dorset line was probably a low priority with the LSWR, which had little incentive to provide it on a thinly populated route from which it received only 45 per cent of the gross revenue. Unfortunately the deployment of old, short wheelbase carriages would be a factor in the tragic derailment at Downton six years later.

The Salisbury & Dorset found the South Western was more willing to assist with modest investment in the line's infrastructure, particularly when the LSWR could make money directly from the projects concerned. In April 1877 the Salisbury Directors asked the South Western to erect a waiting shelter on the down platform at Breamore, offering to reimburse the £50 cost at 4½ per cent interest. This was agreed in June. Later that year a Mr Paget, who had a brickworks near Daggens Road station, offered to pay £25 per year for the use of a siding if the Salisbury & Dorset would provide one. Archibald Scott, anticipating that the Salisbury company could not afford to install the siding, advised that the LSWR would pay the £500 cost provided it received the £25 rental. These terms were accepted by the Salisbury & Dorset on condition that the £25 related to the rent of the siding only [1].

The South Western may have relaxed its policy on the routeing of through ticketing via the Salisbury & Dorset because of Great Western interest in the line. The latter company had converted its Salisbury branch to standard gauge in 1872, and soon realised it had created a potential gateway to Bournemouth from Bristol and the West of England. From Bristol and Bath such a route would be considerably shorter than via Reading and Basingstoke. It would also enable the GWR to compete for Bournemouth traffic with the Somerset & Dorset, which had started building its Bath extension the same year. Scott appears to have been very aware of this threat, for in a letter to the Salisbury & Dorset Board early in 1878, he sought to play

FRUSTRATION AND TRAGEDY

down Great Western support for through bookings by claiming that James Grierson, its General Manager, had accepted the LSWR view that "the train service over the Salisbury & Dorset line could not be altered and passengers would be certain to travel over the quickest route." [2]

Undaunted, the Salisbury & Dorset wrote to Grierson pointing out the savings in time and distance afforded by its line for journeys to Bournemouth from stations on the GWR system. In June he replied that he had been in touch with the South Western, who had no objection to through bookings being arranged from the Bristol direction to Bournemouth via Fordingbridge. The Salisbury & Dorset's Secretary then wrote to Scott, asking him to make the necessary arrangements, but the latter dragged his feet, for in October Grierson advised that he and Scott were still in correspondence on the subject [3].

At its half yearly meeting on 23rd August, the company reported that fares for through traffic between Salisbury, Ringwood, Christchurch and Bournemouth East had been considerably reduced. This was remarkable in view of the South Western's refusal to even issue such fares less than two years previously.

Unfortunately the apportionment of receipts between the two companies remained a sticking point and on 4th November 1878 the Railway Commission heard evidence from both parties concerning the Salisbury & Dorset's formal complaint that its share of revenue had not been properly allocated. Under the terms of its lease of the line, the LSWR had been required to account for all receipts from working it and to allocate them between both companies on a mileage basis, less certain terminal charges allowed by the Railway Clearing House. The crux of the complaint was that the South Western had awarded itself a much higher proportion of the income than it was entitled to.

The Salisbury & Dorset claimed there was an error averaging 19 per cent in the South Western's favour. The latter, it said, had sent both passenger and freight traffic via its own metals in order to maximise its own share of revenue from through journeys, even though one of the main reasons for building the line had been to shorten the distance between Salisbury and Bournemouth, Dorchester, Poole, Ringwood and Weymouth. For instance, people and goods were being routed from Salisbury to Wimborne instead of being transferred at West Moors. Traffic from Salisbury to destinations on the Corkscrew was being routed via Bishopstoke (the present day Eastleigh) and Brockenhurst rather than via Fordingbridge.

In reply, Scott reiterated that his company always worked traffic by the most expeditious, not necessarily by the shortest, route and that the Salisbury & Dorset had not

The level crossing at West Moors, probably taken around 1910. The characteristic crossing keeper's cottage, which still stands, is prominent in this view (see page 112). (Lens of Sutton Collection)

provided sufficient facilities for transfer at Alderbury Junction and West Moors.

Philip Dawson, Secretary to the Railway Clearing House, appeared as a witness for the Salisbury & Dorset, and confirmed that the latter's table of mileages was correct. He added that the company was entitled to a terminal charge of 9d per ton for coal traffic [4].

A week later, on 11th November, a public meeting in Bournemouth discussed proposals for a West Moors Railway which would branch off the Salisbury & Dorset about half a mile north of West Moors from a junction facing Salisbury, and head south to a new terminus on the north side of Branksome Wood Road, Bournemouth, near to its intersection with Richmond Hill Road. The scheme's promoters envisaged that their line could be worked jointly by the South Western and the Great Western, although the practicalities of such an arrangement do not appear to have been thought out.

When a Bill for the proposed line was deposited five days later, it was entitled "Bournemouth Direct Railway". The new line would have shortened the distance between Salisbury and Bournemouth by about six miles compared to the existing route to Bournemouth West via Wimborne and Poole, but even the Salisbury & Dorset Board seems to have been lukewarm, making a conditional offer of £500 towards the promoters' Parliamentary expenses. The LSWR would have resisted the Bill's provisions for the Great Western to be involved in operating the line. The Salisbury & Dorset depended on the South Western for its train services and timetabling so had to tread a diplomatic course. It could not invite the Great Western on to its line unilaterally because the GWR would still need running powers over the LSWR from Salisbury to Alderbury Junction. Given the inter-company politics of the time, the scheme was a non starter. Five years later the South Western would be promoting a Bill with a similar title for a new main line to approach Bournemouth from the east.

Soon afterwards, Scott complained to the Salisbury & Dorset that placards and advertisements it had placed around Bournemouth, Christchurch and Ringwood to promote the Fordingbridge route were "interference which could not be permitted". It appears that 200 placards had been produced at a cost of £2 10s. To its credit, the Salisbury company refused to be intimidated, and placed further adverts in the *Bournemouth Observer*, *Salisbury & Winchester Journal* and the *Morning Post*. For good measure, it again asked the South Western to provide a through service from Salisbury to Bournemouth West [5].

After some prompting, Scott replied that the suggested through service was "deemed inadvisable", but the Salisbury & Dorset was not going to give up easily. It wrote back quoting instances of passengers being dissuaded from travelling to Bournemouth via Salisbury, which Scott had repeatedly denied. His subsequent reply of 30th May 1879 claimed that his staff at Waterloo were not likely to act in an antagonistic spirit towards the Salisbury & Dorset because they were not aware of any separate interest. Perhaps the reality was that some LSWR officials were more partisan than their company intended them to be. Elsewhere in Wiltshire, the Berks & Hants Extension Railway, which ran from Devizes to Hungerford, and was worked by the GWR until the latter absorbed it in 1882, had raised similar complaints that some through tickets were being routed to maximise the distance over Great Western metals rather than to suit the wishes of passengers. People may criticise the privatised Train Operating Companies in Britain today, but their staff are required to offer impartial retailing. This was not the case in the 19th century, and it seems there were many front line officials then who did not regard the railway network as a unified system.

In dealing with the Salisbury & Dorset, the South Western's strategy was always to make selective concessions while firmly resisting demands that might increase the independence of the smaller company. The LSWR was often willing to assist with the improvement of facilities on the line itself, as it stood to gain 45 per cent of any increase in revenue. It was much less ready to make long distance travel via the Fordingbridge line more attractive, not only because passengers might take this route in preference to its own system, but also to discourage Great Western interest in through services.

The Salisbury & Dorset's sense of grievance had intensified in 1878 when the South Western opened a separate station at Salisbury for up trains on the opposite side of Fisherton Street from its originally one-sided station. Trains from Wimborne now ran into the down station, but passengers travelling in the Andover and London direction then had to walk along the station approach and into Fisherton Street to access the up station. This made connections risky if an incoming Salisbury & Dorset train was late, so a full ticket examination was introduced at Downton on three up trains that had tight connections. That station then had to telegraph Salisbury as to whether or not there were any passengers for destinations east of Salisbury, so that the up train could be held if necessary.

The walk between the down and up stations evidently deterred some of the local gentry from using the line to reach the capital, for in April 1880, the Salisbury & Dorset wrote to Scott highlighting the case of a regular traveller who went by road (presumably in his carriage) to Totton and thence to Waterloo. Complaints were also received from Earl Nelson, the Honourable Evelyn Ashley and a Mr Turnbull of Downton. The Salisbury & Dorset took the opportunity to highlight the inconvenience of changing stations at Salisbury as a stronger argument for through carriages between Bournemouth West or Wimborne and Waterloo but Scott was unmoved.

Turnbull, incidentally, tried to persuade the Salisbury & Dorset to erect a crane at his local station, claiming this would generate additional goods traffic. Scott went further, writing to the Salisbury & Dorset on Christmas Day (!) to suggest that Downton needed a small goods shed. Nothing further appears in the Minutes about either facility, and it may well be that the expense was too challenging for the

Salisbury company. Its gross revenue for the six months to 30th June 1880 was only £5,207, but according to Scott the goods shed alone might cost £1,000 [6].

Events were to move rapidly for the company in the next two years. In January 1881, Matthew Marsh died at the age of 70. Latterly he had lived at Bournemouth and had not attended Board meetings since 1878, with the exception of May to October 1880. He was succeeded as Chairman by Thomas Pain, by now an Alderman of Salisbury City Council. George Morrison, one of Downton's main landowners, became the new Vice-Chairman, and the vacant Directorship was filled by Henry Notman of London.

A milestone was reached on 1st September 1881, when the Salisbury & Dorset gained a Sunday service. Although confined to a morning train each way, both were direct between Bournemouth and Salisbury, the up train starting from the West station at 7am, and returning from Salisbury at 8.55. The up train offered connections from Salisbury to Southampton and London.

The Salisbury & Dorset had won an important battle, but the South Western still regarded the Fordingbridge route as a branch line. The new Sunday trains called at all stations and a request to Scott early in 1882 for further improvements received the rebuff that the South Western could recognise no right of the Salisbury & Dorset to call on it to run fast trains between London and Bournemouth via the latter company's line. Yet by March there were distinct signs of a warmer front from Waterloo. In reply to a letter from the Salisbury & Dorset concerning the arrangement of the platforms at Salisbury, Scott noted that through carriages were now operating between Bournemouth West and Salisbury on certain trains, adding that the LSWR was considering whether these could be attached at Salisbury to London bound trains [7].

The thaw in relations between the two companies had come about because the South Western had finally made up its mind to acquire the Salisbury & Dorset. As early as October 1879, the latter's Board had agreed to watch the progress of the LSWR (Various Powers) Bill, which contained provisions for the purchase of the Salisbury company. Then in March 1880 the Board had noted that clauses affecting it had been struck out at the Committee stage as no definite arrangements had been made. It was not until 31st May 1882 that Squarey and Notman met with LSWR Directors at Waterloo to discuss terms for a possible amalgamation.

The South Western may have concluded that an independent Salisbury & Dorset company could undermine its domination of Bournemouth traffic, but a greater threat was probably the Didcot, Newbury & Southampton Railway's plans for a Bournemouth extension via Lyndhurst and Burley, which many of the resort's businessmen and politicians were eagerly supporting. The Salisbury & Dorset still had a modest income, but its long term prospects were brighter with the steady growth of the resort. The South Western's own route between London and Bournemouth was via the Corkscrew, but it now decided to take over the Poole & Bournemouth Railway, with effect from 31st October 1882, with a view to linking it to the new main line it was planning from Brockenhurst via New Milton to Christchurch, whence the existing line to Bournemouth East was to be upgraded. This would take some years to materialise, and involved difficult engineering works at Sway and Christchurch; in the event it did not open until 6th March 1888. From an 1882 perspective the LSWR was acting in its own interest by proposing a merger that would give it the whole of the revenue from a promising line, and forestall any ideas the smaller company might have about closer ties with the Great Western.

On 3rd June the Salisbury & Dorset Board agreed to accept the South Western's terms, subject to the agreement of its shareholders. These were:

- £56,140 debenture stock exchanged for an equal amount of LSWR stock.
- £27,037 ordinary stock exchanged on the basis of £92 of LSWR for every £100 of Salisbury & Dorset stock, or £117 of LSWR 4 per cent preference stock.
- £141,010 ordinary shares exchanged on the basis of £52 10s of LSWR ordinary shares, or £65 of 4 per cent preference shares, or £70 cash, for every £100 of Salisbury & Dorset ordinary shares.
- £10,730 preference shares exchanged on the basis of £88 of LSWR for every £100 of Salisbury & Dorset, or £111 of LSWR preference stock.

60 per cent of the Salisbury & Dorset's capital was being traded for no more than 70 per cent of its nominal value. The South Western had driven a hard bargain.

After an Extraordinary Meeting of shareholders on 29th November, the acquisition was signed and sealed on 11th December. Thomas Pain attended no further meetings of the Salisbury & Dorset Board, although the Minutes make no reference to any resignation. The final recorded meeting on 19th March 1883 was chaired by Elias Squarey. The company, now 21 years old, was ending its existence in reasonable financial health. The Traffic Account had increased by £613 11s 8d over the previous year, and the net revenue account had a closing balance of £646 10s 10d. In the circumstances the Board proposed to pay a dividend of 3 per cent on the preference shares, and awarded the Secretary £250. After paying the legal expenses of amalgamation, and estimating the costs of administration since 1st January, there remained a balance of £315, which was offered to the Directors in recognition of their work in concluding the terms of the merger, which took effect from 20th August [8].

On the same day, Royal Assent was given to the Bournemouth Direct Railway Act (also known as the South Western (Bournemouth etc) Act. This bore no resemblance to the short-lived 1878 proposal of the same name. Instead, its main provisions were for a new main line from Brockenhurst via New Milton to Christchurch; upgrading of the RCBR thence to Holdenhurst, near Bournemouth East station; and a new main line from Holdenhurst to

THE SALISBURY & DORSET JUNCTION RAILWAY

Bournemouth West, involving a new central station and creating a faster route to the resort from London and Southampton. Also authorised was a chord from Corfe Mullen, west of Wimborne on the Somerset & Dorset, to Poole Junction & Broadstone, enabling that company's trains to reach Bournemouth West without reversal at Wimborne. This spur opened in 1885, and reduced the role of Wimborne as a junction. A West Moors Junction Railway, involving a short curve from the Salisbury & Dorset just north of West Moors to a junction facing Ringwood on the Old Road, was authorised in the same Act. This would have created an alternative route between Salisbury and Southampton. Yet it was never built, possibly because the same function was offered by the Andover & Redbridge line, which was being doubled and upgraded between 1883 and 1885.

Early Days of South Western Ownership

Three months after the line passed into South Western ownership, the train service remained meagre, consisting on weekdays of five down and four up passenger trains, one freight each way and one up mixed train. On Sundays there was still only a morning round trip. Three weekday trains each way were through Weymouth services including the 7.20am Weymouth–Salisbury mixed. The down goods left Salisbury at 8.15am, and shunted all the yards on the branch, being overtaken at Fordingbridge by the 9.55 Salisbury–Weymouth, and did not reach Wimborne until 12.13.

The weekday timetable still lacked through trains between Salisbury, Poole and Bournemouth, but connections were available at Wimborne. The 9.55 Salisbury connected well, so that a 17-minute wait at Wimborne gave arrivals of 11.30 at Poole and 11.43 at Bournemouth West. The final return service was via the 6.10pm Bournemouth West (6.22 Poole), a Somerset & Dorset Railway train to Wimborne, where there was a 12-minute connection into the 6.49 to Salisbury. Several of these connecting services were provided by the Somerset & Dorset, whose southern extremity and junction with the LSWR was then at Wimborne. The line from Broadstone (then still known as New Poole Junction) to Corfe Mullen, which would allow Somerset & Dorset trains to run directly between Bath and Bournemouth West without reversal at Wimborne, did not open until 1885. Thus in its independent years the Salisbury & Dorset had linked into a Dorset railway system that converged on Wimborne.

Despite the sparse train service on the Fordingbridge line, a day trip to London was perfectly feasible, with an earliest arrival at 10.35am by changing at Salisbury from the 5.35 Weymouth. The last connecting service from Waterloo was at 5pm, with a 9-minute connection at Salisbury. The Downton Station Master still had to telegraph Salisbury as to whether there were any passengers for destinations east of the city on the 5.35 Weymouth, 11.20am and 6.49pm Wimborne,

Downton station around 1910, looking towards West Moors. (Lens of Sutton Collection)

14

which all had tight connections into up London trains. Although the line was awkwardly placed for travel to or from Southampton, the last up train (6.49pm Wimborne) offered a 15-minute connection from the Southampton direction, provided that intending passengers on the 5.26 Bishopstoke–Weymouth notified the Guard to stop at West Moors to allow them to transfer.

The South Western no doubt had aspirations to exploit its newly acquired line which provided another gateway to the rapidly developing Bournemouth conurbation. A sensible course would have been to have upgraded the track by realigning the sharpest curves as the company was doing with its Andover & Redbridge line, so that longer trains could run comfortably at higher speeds. It chose instead to accelerate the service with little or no investment in the line or its rolling stock. This would soon prove to be a tragic error of judgment.

Disaster at Downton

The safety of rail travel had become a subject of heightened concern amongst the public and the Board of Trade since the Tay Bridge disaster of December 1879. In an effort to restore the reputation of railway transport, the BoT's accident statistics emphasised that, as a proportion of rail passenger journeys, the number of persons killed on Britain's railways from causes beyond their own control was remarkably small. In 1879, the incidence had been one fatality per 7.5 million journeys. The next four years produced a steady improvement, and even when the trend reversed in 1884, accidental deaths to rail passengers represented only one fatality per 22.4 million journeys [9].

Passenger casualties on Britain's railways rose from 11 killed and 662 injured in 1883 to 31 and 864 respectively in 1884. Unhappily for the South Western, it accounted for a quarter of the rise in fatalities, but more significantly its reputation was seriously damaged by one accident which exposed serious systemic weaknesses in the company's management and operations. This was at Downton on 3rd June 1884, its third derailment in nine months. On that fateful day, the 4.33pm Salisbury–Weymouth consisted of two tender locos and six four-wheeled carriages, plus two brake vans. The formation had been strengthened because it was a Tuesday, Salisbury market day, and was marshalled as follows: brake van, two third class, two first, a second and another third class vehicle, brake van. All the rolling stock had been built between 1860 and 1865. The pilot engine, No 113 *Stour*, was an 0-6-0 of the Lion class built at Nine Elms in 1869, while the train engine was No 294, a 2-4-0 of the Vesuvius class, designed by Beattie for express passenger work and built in 1873, also at Nine Elms. The double heading was to enable *Stour* to work a goods train back from

The train engine involved in the Downton disaster, Vesuvius class 2-4-0 No 294, seen here in the engine shed at Bournemouth Central in July 1896. It is carrying the headcode for trains between Dorchester and Bournemouth Central, although coincidentally, this code was later used by Salisbury and Bournemouth West trains. (BL Jackson Collection)

Verwood. The train was described as "moderately well loaded". Among the regular passengers was Lilian Chandler, 14, daughter of the Fordingbridge Station Master, returning from Montague House, an independent school in the city. Charles Chandler had previously been SM at Downton [10].

That Tuesday was the day after the Whitsun Bank Holiday, and there was congestion in the station, with two other trains booked to depart within two minutes of the Weymouth service. After being shunted it was at least five minutes late starting, and some passengers were perturbed by the speed of its departure and progress to Downton. Mr E Hillier, a Salisbury bookseller, later described the vibration through the cutting north of Downton tunnel as so great that he was surprised the chalk was not shaken down. He was sitting next to Thomas Sutton who, on arrival at Downton station, spoke to Station Master John Lever about the speed of the train. This might just have presented a last chance to avert what followed, but unfortunately Mr Lever did not realise that Mr Sutton was alarmed.

A mile and a quarter south of Downton, the train was running on a falling gradient of 1 in 78 on the approach to the pile bridge over the Avon. The track across the bridge was straight, although within a reverse curve. Driver Robert Miles, on the train engine, noticed it was gathering speed and the leading brake van was jumping. He shut off steam and then moved to the fireman's side to discover that the train had detached from the engine and had disappeared behind a cloud of dust. When the dust cleared, Driver Thomas Butler on the pilot loco saw the carriages fall off a low embankment opposite Downton Agricultural College. Both drivers brought their engines to a stand about 30 or 40 yards short of South Charford level crossing. Driver Miles, whose engine was off the rails, ran to the scene of the accident while Driver Butler uncoupled *Stour* and drove it to Breamore to raise the alarm.

All the carriages came to a halt in marshy ground beneath the embankment. Some had their roofs or their sides crushed in. One lost all its bodywork apart from the floor. The descent of one of the rear carriages was halted by a tree, which a Mr Withers, a Fordingbridge wine merchant, later claimed had saved his life. Unluckily, another carriage was upturned and partially embedded in a ditch about three feet deep and it was in this vehicle that three passengers died from drowning. Another died as a result of concussion and 41 were injured, *The Times* remarking that it was little short of a miracle that so few lives were lost.

The death toll probably would have been greater had it not been for the prompt reaction of the train crew and others who saw the accident happen. Gatekeeper William Witts at North Charford level crossing, just north of the pile bridge, had thought something might be amiss when he noticed that the carriages were swaying and apparently running into one another before leaving the rails. He rushed to the scene as did James Porton, a shepherd employed by the College, who had seen the derailment from a nearby field. He found his brother in the train and helped him get out. At North Charford, 14-year-old Emily Herridge had observed the rocking of the carriages, and on hearing a great crash ran to a farm where she alerted Benjamin Croon, a dairyman working for the College. He dashed to the scene and helped some passengers off the train. Before long College staff and students, led by the principal, Professor John Wrightson, were helping to extricate the wounded from the wreckage.

Professor Wrightson had founded Downton Agricultural College only four years earlier. He was a strong exponent of the scientific approach to farming, and had resigned from his previous post at the Royal Agricultural College, Cirencester because of that institution's lack of interest in agricultural science. Ironically, Downton College was closed after many universities and colleges established similar courses to the ones it had pioneered.

In an age when there were no motor ambulances and the fastest means of conveyance to hospital were by train, horse-drawn vehicle, or a combination of the two, some of those injured at Downton may well have owed their lives to the proximity of the College and first aid at or near the scene. This way of dealing with casualties was perhaps more in tune with present day thinking about stabilising their condition before removal to hospital, than with the mid-20th century philosophy of the fastest possible hospitalisation. The large rescue force from the College and the early arrival by rail of local surgeons, almost certainly reduced the severity of shock, which is recognised as a major factor in traumatic death. On the other hand, the fact that three of the four deaths in the accident were from drowning may reflect less

The aftermath of the Downton disaster as depicted in the "Illustrated London News" of 14th June 1884.

advanced knowledge of emergency resuscitation, or it might simply be that these victims had been immersed for too long.

Passengers who gave evidence to the inquest at Breamore three days later all described their alarm at the speed and oscillation of the train after it left Downton station. Their statements suggest that the actual derailment was not unexpected in the last few minutes before it occurred. This may have sharpened the presence of mind of those who were able to get themselves and others out of the wrecked train. One was Charles Coward who later described how he had found himself up to his neck in water but had managed to free Miss Watson, daughter of the Vicar of Gussage All Saints. He had not realised at the time that he had a cut head and two broken ribs, attributing this to the excitement of the accident. Others thrown into the water included James Coventry, of Burgate House, who extricated a Mrs Lush, although she died in his arms, and William Neave, son of the Fordingbridge cereal miller, who had to change his clothes at the College. William had a very eventful week, for the following day he and his brother were thrown out of their coach when the horse shied. The Neave brothers escaped injury, although the coachman broke both arms [11].

When Driver Butler reached Breamore, he got the station to telegraph to Salisbury, Fordingbridge and Wimborne for help. Salisbury Station Master Samuel Davis and his two daughters boarded a special train to Downton, conveying surgeons and all the staff he could muster. This returned with the more seriously injured who would be taken on stretchers to the Infirmary. A large crowd, estimated at over 500, gathered outside Salisbury station to await this train and news of friends or relations who might have been on the 4.33. Meanwhile, Driver Butler had driven *Stour* on to Fordingbridge to collect Station Master Chandler and two surgeons. Mr Chandler arrived to see the lifeless body of his daughter yet "displayed great fortitude and bravery" according to *The Times*. She had drowned in the upturned coach, along with Mrs Emily Corbin, wife of a Ringwood bird stuffer, and Mrs Mary Lush of Godshill. George Waters junior, 33, of Toyd Farm, near Rockbourne, was considered to have died almost instantly from head injuries after being thrown out of a window.

A gang of 40 to 50 men worked through the night to repair about a quarter of a mile of damaged track. The branch reopened as a through route early in the morning, and the wreckage was removed from the ditch and meadow at intervals between service trains by a steam crane sent from Nine Elms, working under the direction of Mr F Higgins, Locomotive Superintendent. Also on site were Mr EW Verrinder, Traffic Superintendent at Waterloo; Mr W Jacomb, Chief Engineer of the company; Jesse Dradge, District Engineer based at Southampton; and Henry Colson, Permanent Way Superintendent based at Ringwood. All the fragments of rolling stock that could be found were transported to Salisbury, but this drew criticism at the Breamore inquest that vital evidence concerning the cause of the derailment might have been lost. Restoration of the line also attracted sightseers from far and wide, according to newspaper reports.

Other senior officers of the LSWR arriving at Downton on the Wednesday included William Adams, Locomotive Superintendent; Wyndham Portal, Deputy Chairman; and Lieutenant Colonel Campbell, a Director. The two last mentioned visited the College to convey their thanks for the rescue efforts and to visit survivors who were treated there. Benjamin Croon, the dairyman, took two others from Dorchester to his house. Some of the walking wounded had gone home by a later train, among them a Mrs Brufford, wife of a Somerset & Dorset engine driver based at Wimborne. Those detained in Salisbury Infirmary were visited by Mr Passmore Edwards, one of the city's two MPs, and who gave the hospital 50 guineas in recognition of its humane assistance. Queen Victoria sent a telegram from Balmoral to the LSWR Directors asking how the patients were progressing.

The first inquest was held in the lecture hall of the Agricultural College on the Wednesday because the Coroner, Mr J Hannen, wanted the earliest possible release of the bodies for burial. After formal identification of the dead, the proceedings were adjourned to the Bat & Ball Inn, Breamore, on Friday 6th June to hear witness statements. A separate inquest was convened at Salisbury on 11th June relating to Matthew Dent, a hotel keeper from Bournemouth, who had died in the Infirmary from his injuries the day after the accident.

At the start of the Breamore inquest, the LSWR's barrister, Mr Noble, said it was the company's most earnest desire to provide any information which would assist the Coroner and jury in reaching conclusions as to the cause of the tragedy. In view of the imminent inquiry to be held by the Board of Trade, he said he thought it hardly necessary for the inquest to examine any evidence beyond that from the operating staff in charge of the train.

In their evidence the front line staff all denied that the train was being driven above its normal speed of about 35 mph during the minutes before the accident. This was in contrast to the testimony of passengers, who were convinced that the train had been travelling faster than usual, some claiming that the crew had been trying to make up time. Opinion on this question from bystanders was divided and probably inconclusive, as they may have seen the train for less than a minute before it derailed. After some survivors had hinted that the affected stretch of line was dangerous, witnesses from the Permanent Way staff were at pains to point out that the track had been well maintained and regularly inspected. Albert Nichols, a ganger living at Charford, testified that the portion of line damaged by the derailment had been reballasted with gravel the previous day and was in perfect order just prior to the accident.

One of the final witnesses called was William Adams. He explained to the jury the nature of a flaw found in the coupling between the front leading brake van and the leading carriage. He maintained that the breaking of this coupling had caused the train to leave the rails. After all witnesses had given evidence, the Coroner adjourned the inquest to 4th July so that it could reach its verdict after the BoT inquiry had taken place.

Funerals, Verdicts and a Damning Conclusion

At least two of the victims were buried on Saturday 7th June. Lilian Chandler was laid to rest at Fordingbridge Parish Church in a grave decked with many wreaths and crosses as well as a floral tribute from the Headmistress, teachers and fellow pupils of her school. Mourners included Mr Edwards, Station Master at Wimborne, and Mr Holliday, District Superintendent at Dorchester.

George Waters, who had served as a volunteer in the Royal Wiltshire Yeomanry Cavalry, was buried with military honours at Martin church. The Salisbury troop of the regiment set out from the city shortly before midday, and reached Toyd Farm by 1pm. A procession was formed for the 1½-mile journey to the service. At its head were the firing party, followed by the band and then the hearse. The coffin was draped with a Union Jack, and on it were placed his busby, caribine and sword. Next came two troopers attending his horse, which carried Yeomanry saddlery, sheepskin and military boots with spurs reversed, and finally came the mourning coach and carriages.

The cortege departed to the strains of the funeral march, but as it passed over Martin Down, a thunderstorm broke out with flashes of lightning. Despite the appalling weather, a crowd estimated at three to four hundred was waiting at the church, reflecting the high local regard for Mr Waters, who had managed the farm for his crippled father. Three volleys were fired over the grave.

On the Sunday prayers were said for the victims in churches across Salisbury, and nearly 100 railway employees attended the service at Fisherton Church, close to the station.

On 11th June the inquest into the death of Matthew Dent opened at Salisbury. A house surgeon from the Infirmary confirmed that Mr Dent had died from a punctured lung caused by the penetration of a broken rib. The solicitor acting for his family claimed that they had not received a telegram advising he was in hospital until the morning after the accident. Moreover, they had been led to believe his injuries were not life-threatening because the message had read, "Brother injured in accident. Will be home tomorrow if possible."

Station Master Davis replied that he had tried to get postal telegrams to all the families of those detained in the Infirmary, but in some cases the best he could do was to telegraph Wimborne station, and ask for the message to be conveyed by train. It was possible that the message concerning Mr Dent had come too late in the evening to catch the post. As to the wording, some of the injured had told him they did not want their relatives to become too agitated. Mr Davis suggested that the messenger may have mistaken news of a less seriously hurt person for that of Mr Dent. My impression, from reading early reports of the accident that listed his injuries as a cut to the face and head, is that surgeons may have failed to discover the broken rib until it was too late. Some reports had named a Mr RC Allen of Poole as the most seriously hurt passenger, the *Wareham & Isle of Purbeck Advertiser* describing him as "seriously injured, hand and chest". It may be that the reporters or even the hospital had initially transposed details of Mr Dent's injuries with those of Mr Allen.

Proceedings were adjourned until 18th June, when the inquest heard the testimonies of many of the same witnesses who had given evidence at Breamore. Similar questions were asked about the speed of the train and the condition of the track. William Adams stated that trains could run safely over the line at 40 or 50 miles an hour, provided the track was in good order. He again asserted that the accident was caused by the breaking of a coupling between the front brake van and the leading carriage. The jury decided otherwise, and after returning a verdict of accidental death on Mr Dent, denounced the operation and maintenance of the line between Downton and Breamore, claiming it to be "in a very weak and faulty condition" and unfit for the passage of a train at the speed at which the jurors believed it had been travelling. In their view the breaking of the coupling had been a result of the derailment, not the cause of it as claimed by Mr Adams. Also condemned was the practice of making up time between stations.

The inquest at Breamore for the other four victims had been adjourned until 4th July pending the completion of the Board of Trade inquiry. This third Breamore inquest concluded that the accident had been due to the train running at excessive speed over a line which it claimed was in a very unsatisfactory condition. The jury also castigated the decision to remove the debris from and around the line at a very early stage, adding that it wished to express publicly and emphatically its view that railway companies should be compelled to leave the site of any injurious accident undisturbed until a Board of Trade inspection had been carried out.

Colonel JH Rich, RE of the Board of Trade had opened the BoT's inquiry into the disaster on 9th June, first visiting the site and then examining the wreck at Salisbury. He appears not to have been too impressed with the traincrews' evidence. For instance, Richard Scadding, fireman of the train engine, described the train as gathering speed over the pile bridge. The Colonel interposed that he thought it strange that a train should be travelling faster on a level stretch of the route than on the preceding downward gradient. In his subsequent report he also criticised the traincrews for claiming they had noticed nothing abnormal until the train had reached the river bridge. This, he pointed out, had been 200 yards beyond where the first disturbance of sleepers had occurred.

The inquiry also examined the question of whether the line had been properly maintained. Inspector Colson testified that the line between Downton and Breamore had been relaid, resleepered and reballasted about three weeks prior to the accident. He had examined the work on 29th May and found the ballast to be at a good level. He had then instructed the ganger to cover the formation outside the rails with chalk to prevent the ballast from spreading.

The proceedings continued in London and the report was published on 9th August. By this time, the LSWR Board may have had been bracing itself for a highly critical report as the two inquests had rejected the company's version of events, and concurred with local opinion. It may not have been prepared for the report's uncompromising description of what it saw as grave corporate dereliction of duty.

The Colonel rejected Adams' theory that the train had left the rails because of a broken coupling, and said that he had no hesitation in deciding that the derailment was due to excessive speed over weak permanent way. A train of two locomotives and eight short-wheelbase carriages could not, he said, run steadily at speed over such a lightly-laid, steeply-graded and curvaceous line. He added that he was in no doubt that the force and weight of the engines had initially displaced the rails to derail the train.

Colonel Rich described the line from Downton towards Breamore as falling on a gradient of 1 in 78 for about a mile. It was then level from the pile bridge across the Avon for about ¼ mile before descending at 1 in 172 for a further half mile. The line curved south from the foot of the 1 in 78 incline on a radius of 40 chains, then was straight for 100 yards across the bridge. It then turned north on a curve which, according to the Parliamentary papers sent to the BoT at the time the line opened, was of 45 chains radius. However, he found the curve to be of only 30 chains radius at the point of derailment.

The damaged sleepers had all been removed by the time of his site visit, but a sketch made by a survivor immediately after the accident and forwarded to the inquiry by the Rev TH Bunbury gave what the Colonel considered to be a very good indication of the course of the train and, together with the evidence of both LSWR and independent witnesses, "pointed pretty clearly to what caused the disaster".

He found the time of departure from Salisbury to have been 4.39, six minutes late, and the passing time at Milford Junction 4.41. Allowing for differences between clocks, a half minute margin of error and slight mistakes by people who had observed the time, he believed that the train had regained at least two minutes in running to Downton station. From this he calculated that it must have been travelling at a speed of 43 to 44 mph, yet the company's timetables showed that the average speed on this section should have been about 35 mph. Given that the route was more favourable for fast running south, rather than north, of Downton, he concluded that the speed of the train could not have been less than 40 mph at the time of the accident.

Colonel Rich noted that the track, although of light construction, had been well maintained. "It had been thoroughly overhauled, all defective sleepers removed and the ballasting had been completed about three weeks before the accident." He discounted the suggestion that defective keys had caused the rails to spread, noting that all loose or worn keys had been made good when the track was overhauled. The ganger (Mr Nichols) had walked the stretch of line two and a half hours before the derailment, as did the Assistant District Engineer and the Inspector (Mr Colson) five days earlier.

"I consider", wrote the Colonel, "that the line was in as good running order as it was possible to maintain a railway of this class." This statement led on to the heart of the matter: the line had not been fit for fast or heavy trains. The rails, when first laid down, had weighed about 70 lbs per yard, were joined with fishplates, and fixed by wooden keys in cast iron chairs weighing 22¼ lbs each. Yet when the line had been completed in 1866, the Salisbury & Dorset company had advised the BoT that the chairs weighed 24 lbs each! Many of the rails had been turned and in his view such lightly laid track was not strong enough to carry trains safely at 35 mph, particularly in view of the numerous curves and steep gradients. Drivers would frequently have to attain speeds of 45 mph or more down the inclines to keep to the company's schedules. He pointed out that a line with so light a permanent way would not now be allowed to open for ordinary passenger traffic.

His comments imply that the Salisbury & Dorset may have deceived the BoT in its effort to get the line authorised and that the South Western had adopted or continued schedules aimed at maximising connections or rolling stock utilisation at the expense of safety. In fairness this policy had probably been in response to a steady stream of complaints from the Salisbury & Dorset and its users for more convenient services. This might not have mattered if higher grade rolling stock with longer wheelbases had been deployed on the line.

The report certainly emphasised that much of the company's rolling stock, including that used on the Fordingbridge line, was singularly ill-suited to fast running, being of old and poor design. Colonel Rich drew attention to another derailment on the LSWR on 15th January of the same year at Fort Brockhurst on the Gosport branch. This too had been caused by inferior rolling stock being driven too fast over weak permanent way. He also referred to numerous complaints received about passengers on the LSWR being subject to violent shaking inside the carriages. He believed bad driving, poor stock and inefficient coupling to be the root causes.

The Colonel accepted that not all of a Railway company's lines and stock would be of high grade but said it was unacceptable that passengers should be conveyed in inferior stock at speeds that made their journeys unpleasant and dangerous. He therefore urged the South Western to introduce a system whereby all its routes, locomotives, stock, trains and drivers would be classified. The need for some kind of classification had been demonstrated by the trials he had carried out with the two locomotives involved in the Downton accident. Whilst *Stour*, the pilot engine, had been found to run steadily, the train engine was unsteady, steamed poorly, and in his view, was quite unfit to work a train at the speed it was timed to run. He noted that had the train been fitted with an efficient continuous brake, this might have checked the speed and oscillation of the train.

Col Rich found evidence of confusion as to the mode of

operating the line. In 1874, to comply with the 1873 Regulation of Railways Act, the South Western had informed the BoT that as at 31st December 1873, the Salisbury–West Moors line was worked by "electric telegraph, in addition to the train staff system", but not by either Absolute Block or Permissive Block. A year later, the return showed the line as worked by the Absolute Block system. He also censured the practice of amending crossing places for trains by the use of telegraphic messages. He regarded this as unsafe, and considered that if the line had been worked by train staff, the pilot loco could have worked light engine to Verwood instead of being attached to the passenger train. In his view a second engine had been both unnecessary and a source of danger.

The report was forwarded to the Secretary of the LSWR by Mr HG Calcraft, Secretary of the Board of Trade. His covering letter said the BoT wished the Directors to pay very serious and special attention to Col Rich's observations about the general condition of the LSWR and its rolling stock. Referring to the three recent derailments on the LSWR and the numerous complaints about violent shaking of passengers, Mr Calcraft said the Board supported the Inspector's conclusion that these facts left no doubt about the need for reform in the management and improvement in the operation of the railway. He added that the BoT would particularly draw the Directors' attention to the suggestion that Drivers, stock and various parts of the system be classified. The BoT would be glad, he said, to receive early confirmation that the Directors had given the necessary instructions for the reforms in the conduct of their system which would ensure the level of safety which the travelling public had every right to expect.

Interestingly, the South Western received less hostility from the local press than might have been expected after publication of Col Rich's report. Whereas *The Times* commented that, "it revolts one to think that under the state of things which Colonel Rich denounces as existing on the South Western Line accidents may be looked for as the natural evolution of effect from cause", the *Salisbury & Winchester Journal* editorial was more measured. It considered that the LSWR was being singled out unfairly when the same bad practices might be widespread on other railways [12]. *The Times* also published (and the Salisbury paper reported) a letter from John Graham, who considered that the report's suggestion that engine drivers be classified did less than justice to their profession. He argued that they had all been carefully selected and that classification was simply a means of keeping down wages.

It is hard not to feel some sympathy for the drivers implicitly criticised in the report. Insofar as they were trying to keep to tight schedules, they were doing only what was expected of them. Driver Miles was asked at the first Breamore inquest whether he had ever been reprimanded for faulty driving. He replied he had not but had twice been rewarded for meritorious conduct; in one instance he had reported bad track on the Alderbury–Downton section, which was later rectified [13]. He had told the inquest on Mr Dent that drivers were not allowed to make up time by going faster downhill, but that in fact, some had been fined for not regaining time [14].

The South Western Directors rightly took the greatest share of the blame for the accident, and may have become indifferent to criticism of the travelling experience on their secondary services. Tales of luggage flying off racks onto passengers on lines such as the Andover & Redbridge had been shrugged off; indeed one LSWR Director is believed to have remarked that some of the curves on the A&R (prior to its realignment and upgrading in 1883-5) were more like angles! [15] Sudden tragedy on a branch line put things in a different light. The South Western now realised it had to try and restore public confidence in the safety of its network and that of the Salisbury–West Moors line in particular. Some lines such as the A&R were already in the process of being upgraded, in this case to create a through route between Southampton and the Midlands via the Midland & South Western Junction Railway. For lines such as the Salisbury & Dorset, where no such investment was in prospect, the immediate future had to be one in which speed and journey opportunities were curtailed in the interests of safety.

Perhaps the only aspect of the tragedy to have generated any pride and satisfaction was the presentation of a solid silver goblet by the LSWR Directors to a deputation from Downton College in the Board Room at Waterloo station in late July. The College party consisted of its President (the Hon. D. Lascelles), Professor Wrightson and two students. Mr RH Dutton, the South Western's Chairman, made a complimentary address in which he described the rescue efforts of students and all others connected with the College as like the silver lining to a dark cloud. He then presented the two-handled goblet, shaped like an urn, on which was inscribed, "To the President, Professors and students of the Agricultural College, Downton, by the London & South Western Railway company, in recognition of the assistance rendered by them on 3rd June 1884." [16]

References
1. Salisbury & Dorset Junction Railway Board Minutes, 4.1.1878.
2. ibid, 1.3.1878.
3. ibid, 29.3, 28.6 and 25.10.1878.
4. *The Times*, 5.11.1878.
5. Board Minutes, 20.12.1878, 31.1 and 28.3.1879.
6. ibid, 31.1.1881.
7. ibid, 24.2 and 31.3.1882.
8. *The Times*, 19.3.1883.
9. PRO ref RAIL 1057/73.
10. Shown in Kelly's Wiltshire Directory, 1875 and 1880.
11. *Salisbury & Winchester Journal*, 7.6.1884.
12. ibid, 16.8.1884.
13. ibid, 14.6.1884.
14. *Southern Times*, 21.6.1884.
15. N Bray, *Andover to Redbridge – The Sprat & Winkle Line*, Kestrel Railway Books, 2004.
16. *Bournemouth Visitor Directory*, 2.8.1884.

Chapter 3

The South Western Makes Amends

By September 1884, a 25 mph speed limit was in force between Alderbury Junction and West Moors as part of a revised timetable involving greatly inflated schedules, notably on the first up train. This now started 40 minutes earlier from Weymouth at 4.55am and was allowed 46 minutes between Fordingbridge and Salisbury compared with 35 at the time of the accident. The 4.33pm Salisbury now started at 4.40 and its schedule to Fordingbridge increased from 29 to 43 minutes. Between Downton and Breamore, the section where the accident had occurred, the schedules of down trains were slackened from six or seven to 10 minutes. The 9.55 Salisbury–Weymouth was retimed to start at 9.58 with an additional 28 minutes running time.

Predictably, some connections were broken as a result of slower timings on the Salisbury & Dorset. The 9.58 Salisbury was now due into Wimborne at 11.21, just missing the 11.15 to Bournemouth West, resulting in a wait until 12.15. There was a similar situation with the final down train, 7.20pm Salisbury, which narrowly missed the 8.28 Wimborne, so that travellers did not reach Bournemouth until around 10pm. A quirk of the retimings was that the 4.40pm Salisbury now offered a good connection to Poole and Bournemouth at New Poole Junction. Hitherto, this had not been feasible because trains to Bournemouth West normally preceded Salisbury–Weymouth services away from Wimborne.

There remained some unfinished legal business from the accident. In July 1885, the Western Circuit tried the case of Waters v the LSWR at Salisbury Assizes. George Waters senior, 66, whose son had died in the disaster, was disabled and very infirm. He had relied on his son to manage the remote 1,300 acre Toyd Farm estate, about 5 miles north west of Fordingbridge. The court heard that George junior, a bachelor, had lived with his father and received no regular wages but had made an independent living from hiring out steam ploughs. Unfortunately he had died intestate. The father had received £1,000 from an insurance policy on his son's life, but said he was out of pocket after meeting his son's liabilities, partly because the steam ploughs had been sold at a loss.

Mr Charles, QC, for the South Western, said the company accepted that young Mr Waters had died because of its negligence, but denied any liability to pay even nominal compensation for any consequential losses as Mr Waters senior had not suffered any financial loss directly arising from his son's death. The jury decided otherwise and damages of £1,000 were awarded to the father, although Mr Justice Field granted a stay of execution without expressing an opinion on the verdict [1].

No mishap on the LSWR featured in the Board of Trade's Accident Reports for 1885. Perhaps the severity of Col Rich's remarks had made an impression on other railway companies also, for in that year the proportion of passenger deaths in rail accidents fell to 1 in 116 million journeys.

By January 1886, the 25 mph speed restrictions on the Fordingbridge line no longer appeared in the service timetable. Schedules had tightened, although in most cases not back to pre-accident timings. All passenger trains were now allowed eight minutes between Downton to Breamore, except for the 6.43pm Wimborne, which was expected to cover this section in seven. A more significant change was the reduction in through Weymouth trains from three to two each way, including the 7.20am Weymouth mixed train.

There was still a warning about excessive speeds in the May 1887 service timetable, which advised that "time must not be made up running down inclines". Mixed train working over the line had now ceased, although it recurred by 1893 on Tuesdays because of increasing freight traffic. The 1887 weekday service now comprised one goods and five passenger trains each way. The down freight started from Salisbury at 8.10am, reaching Wimborne at 12.13, whence it returned at 4.25pm. All goods yards on the branch were served in both directions, as was Milford Goods station, on the south eastern outskirts of the city, and served by a spur from Milford Junction between Salisbury Tunnel Junction and Alderbury Junction. Dwell times at stations were much shorter than in the 20th century, which suggests that local freight business was nowhere near its eventual peak. The Sunday passenger service now involved a morning down train and an evening return, instead of a morning round trip. This created an excellent connection into the 7.5pm Yeovil–Waterloo, useful for people returning to the capital after a weekend in the New Forest. Another significant change was that the final down weekday train, 7.15pm Salisbury, now ran through to Bournemouth West. Two trains each way continued to run between Salisbury and Weymouth.

Working of the Line by Train Tablet

The South Western lost little time in introducing the Train Tablet mode of working the line, initially between Alderbury Junction and Fordingbridge; the whole line was under this system by March 1885. It may well be that the Board of Trade and the South Western had decided to make the Fordingbridge line an early candidate for the new method in order to restore confidence in the route and the company.

Under this system, the normal position of semaphore signals was "on" and they were lowered only to admit a train or light engine into a section, after which they would be restored to danger until the signal box had received and acknowledged a bell or gong signal from the box to its rear, and the section ahead was clear. The bell in each box was used to send and acknowledge messages concerning up trains to Salisbury, whilst the gong was used to communicate the progress of down trains towards West Moors.

When a train or engine arrived at a station, the signalman had to send the arrival signal (three beats on the bell or gong) to the box to its rear. He then had to restore the

London & South Western Railway.

INSTRUCTION No. 126, 1885

SALISBURY AND DORSET LINE.

Revised Instructions to Station Masters, Inspectors, Enginemen, Guards, Signalmen and all concerned

AS TO

WORKING THIS SINGLE LINE THROUGHOUT

BY

TRAIN TABLET.

In substitution for the present Single Line System.

The Tablet Stations will be as follows:—
Alderbury Junction.
Downton.
Breamore.
Fordingbridge.
Verwood.
West Moors.

On MONDAY, 23rd March, at 12.0 noon, the second portion, viz.: from Fordingbridge to West Moors inclusive will be opened, which will complete the whole Single Line to be worked by the Train Tablet.

1. A Train Tablet must be carried with each Train and Light Engine, and no Train or Light Engine must be permitted to leave any Tablet Station unless the Engine Driver is in possession of the Tablet for that portion of the line over which it is about to travel.

2. Each Tablet has engraved or marked on it the name of the Tablet Station at each end of the Section to which it applies.

NOTE.—When a Train Tablet has been taken out of the Tablet Instrument it cannot be put back again, but must be taken forward to the other end of the Section. Therefore care must be exercised before asking permission to take a Tablet from the Instrument, to be certain that the Train or Light Engine about to proceed to the other end of the Section is ready to do so the moment the Tablet is handed to the Driver, and that everything is all right for proceeding on the journey at once.

3. When a Train or Light Engine arrives at a Station, and the Station Master or Signalman has received the Train Tablet, he must see that the **whole** of the Train is clear of the section, and then deposit the Tablet in the cylinder of the Electric Instrument, **lettered side downwards**.

4. When a Train is assisted by a second Engine, that Engine must be coupled in front, and the Driver of it must carry the Train Tablet.

5. No Engine Driver with a Train or Light Engine must leave a Station until he has received the proper Train Tablet, or has seen it in the possession of the Driver of the Engine assisting him, for that Section of the Line over which he is about to travel. After receiving the Tablet he must not start until the proper out-door Signals have

[TURN OVER.

2

TRAIN TABLET INSTRUCTIONS—(continued).

been exhibited, nor until the Signal has also been given by the Guard of the Train. He must keep the Train Tablet under his own charge (except as explained in Rule 7) until he reaches the end of the Section, when he must give it up to the Station Master or Signalman.

NOTE.—Engine Drivers must be extremely careful not to take the Train Tablet beyond the Station at which it ought to be left.

6. An Engine Driver will render himself liable to dismissal if he leaves a Tablet Station without the Train Tablet, or without seeing that the Driver of an Engine assisting him has the Train Tablet in his possession, for the Section over which he is about to run.

7. In the event of an Engine becoming disabled between two Tablet Stations, the Fireman must take the Tablet to the Station from which assistance is most likely to be obtained, and inform the Station Master of such Station, and hand over the Tablet to the Station Master, who will communicate with Mr. Chandler, Fordingbridge, and await his instructions.

8. Should the accident be of such a nature as to obstruct the Line, and the traffic is likely to be stopped for any considerable time, special arrangements must be made for working the Trains to and from the Tablet Station on each side of the point of obstruction. See General Instructions at foot.

The Train Tablet must be retained to work Trains or Light Engines between the point of obstruction and the Station or Signal Box from which the Train Tablet was issued.

Ballast Trains.

9. The Driver of a Ballast Train that has to do work on the Line must be told when receiving the Tablet to which end of the Section it is to be taken, and at what hour it is to be there, in order to clear the Line for the next Train.

Obstruction in Working of Single Line Section in consequence of Tablet Instrument getting Locked.

10. In the event of the Signalman in charge of the Signals overturning the lower disc, thus preventing the Train Tablet being released, he must immediately telegraph to the Signalman in charge of the instrument at the other end of the Section to that effect, who must, immediately on receipt of such information, ask authority to get a Tablet relieved. When the Train Tablet is released it must be forwarded without delay to the other end of the Section (where the instrument is locked) by the most expeditious means possible, either by Train, Engine, or Special Messenger, as will under the circumstances (taking into account the importance and time of running of the Trains that are likely to be affected by the interruption) cause the least possible delay to the most important traffic, when by the placing of the Train Tablet into the cylinder, the locked instrument will again be put into working order.

General Instructions.

11. In the event of a defect in the instrument in the Signal Box by which a Tablet cannot be obtained, the failure of an Engine, or from any other cause interfering with the regular working, a telegram must immediately be sent to **Mr. Chandler**, of **Fordingbridge Station**, who will give instructions for the working of the traffic in accordance with the rules laid down at page 210 of the Rule Book.

Should the defect or obstruction be at Alderbury Junction, a telegram must also be sent by the Signalman to Mr. Lever, Downton Station, who will communicate with Mr. Chandler and await his instructions.

Salisbury and Dorset Line.

Referring to the Note at the top of page 51 of Service Time Table, this Line is now to be considered a Double Line between Salisbury and Alderbury Junction.

WATERLOO BRIDGE STATION,
March 2nd, 1885.

BY ORDER.

LONDON & SOUTH WESTERN RAILWAY.

INSTRUCTION No. 13, 1887.

SALISBURY AND DORSET LINE.

Instructions to Station Masters, Signalmen and all concerned,

AS TO THE

WORKING OF THIS LINE

BY

PILOTMAN

When means of communication by speaking telegraph with Mr. Chandler, of Fordingbridge Station, have failed, and when the Train Tablet System has broken down.

In the event of the Tablet working between any two Tablet Stations being entirely destroyed, and speaking telegraph means of communication with Mr. Chandler is also interrupted, the working of the traffic over the Section must at once be arranged for by means of a Pilotman, by the Station Master or other responsible official, who must fill up three of the printed forms for establishing Pilot working, and deliver one of these to the Signalman, or person in charge of the fixed Signals at the Station; the other two must be given to the Pilotman, and the Pilotman, when satisfied that the Signalman, or person in charge of the Signals, has received the printed form duly filled up, and that he understands that no Train or Light Engine is to be allowed on to the Section until the Pilotman returns, must walk along the Railway to the other end of the Section, or by conveyance, if obtainable, and if the Section is clear, must deliver one of the forms to the Signalman, or person in charge of the Signals there, retaining the other for himself. The Signalman at each end of the Section must know the man appointed as Pilotman, and must countersign the form for Pilot working held by him, the form held by each Signalman being in like manner countersigned by the Pilotman. Afterwards Trains and Light Engines may be allowed to go on into the Section in accordance with the following regulation.

The Pilotman must, when practicable, accompany every Train or Light Engine, but when it is necessary to start two or more Trains or Light Engines from one end of the Section under his control before a Train or Light Engine has to be started from

[OVER.

PILOT WORKING—continued.

the other end, he must furnish the Engine Driver in charge of each Train or Light Engine, not accompanied by himself, with one of the printed Pilotman's Card Tickets properly filled up and signed, personally start such Trains or Light Engines, and must himself accompany the last Train or Light Engine. The Tickets granted in such cases will apply only to the single journey to the other end of the Section, where they must be immediately given up to the Signalman or other official in charge of the Signals, who must forward the same to the Traffic Superintendent.

The Pilotman must, after issuing a Card Ticket, not permit another Train to enter the Section until he has received intimation by a telegraphic message from the other end of the Section that the Train holding the Card Ticket has arrived; but should telegraphic, as well as tablet communication be destroyed, the Pilotman must accompany every Train over the Section.

When the Tablet apparatus is again repaired and ready for use, the Pilotman must withdraw the notice for Pilot working at one end of the Section, then take the Train Tablet from that end of the Section to the other end, and after delivering it up to the Signalman there, and withdrawing the notice for Pilot working, the traffic will again be conducted in accordance with the Train Tablet regulations.

Signalmen or other officials in charge of Signals must not, on any account, take off their Signals to allow any Train or Light Engine to pass on to any Section that is being worked by Pilotman, except under his instructions, and when he is present.

E. W. VERRINDER.

TRAFFIC SUPERINTENDENT'S OFFICE,
WATERLOO STATION,
January, 1887.

LSWR documents relating to the introduction of Train Tablet working in March 1885, and a supplementary instruction, dating from January 1887, regarding Pilotman working when Train Tablet working was not possible.

tablet instrument to its normal position. A train was not considered to be out of the block section until either it had been signalled into the next section or shunted away from the running lines. Nor was any signal via the tablet apparatus regarded as complete until an acknowledgement by means of the bell or gong had been received from the box to which that signal had been sent.

Before a train was allowed to depart from a station (or on to the branch from Alderbury Junction), the signalman had first to send a train tablet signal (five beats) to the box in advance. Thus Fordingbridge box might send five beats of the gong to Verwood, which would acknowledge this with one beat on its gong. In this example the Fordingbridge signalman would then depress the bell plunger in his tablet instrument until the galvanometer needle fell to zero. He then had to depress the switch plunger immediately, and hold it down until the upper disc turned red and displayed "Out". He then released the switch plunger, lifted the check pin and drew out the tablet slide, gave one beat of the gong and withdrew the tablet to give to the Station Master.

When Fordingbridge box signalled that a train was ready to depart in the up direction, the signalman would follow the same procedure but send the corresponding beats on the bell to his opposite number at Breamore. At the four branch stations with signal boxes (and at West Moors for trains entering or coming off the branch) the instructions stipulated that the Station Master would collect the train tablet from the driver before handing it to the signalman. Likewise the signalman had to give the tablet to the Station Master, who would then hand it to the driver. This was a more specific demarcation of duties than were laid down in the LSWR's General Instructions for the train tablet mode of operation, which provided for either the SM or signalman to perform token transfer. No doubt the South Western had to be seen to be doing all in its power to avoid another serious accident on the line, particularly in view of the severe criticism it had received from Col Rich's report into the Downton tragedy.

Once the signalman had received the tablet he placed it in the cylinder of the tablet instrument. He was required to remain in his box whenever a train or loco was in either section. At Alderbury Junction, however, the signalman received and collected the tablet as the person in charge of operations. In practice, signalmen at the crossing stations would have exchanged tablets with drivers outside the hours when the Station Master was on duty.

Some drivers may have been taking advantage of the lack of supervision at Alderbury Junction because the July–September 1893 WTT contained the following note at the head of the Salisbury–Wimborne table: "The speed of all trains must be reduced when passing Alderbury Junction to allow for the changing of the train tablet without danger to the signalman. The present speed of trains on passing the junction is far too high and Enginemen must give this matter special attention." This warning note still appeared in the October 1902 Working Timetable.

All bell or gong communications sent and received at each signal box had to be recorded in the Train Signal Book.

Station Masters were required to deploy a "competent signalman" in their respective boxes at least 15 minutes before the scheduled arrival or departure of the first booked train in order to attend to the tablet instrument, bell and gong, starting with the opening signals (four beats, pause, five beats) to the adjacent boxes. Station Masters also had to ensure that the signalman remained on duty until the closing message (five, pause, four) had been exchanged with the next box in each direction and recorded.

The Fordingbridge Station Master, who in 1892 was John Judd, was empowered to manage the line in the event of the tablet system failing or a train (or engine) becoming disabled between two tablet stations. In the latter case, the fireman had to take the tablet to the station more likely to be able to provide assistance and hand it to the Station Master, who would then await orders from Mr Judd. In all cases of disruption, whether from train failure or a defective tablet instrument, a telegram had to be sent to Mr Judd, who would give instructions for working the traffic on each side of the obstruction. If the failure or defect was at Alderbury Junction, the signalman had to telegraph Mr Lever, the Downton Station Master, who would then take orders from Mr Judd.

If, in addition to failure of the tablet system between two stations, the electric telegraph communication with Mr Judd broke down, pilot working then had to be introduced at once over the affected section. The Station Master or person in charge completed three printed forms, one being given to the signalman and two to the pilotman. No train movements were then permitted until the pilotman had returned from inspecting whether the section was clear, either by walking along the line or in a road conveyance.

New Routes and their Effect on Train Services

Meanwhile, the LSWR had created a shorter route from London to Bournemouth with the opening of the Bournemouth Direct Line from Brockenhurst via New Milton to its new Bournemouth Central station on 6th March 1888. This reduced the importance of the Corkscrew, which offered more circuitous routes to the resort, either via the branch from Ringwood or by way of Broadstone and Poole to Bournemouth West. The Corkscrew and the Salisbury & Dorset remained the South Western's two routes from London to Weymouth, although naturally most of this traffic used the former which, being double track, provided a more frequent service than was possible via Fordingbridge.

Now that the South Western had a faster and more convenient route between Bournemouth and the capital, it turned its attention to the need for a direct link between Bournemouth, Poole and Weymouth. At that time a journey to Weymouth from either Bournemouth or Poole involved a change of train at Broadstone Junction [2]. The fast growing population and economy of Bournemouth was reducing the relative importance of inland towns such as Wimborne and Ringwood, a process likely to favour settlements such as Christchurch and New Milton on the newly-opened main line. Weymouth remained a popular resort so it made commercial sense for the LSWR to develop a main line linking Southampton with the three main centres of population west of that port, that is, Bournemouth, Poole and Weymouth.

Accordingly, the company sought Parliamentary powers in 1889 to construct a new line, to be carried on a causeway across Holes Bay, between Poole and Hamworthy Junction. This was authorised on 4th July 1890, and work began in 1891. The new line opened on 19th May 1893, direct passenger services commencing between Bournemouth and Weymouth on 1st June.

The LSWR Working Timetable for July–September 1893 shows the table for the Salisbury & Dorset line still headed "Salisbury and Weymouth Line". Of the five down weekday passenger trains, one (the 5pm ex-Salisbury) ran through to Weymouth calling at all stations to Dorchester. Two others had Weymouth connections at Wimborne, because many of the trains between Southampton and Weymouth continued to run via the Corkscrew. In the up direction, two out of five weekday passenger trains to Salisbury started from Weymouth. Of these two, the 7.20am became a mixed train from Wimborne northwards on Tuesdays (Salisbury market day), when its schedule was slackened by 10 minutes to allow attachment of wagons. Despite the growing importance of Bournemouth, only one weekday train from Salisbury served it directly, this being the 7.15pm to Bournemouth West.

Growing local freight traffic is suggested by the very long dwell times at some intermediate stations served by the 8.5am Salisbury–Wimborne pick-up goods. It was allowed 50 minutes at Downton, 90 at Fordingbridge, 15 at Daggens Road and 28 at Verwood.

At the start of the new century, the basic weekday passenger service was five trains each way, but in the evening there were one up and two down through trains between Salisbury and Bournemouth West. The last down train of the day was retimed to leave Salisbury at 7.53pm, giving a significantly later connection from Waterloo at 5.50, and making it easier for City gentlemen to take a weekend break in the Fordingbridge area straight from their workplaces. The earliest arrival in the capital was at 10.5am, using the 6.30 Wimborne, which had a nine minute connection at Salisbury. The evening train from Wimborne to Salisbury now started from Bournemouth West at 6.15pm.

By contrast, travel between Salisbury and Weymouth was becoming less convenient. The 1.25pm Weymouth was the resort's only direct train to Salisbury in the January 1900 timetable, by which time there were no through trains from Salisbury to Weymouth. The 7.25am Weymouth–Salisbury of 1893 now started from Hamworthy Junction at 8.25, with a connection from Weymouth at 7.20. In some cases a journey between Salisbury and Weymouth now involved changing at both Wimborne and Poole. This was a farce on Sundays, when the 9.5am Salisbury involved a wait of over four hours at Wimborne. The South Western may have realised the unpopularity of these alterations because from June it introduced a through excursion, running initially on Mondays only "when required", departing Salisbury at 1.50pm and calling at all stations to reach Weymouth at 4.36. The train returned at 5.5 so it was of no use for day trips; indeed the last connection from Weymouth, via Poole into the 6.15 Bournemouth West, was at 5.30.

From July 1900 through to May 1901 there was a timetable path for the excursion to run twice weekly, Mondays and Thursdays down, returning from Weymouth Mondays and Fridays. If it did indeed run on all those possible dates, it might have attracted those unable to stay for a whole week, as well as the more genteel holidaymaker able to do so. Connections to and from Waterloo were good, which suggests there was a market for the service east of Salisbury, for instance at Andover. The service timetable shows arrival and departure times of the outward train at Alderbury Junction, suggesting that it stopped at the staff platforms for the benefit of local railway families.

By June 1902, a dated excursion was running on Wednesdays from Salisbury to Bournemouth West, out at 8.35am and returning at 8.25pm. The basic weekday service was now six trains each way, including a second direct train from Bournemouth West at 2.50pm, which was retimed in 1903 to 4pm. The October 1903 timetable brought a dramatic change in that half of the 16 weekday trains (five down and three up) were through services between Salisbury and Bournemouth.

The Tuesday mixed train had gone by 1900 and in its place was a 7.20am Fordingbridge–Salisbury cattle train, formed by a 6.15 from Salisbury. Mr Lawrence, the Fordingbridge Station Master, was to advise all concerned when this Tuesdays-only working was required. It could also be extended if necessary to Verwood to take up cattle traffic there and at Daggons Road.

Bournemouth Becomes the Goal

The transformation of the timetable was complete from summer 1904, when nearly all passenger services via Fordingbridge were direct between Salisbury and Bournemouth West. The exceptions were the morning train from Hamworthy Junction to Salisbury, possibly to maintain route knowledge over the Old Road, and the 2.25pm Sundays Salisbury–Wimborne. The Wednesday excursion train continued to run, leaving Salisbury at 8.35am and departing Bournemouth West exactly 12 hours later. This continued during the summer months for the rest of the decade. By 1907 the outward leg of this train started from Wilton.

Despite having opened more direct routes from London to Bournemouth and Weymouth in 1888 and 1893 respectively, the South Western did not neglect promotion of the Salisbury & Dorset line. Evidence of a determined effort to promote it as a gateway to Bournemouth and the New Forest is demonstrated by its public timetables, which now showed connections at Salisbury not only from the London, but from the Yeovil, Exeter and Plymouth directions also. Naturally it suited the LSWR to route passengers from Devon

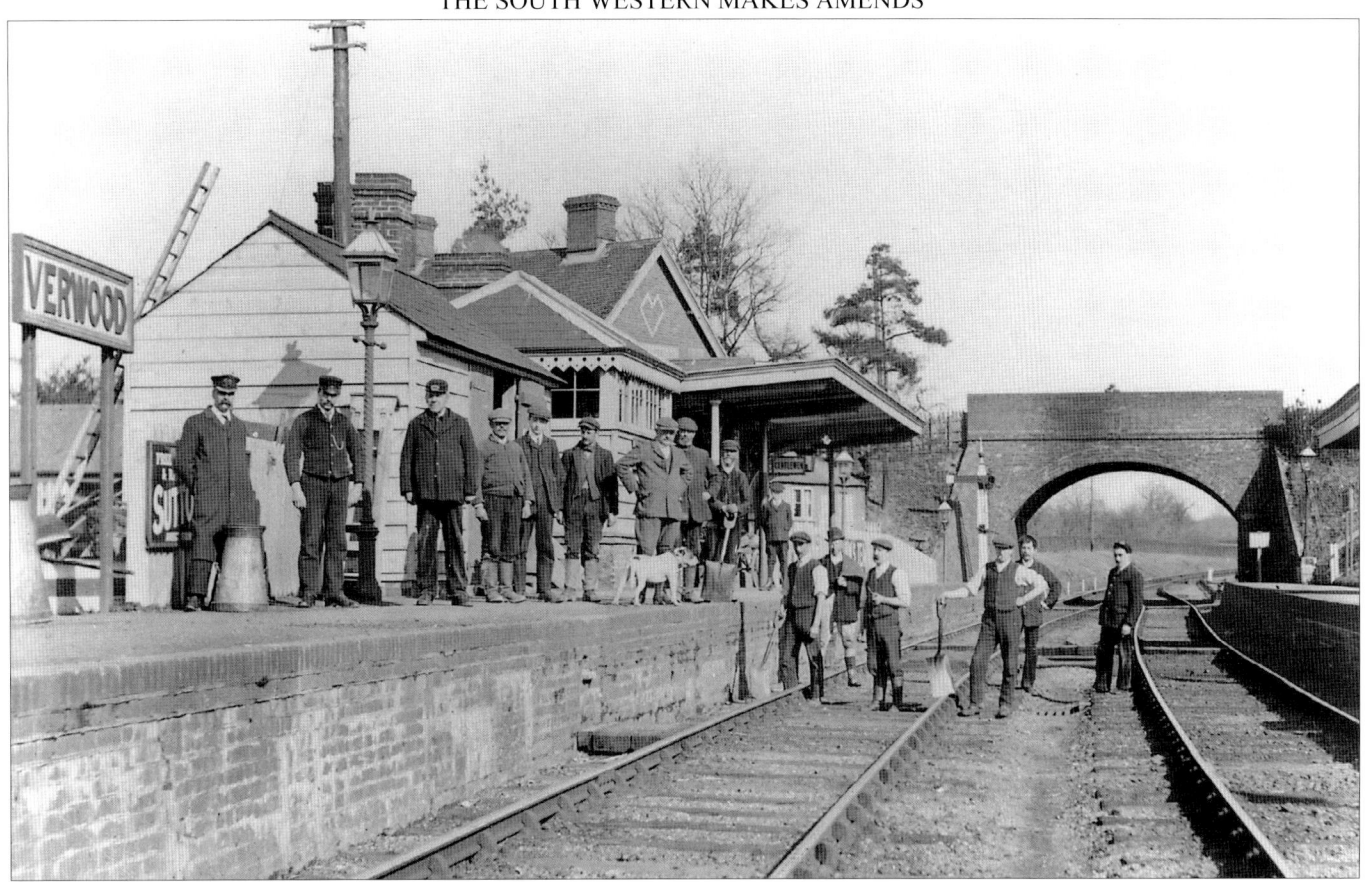

Two fine views of Verwood station, believed to have been taken around 1914. The large complement of men in the first photograph would suggest that if the First World War had begun by the time the photograph was taken, it must have been in its early stages. (Both, Lens of Sutton Collection)

to Bournemouth via Salisbury rather than via Templecombe and the Somerset & Dorset, as the latter was a joint company whose revenue would be shared between the South Western and the Midland Railway.

Sunday passenger services now involved a round trip from Bournemouth West to Salisbury and back in the morning, with nothing else until a pair of mid-afternoon trains. These were the 2.25 Salisbury–Wimborne, which had a good connection from the 12.30 Waterloo, and the 3.42 Bournemouth West–Salisbury, which involved a 25 minute wait for an express due into the capital at 8pm. The branch had no Sunday evening trains and its signal boxes almost certainly operated split shifts. It may well be that the South Western chose to pacify the church authorities by giving staff the opportunity to attend morning or evening worship, as well as keeping down the wages bill.

Despite steadily improving the timetable in terms of direct Bournemouth services, the South Western did not provide more capacity on the Salisbury & Dorset. The line's lack of operational flexibility was exposed by another accident at Downton, on 2nd November 1904 that, unlike the one 20 years earlier, resulted in no fatalities or serious injuries. This time the final down passenger train, 7.58pm from Salisbury ran into wagons that had broken away from an up goods train.

The 31-vehicle freight train included three brake vans, of which two were at the rear of the train and the other next to the engine. The train was about 225 yards long, but the loop line within the station amounted to only 130 yards. This would not have been a problem if this train had been running to time, as it would then have been well ahead of the 6.35 Bournemouth West–Salisbury, and would also have passed Alderbury Junction before the 7.58 Salisbury approached the branch.

Unfortunately the freight was 25 minutes late into Downton, risking delay to both up and down passenger trains. The former was due away from Downton at 7.58 and into Salisbury at 8.13, with connections at Salisbury for London and Yeovil. When both passenger trains were punctual, they would pass on the double track between Salisbury Tunnel Junction and Alderbury Junction, but on this occasion the progress of the 6.35 Bournemouth West was checked by the late running freight. In the absence of any siding at Downton long enough to recess the freight, a decision was made to shunt it in and out of the station with the intention of minimising delay to the passenger trains and hopefully maintain connections.

The first stage of this manoeuvre involved sending the freight train into the Downton–Alderbury Junction section north of the station so that the 6.35 could enter the up platform. Once the latter train had arrived, the freight reversed through the down platform and came to a stand south of the station, outside the up home signal. It remained there while the 6.35 Bournemouth proceeded to Alderbury Junction.

Once the 6.35 was on the main line, the 7.58 Salisbury could enter the branch. It reached Downton at 8.19, only two minutes late, which suggests that the plan was fine in theory. The second stage, to route the freight through the up platform and on its way to Salisbury while the 7.58 stood in the down platform, could now begin. Unfortunately the freight had been standing for half an hour on a gradient of 1 in 78 with the loco at the higher end.

When Signalman Summers cleared the up home signal after obtaining the tablet from the driver of the 7.58, the freight train moved forward into the up loop. As it did so, the coupling between the 16th and 17th vehicles broke, causing the rear 13 wagons and two brake vans to start rolling down the incline. After some 50 yards they were checked by brakesman Ingram, who applied the hand brake from his van.

Summers made a critical mistake in not waiting to see the tail lights of the freight train before handing the Downton–Breamore tablet to the fireman of the 7.58 Salisbury. Returning to his box, he cleared the signals for the passenger train, which then departed and hit the stationary wagons at 20 mph. Two passengers complained of injury.

Major JW Pringle, RE, in his report to the BoT, concluded that the accident would not have occurred if the signalman had carried out his duty to ensure that the freight train had passed him in its entirety before allowing the down passenger train to proceed. Driver Dart and guard Wisdom, the latter travelling in the leading brake van, were criticised for being slow to discover that their train had become divided.

Guard Wisdom had only become aware that the train was unusually light when it gathered speed after entering the up platform. It was his duty to exchange signals with the rear guard to ascertain that the train was complete, but the absence of an "all clear" signal from the latter should have alerted Wisdom to the possibility that something was amiss. It was not until the train had run about 100 yards beyond the signal box that Wisdom displayed a red light to Dart, who stopped the train.

Major Pringle accepted that it had been necessary to shunt the goods train in and out of the station because it was too long for the station loop. He considered, however, that the accident proved there was a danger of couplings breaking because of the gradients at either end of the station. He therefore advised the company either to lengthen the loop or provide a refuge siding capable of accommodating long freight trains [3].

In the summer 1909 Working Timetable, the 10.28am Bournemouth West and 3.5pm Salisbury were booked to call at Alderbury Junction platforms to allow "wives of the company's servants" to go shopping in Salisbury, where they had exactly three hours at their disposal. Similar footnotes to this effect appeared in Southern Railway WTTs, although the designated trains varied over the years. Certain trains, passenger or freight, were booked to call at Alderbury Junction and some of the manned level crossings for the delivery of coal, stores and internal mail.

Connections to and from London at Salisbury remained generally good, notably from the 2.35 Wimborne, which offered Fordingbridge its fastest service of the day (2hr

36min) to the capital. Three down afternoon trains (1.20, 3.5 and 4.54 ex-Salisbury) all provided a 2hr 41min journey from Waterloo to Fordingbridge.

At this time all down trains were timed to pass Alderbury Junction after an up train had cleared the branch. In most cases, up and down services were scheduled 20 to 90 minutes apart at this point, so that conflicts were infrequent, but the policy was to regulate down trains there if necessary in the interests of maintaining connections at Salisbury from up trains. Very probably there would have been clashes between the 6.36pm Bournemouth West and the 7.58 Salisbury, due over the junction at 8.2 and 8.12 respectively. The up train was the final weekday service with a connection for Waterloo at Salisbury, where the margin was only five minutes, so this regulation in its favour was essential from a commercial standpoint.

At West Moors, down branch trains had priority over up branch (though not of course over main line) services. This may have been to minimise delay to holidaymakers or to offset reactionary delays from any regulation at Alderbury Junction. One pair of afternoon trains was timed to cross at Downton but its role as a block post appeared to be in decline.

There were then two freight trains each way on weekdays. The earliest, 5.30am Branksome–Salisbury, was overtaken at Poole by the first up passenger train (5.50 Bournemouth West). The only booked stop on the branch by this freight was at Fordingbridge, but on Tuesdays it would call as required at other branch stations to take up cattle traffic for Salisbury. Additionally, it would stop at Downton if there were wagons to attach or beer traffic to unload.

The down pick-up goods departed Salisbury at 9.20am, and serviced all stations from Milford Goods to Wimborne, where it was not due until 3.39pm. Its station dwell times were long, the shortest on the branch being of 22 minutes at Breamore. It crossed the 10.28 Bournemouth West at Breamore and the 2.35 Wimborne at Verwood, but was also overtaken by the faster 11.50 Milford–Bournemouth West freight at Fordingbridge and the 1.20 Salisbury passenger at Verwood.

The up stopping freight started from Wimborne at 4.51 pm, probably returning the Salisbury engine of the inward service. This crossed the 4.54 Salisbury at Verwood and was somewhat faster than the down pick-up, reaching Salisbury at 8.33.

The early 20th century saw an expansion of traditional brick, ceramic and tile industries at Daggons Road and Verwood because the railway offered access to markets outside the region. No longer did local potters have to rely on "higgling" their wares by horse and cart within a small catchment area, although many continued to do so. Hopkins' tile yard opened in 1906 north of Verwood station. In the same year sand extracted at Verwood sandpits, on St Stephen's Hill north east of the station, started being railed to South Wales for use in the glass making industry.

By the eve of the First World War, passenger services had been accelerated by as much as five to seven minutes between Salisbury and Bournemouth, particularly in the up direction. Travel between the Fordingbridge area and London was now a more attractive proposition because branch trains were timed to make good connections at Salisbury. Three of the six up weekday trains connected into expresses which were non-stop to Waterloo and conveyed restaurant or dining cars, as did the last down connection (5.50pm Waterloo). Not surprisingly, the South Western tried to develop leisure travel to the New Forest by promoting the line (and neighbouring routes) in its magazine, and offering cheap weekend fares.

An interesting development in the October 1913 timetable was that the 8.25am Hamworthy Junction–Salisbury now started back from Swanage at 7.30, although there was no corresponding down train. The following summer service provided a Weymouth portion of the 10 am Salisbury–Bournemouth West, which was detached at Wimborne and catered for leisure travel to the Dorset coast. It is likely that the stock off the Swanage–Salisbury train returned to Weymouth with a crew who had route knowledge via Hamworthy Junction. This route knowledge would be needed for freight traffic using the Fordingbridge line during the Great War, which may explain why the 7.30 Swanage continued to run after the 1918 cuts to the passenger timetable.

By October 1913, an express freight was running in the small hours. This left Salisbury at 3.55am, calling at Milford Goods, Wimborne, Broadstone and Poole. Milford was required to advise Wimborne as to the number of wagons for Broadstone, Poole and the Bournemouth line, probably to expedite shunting. There was also a path for an 11.50am Milford–Fordingbridge freight, to run if required, with a path for the light engine to return from Fordingbridge at 12.55pm. The northbound pick up goods (5.20pm Wimborne) now had longer station allowances, including a stop at Milford, not being due in Salisbury until 10.5.

World War One

Despite the introduction of conscription in 1916, the line was still offering six weekday passenger trains each way in November of that year. Three freight services were booked to run in each direction, compared with two each way in 1909. The 3.55am Salisbury now ran to Hamworthy Junction instead of Poole, returning at 2.30pm. The back working was a pick-up goods, overtaken at Fordingbridge by the 4.25 Bournemouth West passenger.

The early morning freight from Branksome continued to collect cattle wagons from the branch stations on Tuesdays, while Downton was served if required on all weekdays to attach wagons or unload beer barrels. Kelly's Directory noted that Downton's market was long discontinued, but that it still held two annual fairs in April and October, principally for sheep, cattle and horses. Downton also had a major tannery, which received hides by train. By 1918, the Downton stop in the early freight from Branksome had become unconditional, perhaps reflecting a boom in produce being sent to London and other major cities. Another local source of freight helping the war effort were trench props manufactured by Robert Thorne Ltd, based at Romford Mill, west of Verwood.

The effect of depleted manpower really began to bite in 1918, after men aged up to 50 were called up. On weekdays one up and one down passenger trains were withdrawn, leaving a gap from 1.20 to 5.27 pm in departures from Salisbury; the up train cut was the 2.45pm Wimborne. Also removed was the Sunday morning Bournemouth–Salisbury round trip. The remaining Sunday services were the 2.25pm Salisbury and 3.39 Bournemouth West. A Sunday afternoon service in these paths would feature in most timetables for another 41 years, partly to convey milk churns.

By contrast the three freight services each way were maintained, indeed the afternoon service from Hamworthy Junction now started from Wareham at 1.45 and was speeded up, no longer calling at West Moors, Verwood, Daggons Road or Breamore. All up freights now terminated at Milford Goods instead of Salisbury proper.

Although leisure travel was discouraged from 1917 by a substantial fare rise, the South Western nevertheless paid special attention to the maintenance of connections at Salisbury. The instruction to Downton station to telegraph Salisbury as to whether there were any passengers on the first and last up trains (5.45am and 6.36pm Bournemouth West) for stations further east remained in force. No doubt this helped reduce the risk that people making essential journeys, such as hospital visits or servicemen returning from leave, would be stranded or delayed by any disruption to a reduced train service.

References
1. *The Times*, 10.7.1885.
2. This was the fourth successive name of the station originally opened as New Poole Junction and applied from March 1888.
3. *The Railway Engineer*, March 1905.

One of the last LSWR timetables for the line, dating from July 1922.

Chapter 4

The Southern Railway Era

The 1920s brought two decisive changes to public transport between Salisbury and Bournemouth, which were to set the pattern of passenger services on the line for the rest of its life. One factor was an increase in holidays for the working population and the other was road competition. After the war many surplus army lorries were sold off and many ex-servicemen who had learned to drive were able to start businesses in road haulage or passenger transport. By contrast, the railways were having to recruit a new intake of men for frontline duties, partly because a significant number of their staff had been killed or badly injured in the conflict, but also because of the reduction in the working day for footplate staff from 12 to 8 hours in 1919. This manpower shortage retarded the restoration of pre-war timetables but also encouraged creative timetabling to maximise rolling stock utilisation and traincrew route knowledge. Hence the continuation of a Swanage–Salisbury service in the 1920 timetable. Coal shortages were another reason why train services did not immediately revert to their pre-war levels. Domestic coal was still rationed in June 1919, when it was being distributed from Fordingbridge station by the town's Fuel Society.

In 1920, the Salisbury & Dorset line had not regained the passenger trains withdrawn two years previously, but it now boasted another freight service. In the long weekday afternoon gap in down trains now ran a 3.20pm Salisbury–Fordingbridge, whence it returned as a freight and milk working at 6.3, calling also at Breamore and Downton. Much of the milk came from the Avon Valley Dairies, served by a loading dock at the south end of Breamore station. If there were no wagons for the outward trip, a light engine was scheduled to leave Salisbury at 3.55 instead. The timings of other freight services suggest a growing importance of Fordingbridge as a source of traffic. As well as coal and general merchandise inwards, watercress from nearby Burgate was despatched by train, as were the products of Messrs Neave, whose cereal food factory was next to the station. The 9.30am Salisbury–Wimborne local freight was now allowed two hours dwell time at Fordingbridge, compared with 68 minutes in 1916. On Sundays there was now a 3.30pm empty van train from Salisbury to Fordingbridge, to form a 4.40 milk train calling at Breamore and Downton. This round trip was slotted in between the one down and one up passenger train.

The sparse weekday passenger service had generally good connections at Salisbury with expresses to and from London. It was possible to reach the capital at 11.6am by taking the 7am Bournemouth West, which reached Salisbury at 8.39. In the down direction the 11am, 3.4 and 6pm services from Waterloo connected into the 12.55, 5.7 and 8.20 departures from Salisbury respectively. Despite providing a relatively fast link with the Home Counties, the line was beginning to become less relevant as a means of local transport. The seeds of bus competition were about to flower and bloom.

From 1st January 1923, Britain's railways were grouped into four companies. The LSWR was absorbed into the Southern Railway, as were the London, Brighton & South Coast, the South Eastern & Chatham and the Isle of Wight lines. The Somerset & Dorset Joint Railway, whose metals joined the Corkscrew at Broadstone, was now jointly administered by the SR and the London, Midland & Scottish Railway. It continued to provide through services between Bournemouth West, the Midlands and the North West so that some interesting connections with the Salisbury & Dorset route were available at Broadstone or Poole.

Grouping brought a few timetable improvements to the Fordingbridge route, notably an additional train each way between Salisbury and Bournemouth on weekday afternoons. The second up weekday train, due into Salisbury at 9.17am, now started from Weymouth instead of Swanage. The final down train, which connected from the 6pm Waterloo, was extended from Wimborne to Bournemouth West. The final up train now left Bournemouth West at 7.40pm instead of 6.55, although this retiming broke the London connection at Salisbury.

The most interesting development in the summer 1923 timetable was a path for a Great Western excursion from Bristol to Bournemouth, Saturdays only and when required. The outward train was due off Salisbury at 9.10am to enable it to pass the 6.40 Weymouth between Salisbury and Alderbury Junction. The excursion ran non-stop to Wimborne and returned from Bournemouth West at 7.30pm, running fast from Poole to Salisbury to keep it well clear of the stopping train to Salisbury, which started 10 minutes later. Five years later, the return leg of the excursion ran on Mondays, leaving Bournemouth West at 11.22am and running to Cardiff.

Even now there was still only one passenger service each way on Sundays. These were the 2.55pm Salisbury–Wimborne and the 3.53 Bournemouth West–Salisbury. In between them was the empty van train to Fordingbridge which returned to Salisbury with milk churns. By summer 1928, this milk working extended to Verwood.

Freight remained heavy enough to justify four down and three up workings plus a light engine from Wimborne at 3.36pm which ran to Downton, returning to Fordingbridge with wagons which were added to a 5.47 service back to Salisbury. Downton had ceased to be a crossing place by 1922, so this trip was tightly timed, having to reach Breamore before the 4.55 Salisbury–Bournemouth West passenger could clear Alderbury Junction. Traffic for Salisbury market was catered for by the longer dwell times at Fordingbridge and Breamore on Tuesdays of the 5.10am from Branksome. An express freight from Salisbury to Bournemouth Central freight was restored but started at 12.15pm instead of the wartime departure of 3.55am.

Meanwhile two bus companies, Hants & Dorset and

Wilts & Dorset, had begun a joint Bournemouth–Salisbury service on 12th July 1920, with three journeys daily. This had doubled to six each way by the summer of 1925, comparable with the frequency of the rail service, but when the bus service became hourly in May 1929, it was able to capture a large share of the market for travel between Fordingbridge, Breamore, Downton and Salisbury. The trains were faster, but in practice the buses provided a quicker journey into Salisbury because its station was (and still is) a good 10 to 15 minutes' walk from the heart of the city. Bus travel to Salisbury became a particularly attractive proposition from Fordingbridge, where the station lay ¾ mile from the town centre via Shaftesbury Street, away from the direction of travel. Additionally, the buses served Ringwood, which was an awkward journey to Salisbury by rail. The lower bus fares were another incentive for people to forsake the railway.

Road competition had also been boosted by the General Strike of May 1926, which most railway workers supported. Nearly 1,000 railwaymen were said to be out at Salisbury (*see Appendix A*) in the first week. Significantly, the *Salisbury & Winchester Journal* commented, "Not one lorry driver in the district has come out on strike". In the second week, in which hundreds of striking railwaymen had asked the Bishop for a special service in the cathedral, a limited number of trains ran on the city's main lines bound for London, Exeter, Portsmouth and Bristol, although there do not appear to have been any over the Fordingbridge route.

With so few staff defying the strike call, and only 20 volunteers at Salisbury from outside the industry, a basic service on main lines was the best the Southern Railway could manage [1].

The Southern Raises its Game

By the early 1930s, bus services were flourishing between Salisbury and Bournemouth, but the Southern rose to the challenge by targeting new markets. It could not relocate poorly-sited stations, nor greatly increase the frequency of the passenger trains without costly expenditure on infrastructure such as additional passing loops. In fact the line had lost a block section with the closure of Downton signal box, officially in 1922, but very probably implemented during the Great War. It proved to be a serious mistake in the context of bus competition, which may not have been foreseen during the war. One result of this reduced capacity was that wagons collected from Downton by the Salisbury–Wimborne pick-up freight had to be attached next to the engine and then remarshalled at Fordingbridge.

A less restrictive economy, introduced at Verwood from 25th August 1931, was the provision of a closing switch in the signal box, so that the block section could become Fordingbridge–West Moors at less busy times. This involved the use of a miniature train staff for the long section, instead of the electric tablet which remained the mode of signalling

Ex-LSWR A12 class 0-4-2 No 652 at Daggons Road in the 1930s with a mixed freight working. (Lens of Sutton Collection)

when Verwood box was in circuit.

The Southern knew it could make more money from the line, with a minimum of additional expenditure, by concentrating on seasonal passenger traffic and freight. Aware of a growing market for holiday travel, it geared the timetable to cater for through traffic, particularly to Bournemouth and neighbouring resorts, from Salisbury and beyond. The two mid-afternoon trains introduced in 1923 were speeded up in the 1930s, when the up train (3pm Bournemouth West) had only one stop on the branch, at Fordingbridge; this incidentally gave the latter town a 2hr 13min journey to Waterloo, possibly its fastest ever connection to the capital. The two trains were timed to pass on the double track between West Moors and Wimborne.

A further development by the summer of 1933 saw more acceleration, particularly in the down direction. A number of schedules were tightened by two minutes between Fordingbridge and Daggons Road, Verwood and West Moors, West Moors and Wimborne, and between Wimborne and Broadstone. The first daytime down train, 7.23am Salisbury, which in 1930 was allowed exactly two hours to reach Bournemouth West, was retimed to start at 7.30 and arrive at 9.6, a gain of 27 minutes. David Vidler has suggested that the saving of nine minutes between Breamore and Daggons Road in this train's schedule may have been the reduction of recovery time which had been used for unloading milk churns and parcels. It may well be that the SR suffered the same drastic fall in milk churn traffic as befell the Great Western at this time, hence the reduction in station time for an early morning train.

I looked for evidence as to whether the faster schedules were the result of more powerful locomotives being cascaded to the line. David Vidler has noted a cascade at Yeovil, where the arrival of Maunsell U 2-6-0s in 1933 displaced T9s and S11s, but this would have been for mostly main line work. DL Bradley noted that Salisbury depot was still using Adams X2 4-4-0s on Bournemouth duties, although most of the class would be withdrawn by 1936. These 4-4-0s, with 7ft 1in driving wheels, had been displaced from main line express work by the T9s. Other trains were speeded up by between 3 and 12 minutes, yet all these improvements were achieved despite the opening on 19th June 1933 of Creekmoor Halt (between Broadstone and Poole), where nearly all Salisbury–Bournemouth trains now called. David Vidler believes that the trimming of the odd minute from running times between stations was evidence of a general sharpening up of operations in response to bus competition.

Another factor was the inauguration of regular through trains from the Great Western to Bournemouth on high summer Saturdays. These had operated as excursions on a few dates from Bristol since 1923, becoming more numerous in 1931, but a major development in 1932 were regular direct trains on peak Saturdays between Cardiff and Bournemouth. These were potentially high earning services for both companies and the Southern realised it had to raise its game if they were to work efficiently over the single track Fordingbridge route.

Bournemouth's growing popularity as an upmarket resort, where a holiday was within reach not only of the middle classes but increasingly for the families of skilled working men, was the reason for the enhanced summer timetable on the Salisbury & Dorset. The LSWR and GWR built on the success of the Cardiff–Portsmouth service that they had begun in 1896, taking advantage of the Severn Tunnel which had opened ten years earlier. With industry still depressed after the slump of 1931, both companies turned their efforts towards holiday and excursion travel. The through trains also attracted people from South Wales who found work in Southern England (where the effect of the depression was much less) and returned home at weekends. Bournemouth's links with South Wales were strengthened by the opening of a convalescent home at the resort for miners, which is still in use.

The Great Western may also have taken its cue from the LMS, which had been running a Saturday excursion from Bristol St Philips via the Somerset & Dorset. In July 1931, this started at 8.30am, reached Bournemouth West at 11.30, and returned at 7.45pm. Later that month the GWR operated a through service to Bournemouth for a few peak Saturdays. The departure time from Temple Meads was considerably earlier, because of the engine change at Salisbury and pathing over Alderbury Junction, but it gave trippers slightly longer at the resort, being due into Bournemouth West at 10.37, and starting back at 7.17pm. In both directions the only intermediate stops south of Salisbury were at Wimborne and Poole. The up train was tightly timed, being booked to pass Alderbury Junction only three minutes before the 8.13 Salisbury down train.

The first regular Cardiff–Bournemouth service ran on Saturday 30th July 1932, starting at 2.50pm and departing Salisbury at 6.20pm, after the customary change of locomotive. An engine change was required for these (and Cardiff–Portsmouth) trains because the Great Western had been denied running powers over the LSWR south east of Salisbury. The 2.50 Cardiff stopped at Breamore to cross the 5.25 Wimborne freight and milk train, and was then non-stop to Wimborne reaching Bournemouth West at 8pm. The stock of the Cardiff train did not return until the following Saturday as the up service was 11.25am ex Bournemouth West, due into Bath Spa at 2.40pm and Cardiff General at 4.10. As well as competing with the LMS for Bristol and Bath to Bournemouth holiday traffic, the Cardiff trains also provided a direct service to the resort from Bradford-on-Avon, Trowbridge, Westbury and Warminster. The Bristol stop was at Stapleton Road, to avoid reversal at Temple Meads.

In 1933 there were three services on Saturdays in the high summer from South Wales or Bristol to Bournemouth West via Fordingbridge. The train from Bristol now ran from early July to late August with similar timings and calling points as in 1931. The second working from the Great Western was a portion detached from the 11.15 Cardiff–Portsmouth. This left Salisbury at 1.54pm, stopping at Fordingbridge to cross the 1.26 Bournemouth West–Salisbury local. Finally, a portion off an early afternoon train

Salisbury Scenes

Right: Class T9 4-4-0 No 30721 simmers before heading down the Salisbury and Dorset line to Bournemouth, in the late 1950s or early 1960s. (David Lawrence/Photos of the Fifties)

Bottom: Q1 class 0-6-0 No 33020 is seen with the 9.20 Cardiff–Pokesdown train on 12th August 1960. (P Cupper)

Opposite page, top: U class 2-6-0 No 31798 prepares to depart with the 9.23 to Bournemouth West on 21st October 1961. (E Wilmshurst)

Opposite page, bottom: Another U, No 31792, stands with its train on the last day of working, 2nd May 1964. (C Whetmath)

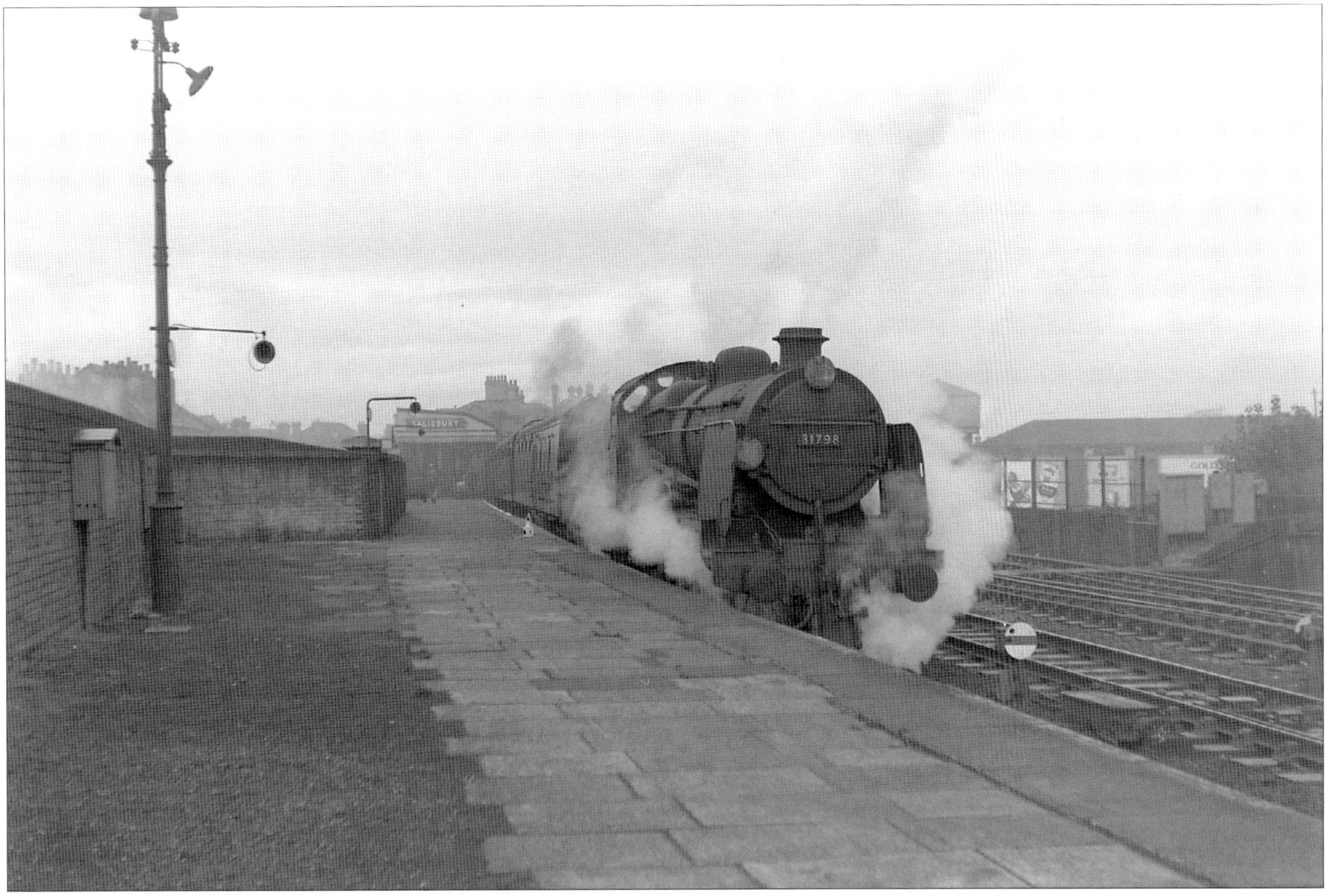
31798

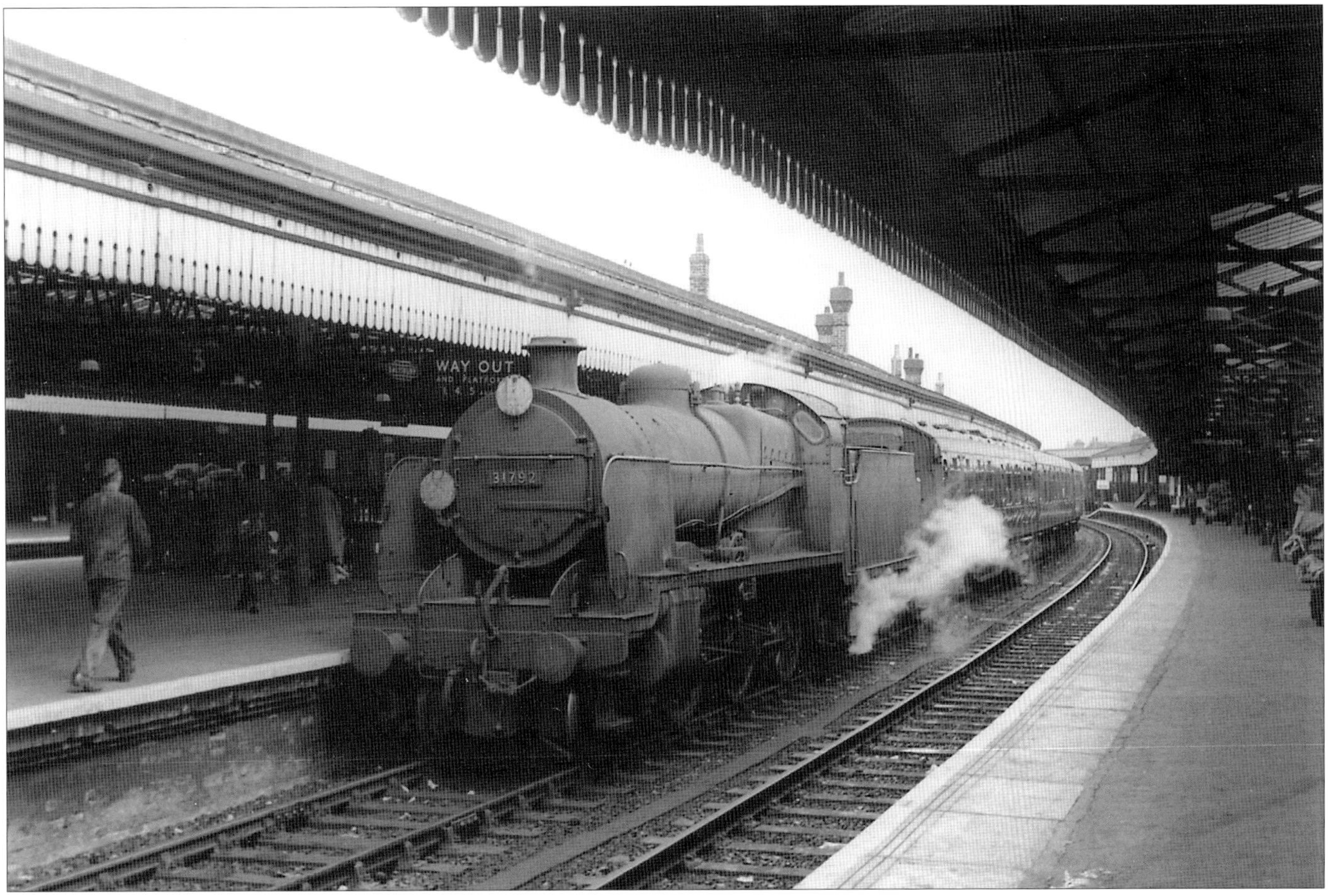
WAY OUT
31792

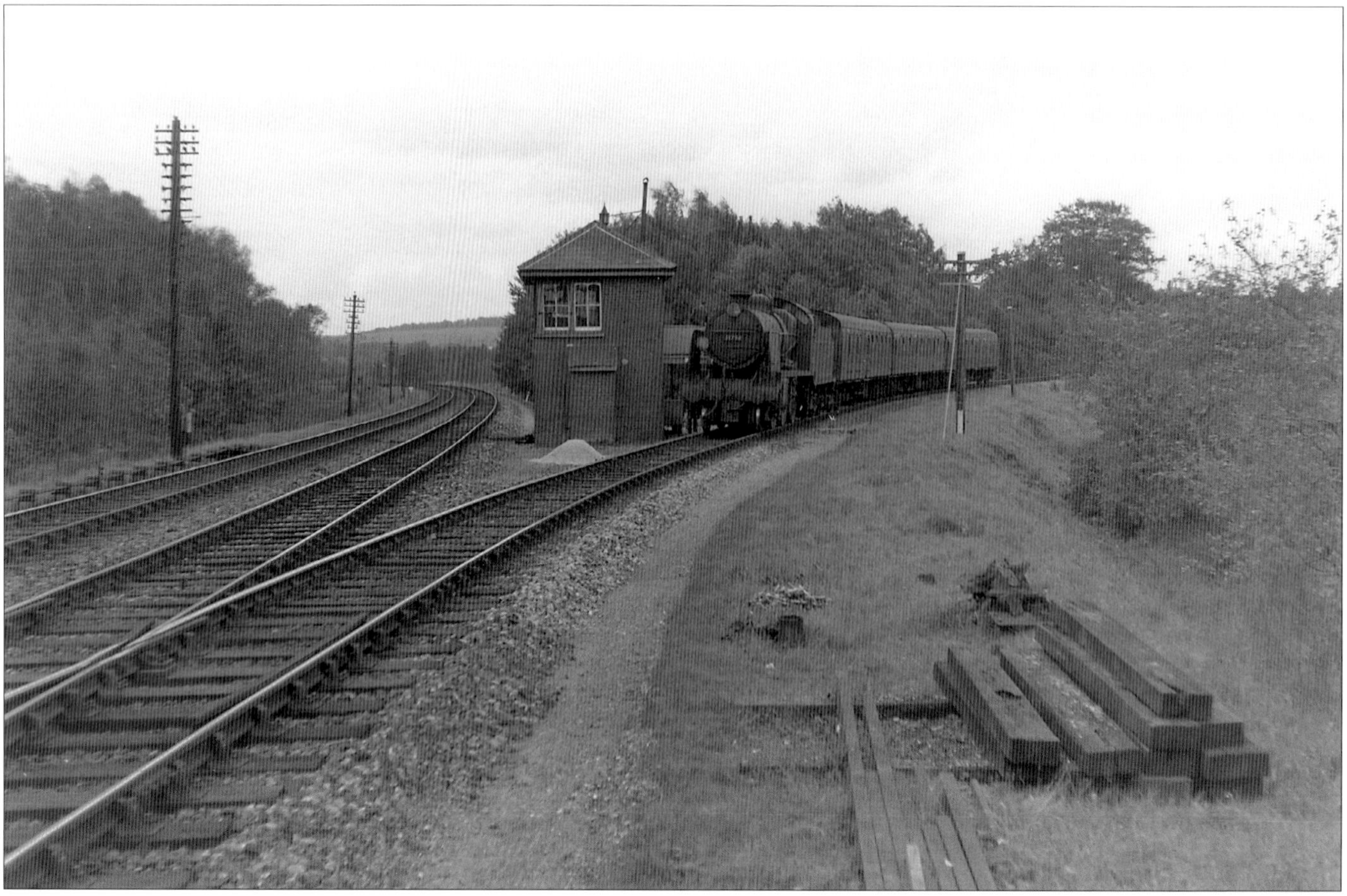

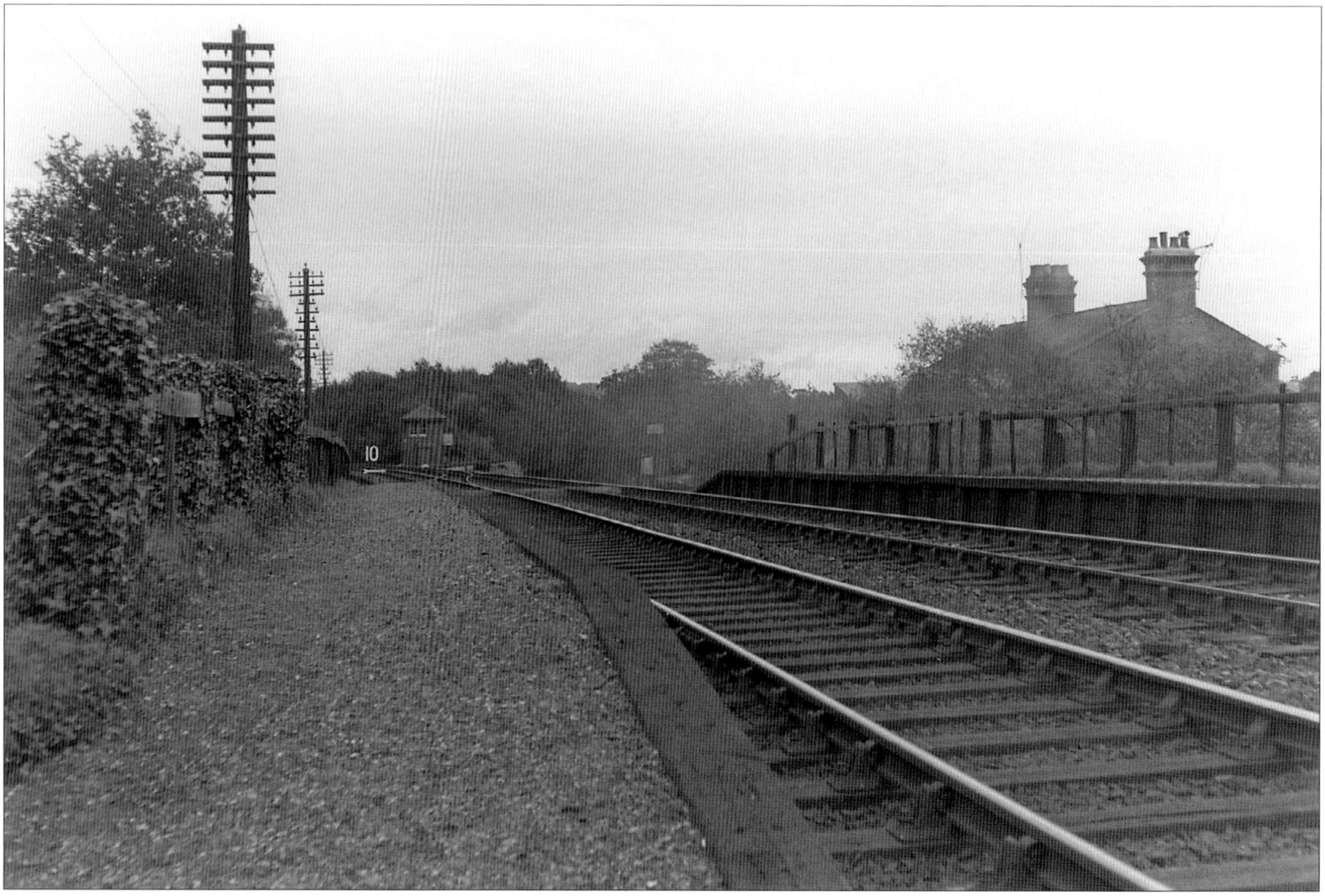
10

Alderbury Junction was where the Salisbury & Dorset met the main line.

Opposite page: The driver of U class 2-6-0 No 31798, hauling the 1.3 Bournemouth West to Salisbury train (top), returns the tablet to the signalman on 21st October 1961, while (bottom) we see a view of the halt looking back towards the junction on the same day. *(E Wilmshurst)*

This page, top: The view from the Salisbury & Dorset line towards the halt on 1st May 1964. *(South Western Circle)*

Right: A closer view of the halt from the east on 17th June 1964. *(Lens of Sutton Collection)*

from Cardiff formed a 5.27 all-stations train from Salisbury, replacing the normal 5.13 Salisbury on Saturdays 22nd July to 9th September.

In the up direction there was only one booked service from Bournemouth to the GW system on these Saturdays, other than the return working of the Bristol excursion. The regular train was a 2.30pm Bournemouth West–Cardiff, calling only at Poole and Fordingbridge before Salisbury.

The line now saw much more activity on Sundays too. In the high summer of 1932, there were up to five Sunday passenger services each way, including a 10.25am Salisbury–Weymouth on three dates in July, August and September, calling at all-stations to Broadstone, then Wareham, Dorchester and Weymouth. Excursionists had eight hours at the resort with the return train due into Salisbury at 10.41pm. Extended hours of Breamore and Fordingbridge signal boxes also enabled a dated excursion to return from Cardiff to Christchurch, due away from Salisbury after 11pm. This day trip, which started from Christchurch at 10am, was repeated on three dates the following year. It ran non-stop between Wimborne and Salisbury in both directions.

Additionally, there were two Salisbury–Bournemouth West passenger trains running on all Sundays from mid-July to late September. In 1933, these started at 9.55am and 1.36pm, calling at all stations except Creekmoor Halt. The latter train conveyed through carriages from the 10.50am Cardiff–Brighton between 23rd July and 10th September. The return trains were 2.30 and 8.10pm Bournemouth West, of which the former included carriages attached at Salisbury to the 1pm Brighton–Cardiff between the same shorter range of dates. All four trains resumed running from 6th May 1934.

The more intensive use of the line on summer Sundays reflected not only an improvement in the national economy but also a growing secularisation of society, a trend strongly promoted by the National Sunday League which provided a great deal of welcome business for the railways. On winter Sundays, however, the only service was one round trip in the afternoon between Salisbury and Wimborne, combining the passenger and milk traffic, which had been conveyed by separate trains in 1923 and 1928.

By October 1934, a Great Western set of four corridor carriages (van third, compo, third and van third) was working from Bristol to Portsmouth on alternate weekday evenings. After overnight stabling at Eastleigh, the set was conveyed to Bournemouth West on an early morning service, and was then attached to the 3pm semi-fast to Salisbury, returning to Cardiff on GW services. This diagram was still operating in summer 1939.

In summer 1938, there were still two through Saturday workings from Cardiff and one return train, but the Bristol excursion was no longer in the timetable. Quite possibly this now ran intermittently as a special. The Sunday service still included through carriages to and from Cardiff for the same duration of the year as in 1933, but the afternoon passenger and milk working between Salisbury and Wimborne now ran from early October to late April only. During the warmer months its return leg now started from Bournemouth West.

Cheap day tickets to London were sometimes offered on the first up train (7.13am Broadstone–Salisbury), which had few local commuters. On Wednesday 15th March 1933, the third class fares were 11s 3d from Fordingbridge and 10s 9d from Breamore or Downton. On Saturdays slightly higher fares were charged but were available by any train.

In 1932 the Great Western had closed its Salisbury terminus, its services being diverted into the Southern station. At first both companies continued to place separate adverts for excursion fares in the local press, but by 1937 the SR had assumed responsibility for local marketing of GW train services at Salisbury. One result was that the Salisbury & Dorset line occasionally featured in promotions for travel to Bath, Bristol and South Wales, for instance on Sunday 23rd May 1937, when a cheap day return was available from Fordingbridge to Bath Spa (6s 0d) and Bristol Temple Meads (7s 6d). Outward travel from Fordingbridge was at 8.7am. The LMSR also had a travel bureau in Fisherton Street, close to the two Salisbury stations, which promoted through tickets on to its system from certain GWR and SR stations.

The SR takeover of local marketing appears to have removed some interesting competing routeings of excursion tickets to the same destination. On Sundays in July 1933, the SR had offered cheap day tickets from Salisbury to Weymouth (12s 9d first and 7s 9d third class) via Fordingbridge and Poole, travelling out on the 9.55am Salisbury–Bournemouth West. This train ran from early May to late September until the Second World War, and in summer 1933 allowed people to travel third class from Breamore to Weymouth for 6s 3d day return. In the same season the Great Western had undercut its rival's Salisbury–Weymouth fare by promoting a half day excursion on 10th July for 5s 0d, despite a longer route of 75 miles, involving reversal at Westbury.

An interesting development in local SR marketing was the reduction in some first class excursion fares. In 1937, these included Fordingbridge–Salisbury for 2s 9d (compared with 3s 3d in 1933), while Fordingbridge–Weymouth was excellent value at 6s 0d, having been 10s 0d in 1933. This fare was now lower by 3d than the third class excursion fare to Weymouth had been in 1933 from Breamore, 2½ miles further back! Very probably these were aimed at the car owning classes who were deserting infrequent and indirect rail services in favour of stylish personal transport.

This probably explains why first class travel to Ascot during the main Race week also became cheaper, while third class fares remained at 1933 levels. The first class cheap day fares in June 1937 from Fordingbridge or Breamore were 11s 3d and from Downton 10s 6d, compared with 12s 6d and 12s 0d respectively four years earlier. In both years, outward travel was via the second up branch train, which started from Bournemouth Central.

The line also brought visitors and tourists into the area. By the 1920s, boys from London and other big cities were staying in the Fordingbridge area as a result of the Fresh Air Fund [2]. Another attraction was Sandy Balls holiday camp near Breamore which opened in the 1930s.

The timetable for July 1938

Freight traffic remained fairly substantial in the inter-war years because the line served not only a large and prosperous agricultural area, but also brick and tile industries at Daggons Road and Verwood. Milk traffic was heavy enough for the early evening freight from Wimborne to be designated "milk and freight". In the late 1930s this service had a 'Q' timing to enable it to convey a milk tank from Poole, which was destined for Devonport and transferred at Salisbury to the 5pm Basingstoke–Exmouth Junction. The 'Q' timing inflated the schedule by six minutes, mostly in terms of a greater allowance between Downton and Alderbury Junction, no doubt to recover any time lost, and secure a path on to the main line.

By 1938, the 4.30am Salisbury–Bournemouth Central express freight already had a 'Q' timing when there were livestock wagons to detach at Downton. The Western Divisional Superintendent's Office had to advise both Salisbury and Downton by 4pm the previous day if this was required. In its normal timings the train's only stops before Poole were at Fordingbridge to set down "general goods wagons" (almost certainly market deliveries) and at Wimborne to detach livestock or other urgent traffic for Wimborne or Ringwood [3].

The line provided a natural route for freight between Bournemouth or Poole and stations on the Great Western system. Wagons for GW destinations travelling via the 6.45pm Wimborne were marshalled next to the brake van to enable them to be transferred at Salisbury after all vehicles for Milford and SR stations had been detached.

World War Two

While Britain was preparing for the possibility of war with Germany, it was business as usual for the line's through services linking Bournemouth with the Great Western. In the summer 1939 timetable, two of the three direct Saturday trains, 2.50pm Cardiff–Bournemouth West and 2.30pm return, were worked on alternate weekends by GWR and SR stock, the latter consisting of a six-coach corridor set. When Southern stock formed the down train, the first class accommodation was in two compos, but the same company's set for the up train included a full first coach and one compo. The 11.15am Cardiff, which had detached a Bournemouth portion in 1933, was now a through train, diagrammed for six GW corridor coaches (van third, third, two compos, third, van third) but ran in August only. The stock returned as the 8.38pm Bournemouth West–Salisbury, the set returning on Monday mornings as a GW service to Bristol.

Through carriages still operated between Cardiff and Bournemouth on Sundays. A SR third corridor brake and corridor compo were detached at Salisbury from the 10.33am Cardiff–Portsmouth, with a similar pair being attached from the 2.25pm Bournemouth West–Salisbury to the 2.35 Portsmouth–Cardiff.

Days before the declaration of war on 1st September, a variety of Drummond motive power was working many of the passenger trains, although on 30th August, Maunsell Q class 0-6-0 No 538, built only the previous year, headed the 5.14pm Salisbury. This class, designed for freight but able to work passenger services by virtue of its steam heating pipes, would have a long association with the line until its closure. K10 4-4-0 No 389 hauled the 9.23am Salisbury on 31st August, but on the day war broke out, this service was powered by L11 No 173. This train was then six coaches from Salisbury, but three were detached at Wimborne to form a 10.33 to Hamworthy Junction, the only scheduled passenger train over the Broadstone–Hamworthy Junction section of the Corkscrew at the time. In summer 1938, this service had been formed by the 9.32 stopper from Brockenhurst.

The T9s, which would outlast the K10s and L11s by a decade, were very much in evidence. No 713 of Salisbury shed worked the 10.7am Bournemouth West–Salisbury, 2.49pm return and 7.43pm Bournemouth West–Salisbury on both 31st August and 1st September. On the latter date, sister engine No 117 was in charge of the 4.47pm Bournemouth West and 8.14pm Salisbury. On the two previous days, a Bournemouth M7 was recorded on the same pair of trains – No 53 on the 30th and 245 on the 31st [4]. One wonders whether the 0-4-4T could manage schedules that had been tightened only a few years earlier.

The need for sufficient stock and manpower to run trains at short notice for the war effort very soon resulted in reduced timetables across the whole system. In the working timetable from November 1939, the basic weekday passenger service via Fordingbridge amounted to just five up and four down trains. In the up direction there was no train between the 7.42 Bournemouth Central, due into Salisbury at 9.10, and the 1.25pm Bournemouth West, arriving at 2.46pm. Four weekday services were withdrawn including the 12.49pm Salisbury and the 3pm Bournemouth West semi-fast. Ironically, the two last mentioned had provided the line with some of its fastest connections to or from Waterloo. Removing the lunchtime departure from Salisbury resulted in a very undesirable gap in down trains between 9.25am and 5.14pm. The only remaining Sunday service was the 2.24pm Salisbury–Wimborne, returning at 4pm. Naturally these cuts restricted the possibilities for leisure travel but in any case the Government, which had assumed control of the railways through the Railway Executive Committee, would soon be actively discouraging such journeys with a 10 per cent fare increase in May 1940.

One train that escaped the cuts was the 3.38am Salisbury–Weymouth newspaper train. On Mondays it started at 3.52, and conveyed a corridor brake composite coach, providing first and third class accommodation, with stops to set down on the branch at Downton, Fordingbridge and Verwood. This train had commenced running in the mid-1920s, initially to carry newspapers only. In summer 1928, it had departed Salisbury at 4.10, comprising a van or two detached from the 2.30am Waterloo–Exeter news train. Routeing the Weymouth portion via Fordingbridge may have been to avoid congestion in the Southampton area, and involved minimal extension of signal box opening because the train was slightly ahead of the 4.30am Salisbury–Bournemouth express freight.

It was at least still possible to make a day trip from the Fordingbridge line to London because the early up trains and the 8.34pm Salisbury continued to run. A day out to Bournemouth or the Dorset resorts was now a less attractive proposition because of the eight-hour gap in down trains.

On 14th May 1940, the line received a visit from a Royal Train, consisting of Great Western stock hauled by T9 No 119. The train had arrived at Broadstone from London behind an LMS "Black 5" 4-6-0 in the small hours, and later that day, after stabling at Blandford Forum, it returned as empty stock to Broadstone, whence the "Greyhound" took it forward to Downton. Here, King George VI and Queen Elizabeth rejoined the train for their journey to Waterloo via Salisbury. It is possible that Their Majesties had visited Breamore House, which was then functioning as a headquarters for Southern Area Command.

T9s continued to make regular appearances on passenger trains, three being observed on 10th September 1943. The following summer, the 7.14am Broadstone–Salisbury, regularly formed of a single carriage, was noted on various dates behind T9s Nos 281 and 719 or L12 No 415 [5]. The latter class, also a Drummond 4-4-0, was several years younger than the T9s, but would be extinct by 1955.

Tim Hale has uncovered evidence of temporary military sidings between Downton and Breamore. These were laid near to the road which led to Breamore House from South Charford level crossing. The sidings were on both sides of the line near the crossing keeper's cottage, and ran parallel with the A338 for a short distance. He believes they were installed as part of the preparations for D-Day. They may have been removed soon after the war as David Vidler cannot recall seeing them when he travelled over the line in 1947. Further south at Burgate, between Breamore and Fordingbridge, a siding was provided to serve a Ministry of Food buffer store in 1942.

Throughout the war, the line sent farm produce to London and other large cities, including milk conveyed on the Sunday afternoon train from Wimborne to Salisbury. Empty churns returned to Wimborne on the outward leg of this Sunday working. Freight services amounted to two trains each way on weekdays. The fast 4.30am from Salisbury had one booked stop on the branch at Fordingbridge, although it called if required at Downton to detach livestock wagons.

By contrast, the traffic from the brickworks at Verwood and Daggons Road declined. Blackout restrictions had made it impossible to fire the kilns continuously, and another reason was that the clay pits at Black Hill, Verwood became exhausted. The private siding to the Station Brickworks at Verwood, latterly owned by the Southern United Brick Co, was removed by about 1945, and the works were sold by auction in 1947.

References
1. *Salisbury & Winchester Journal*, 7.5 and 14.5.1926.
2. ibid, 24.8.1923.
3. SR Southern Division Working Timetable, 2.7.1939.
4. *Railway Observer*, October 1939.
5. ibid, October 1943 and September 1944.

Chapter 5

An Uncompetitive Service

Unhappily for the Salisbury & Dorset line, not all the passenger trains withdrawn in 1940 were restored after the war. Neither of the mid-afternoon trains that the Southern had introduced in the 1920s to fight bus competition was reinstated. The October 1947 timetable, the last under Southern Railway ownership, provided only six trains each way on weekdays and one Sunday afternoon return working between Salisbury and Wimborne. The latter service was worked by a Salisbury M7 0-4-4T of the non push-pull variety. The newspaper train now terminated at Dorchester, but conveyed a passenger coach on all weekdays, giving an overnight connection from the 1.25am Waterloo–Plymouth. During the daytime the gap in departures from Salisbury between 12.55 and 5.20pm did not encourage business.

To make matters worse, connections at Salisbury, Broadstone and Poole left much to be desired as main line services were infrequent by today's standards, and in 1947 had yet to be restored to pre-war levels while demobilisation was in progress. Four of the five daytime trains down the branch had reasonable connections from London, of which the best was from the down Atlantic Coast Express (10.50am Waterloo) into the 12.55pm Salisbury, which also enjoyed good connections from the 8.15am Plymouth–Waterloo and the 10.30 Portsmouth–Bristol. From the Bristol direction, a wait of over an hour was the norm although there was a very risky possible connection due in at 12.53.

Only two of the six up trains afforded good connections to the capital. The 7.42am Bournemouth Central connected into the 7.30 Exeter Central, a fast service reaching Waterloo at 11.46. The 1.18pm Bournemouth West was timed to make a very smart connection into the up ACE, enabling London to be reached in 2hr 21min from Fordingbridge. The Sunday up train also connected well for Waterloo, suggesting that a market had been identified for weekend travel by people with jobs in the Home Counties.

Timings over the Salisbury & Dorset were constrained by pathing at Alderbury Junction and through the busy Bournemouth–Poole corridor, with the added complication of speed restrictions over 18 miles of single track. The loss of some connectional opportunities was therefore almost inevitable. Perhaps the unluckiest involved the 4.47pm Bournemouth West, scheduled to depart Poole at 5.1, one minute before the arrival of an express from Manchester via the Somerset & Dorset, and also missing a connection for London by two minutes at Salisbury, resulting in a wait there of almost two hours for a service to Waterloo.

Other missed opportunities were connections via West Moors and Brockenhurst that might have relieved some of the gaps in services via Salisbury. The Sunday down train was one of the very few to realise such possibilities, offering a 20-minute wait at West Moors for a train to Brockenhurst, which itself provided a good connection to Southampton Central, reached at 5pm. This in turn connected into the up Bournemouth Belle, reaching Waterloo at 6.45 although the up branch train (4pm Wimborne) via Salisbury was more direct, offering a 7.27 arrival in the capital. Ironically the introduction of Brockenhurst–Ringwood–Bournemouth push-pull trains in 1933 had reduced the number of direct Southampton services over the Corkscrew, so that a further change was likely at Brockenhurst for journeys between Southampton and the Fordingbridge line via West Moors.

Nationalisation of Britain's railways from 1st January 1948 placed the Southern Railway system into British Railways Southern Region. In BR's first summer timetable, commencing on 31st May, the weekday passenger service on the Salisbury & Dorset was provided by two T9 and one S11 turns, the latter being a Bournemouth engine that began its day by running light to Broadstone, whence it worked the 7.14am to Salisbury. It then made two round trips between Salisbury and Bournemouth before working the 7.43pm Bournemouth West to Salisbury, where the engine stabled. This and one of the T9 duties were exclusively Salisbury & Dorset line work, whereas the other T9 diagram consisted of one Salisbury–Bournemouth round trip followed by passenger and freight work in the Southampton and Eastleigh areas. The two freight trains each way were worked by two class 700 diagrams, one of which involved some shunting at Poole and Wimborne. The only regular Sunday service on the line was the afternoon trip to Wimborne and back, powered by a Salisbury M7. This turn also had provision for working troop specials originating at Waterloo, from Grateley to Amesbury if required. After passenger services on the Bulford branch were withdrawn in 1952, the M7 was deployed shunting carriages at Salisbury for the remainder of the day.

Restoration of Cardiff–Bournemouth trains on Saturdays was a welcome feature of the summer 1948 timetable, although their absence from the engine workings suggests there had been doubts about whether sufficient manpower and stock would be available to work them. Two sets of carriages were required because both the southbound and northbound services started in the morning, making a round trip with one set impossible. The 10.8am Cardiff–Christchurch service was due off Salisbury at 1.15pm and then called only at Wimborne, Broadstone, Poole, Bournemouth Central, Boscombe and Pokesdown before reaching Christchurch at 3.9pm. The return working started from Christchurch at 9am on the same Saturdays, served the same stations south of Salisbury, and crossed a down stopper at Verwood. Also on summer Saturdays, there was a 'Q' path for a 1.50pm Bristol Stapleton Road–Bournemouth West excursion, departing Salisbury at 3.49, and aimed at people who had to work on Saturday mornings.

1948 revealed a trend towards fewer stops by both freight and passenger services, although on the Fordingbridge line, the normal all-year passenger trains continued to call at all stations. The 3.50am Salisbury was of course limited stop, and this now ceased to serve Downton. The second up freight, 6.40pm Wimborne in 1948, no longer called at Breamore and Downton. Its dwell times at remaining stops became shorter, and there was a WTT instruction that Verwood must not detain this train for shunting. On Saturdays in 1948, when the Cardiff trains were running, the 8am Salisbury–Wimborne pick-up freight omitted the Downton stop. This allowed it to reach Breamore, where the 9am Christchurch could cross it.

Increased manpower from demobilisation allowed the restoration of local trains on the SR's West of England route, which had been withdrawn early in the war. This meant that longer distance services were now making fewer stops, resulting in earlier arrivals into Salisbury. Naturally there were gains and losses for the Salisbury & Dorset line in terms of main line connections.

Favourable changes from summer 1948 included a connection from the 4.47pm Bournemouth West into the 2.25 Plymouth–Waterloo (6.38 Salisbury) which arrived at 8.31. A year later the 7.30am Exeter Central–Waterloo was accelerated to reach Salisbury 20 minutes earlier, and ran faster thereafter. This gave passengers connecting from the 7.42 Bournemouth Central (8.41 Fordingbridge) an arrival in the capital of 11.8 instead of 11.46. Also from May 1949, the 3.50am Salisbury reverted to being a Weymouth service.

The down side of faster main line schedules was that earlier arrivals at Salisbury from the west also broke a few connections, notably into the up ACE, even when the latter ran as separate trains from Padstow and North Devon during the holiday season. Thus in summer 1948, the lunchtime train from Bournemouth West, due into Salisbury at 2.59, narrowly missed both versions of the up ACE, one of which was booked to depart just as the Bournemouth train arrived. When the ACE was duplicated in this way, one train might call at say Sherborne and the other at Templecombe, but the saving of minutes cost connections from the infrequent trains via Fordingbridge. One consolation of increased manpower was the provision of a 3.15pm Salisbury–Waterloo semi-fast, terminating at 5.35. This gave Salisbury & Dorset passengers a useful connection to Andover and Basingstoke, although it reached London an hour after the ACE. Apart from the loss of connections as a result of main line retimings, it was in any case not always feasible to amend the branch timetable because of pathing and speed restrictions. The 10.20 Manchester–Bournemouth West now offered a 15-minute connection at Broadstone for the Fordingbridge line, but most other journeys between the Somerset & Dorset and the Salisbury & Dorset involved long waits at either Broadstone or Poole.

At this time single fares from Fordingbridge to London were 33s 1d first class and 19s 11d third class. Monthly return tickets cost 40s 3d first class and 26s 10d third class. Salisbury was the normal routeing between branch stations and Waterloo, although fares between West Moors and London were the same via Ringwood (a distance of 108¼ miles) as via Salisbury (107¾). For journeys from West Moors, the Ringwood route offered more connections because of its more frequent service, and was generally faster, although one of its best London services was at 8.21 am via the 7.42 Bournemouth–Salisbury.

BR promoted cheap day returns from Salisbury to Bournemouth or Poole, travelling out by the 9.25am or 12.55pm. In March 1951, the fare of 5s 0d was competitive with that of a Wilts & Dorset coach (5s 6d) which ran once daily on specific dates. On summer Saturdays, the cheap ticket could be used from Salisbury on the direct trains from South Wales to Bournemouth, while on certain Sundays an excursion train departed Salisbury at 1.50pm. In the opposite direction, cheap day returns to Woking, Surbiton and London were advertised using any train outwards at or before 11am. Third class fares to Waterloo were 18s 9d from Downton, 19s 6d from Breamore and £1 from Fordingbridge. A Holiday Runabout ticket covering Salisbury, Wimborne, Bournemouth, Swanage and Weymouth was excellent value in summer 1951 at 12s 6d for a week.

For all these marketing efforts, the line got a raw deal in terms of service frequency when viewed against that of the Service 38 Bournemouth–Salisbury bus route operated jointly by Wilts & Dorset and Hants & Dorset. These buses now ran half hourly for most of the day, even on Sundays, and also served the centres of the towns and villages, so that any time saved by taking the train from Downton or Fordingbridge to Salisbury was likely to be cancelled out by walking to and from the stations involved. Relatively few people had cars to reach their local stations in the early post-war years and the buses ran on largely uncongested roads. One of the few markets in which the line could compete was for travel to Bournemouth because the journey (around 1½ hours from Salisbury and an hour from Fordingbridge) was 15 to 20 minutes quicker than by bus. Another was for travel to Poole because Service 38 ran via Christchurch whilst Service 97 (Fordingbridge–Poole) took a devious route via Cranborne. The line did not exploit its potential for long distance travel from the area, partly because most people could not afford the time and expense. Families were less dispersed and fewer people went to higher or further education in 1950 than nowadays. Some people relied on the railway for what would become natural car or taxi journeys in a more affluent age. Don Hibberd has recalled how he and his mother used to take the early evening train from Daggons Road to visit Fordingbridge cinema. The sparse trains and long walk from the latter station meant that they usually missed the start and end of the programme, travelling home on the 8.24pm Salisbury [1].

Panic Driven Cuts

As early as 1949, return halves of rail tickets between Salisbury and Bournemouth or Salisbury and Fordingbridge were accepted for travel on Hants & Dorset and Wilts & Dorset bus services. Rail tickets between Bournemouth and Verwood also were valid for return by Hants & Dorset buses. Holders of bus return tickets could return by train on payment of a supplementary fare, although the supplements were much higher on the Salisbury & Dorset line than on neighbouring routes where similar arrangements existed. In summer 1951, it cost an additional 2s 2d for an adult holder of a bus ticket between Salisbury and Fordingbridge to return by train, although the road distance was 11 miles, and there were few trains. By contrast, the supplementary road to rail charge between Andover Town and Horsebridge, an 11-mile rail journey with more frequent services, was 10d per adult and 4½d per child. Between Salisbury and Bournemouth West (38½ miles by rail) the road to rail supplement was 5s 1d adult and 2s 6½d child, nearly as high per mile as for Fordingbridge to Salisbury [2].

It is tempting to suggest that, by offering little incentive for people to trade up from bus to train, BR was not eager to win additional business on the Salisbury–Bournemouth route. If this was indeed the case, it may help explain why the train service was severely cut a few months later with the start of the winter timetable on 10th September 1951.

The line may have been a soft target for cuts because its winter patronage was undoubtedly light, as David Vidler has recalled in finding himself the only occupant of his carriage after Downton when returning to Salisbury on the 7.43pm Bournemouth West. The crisis that precipitated the cuts was a national coal shortage, bad news for an overwhelmingly steam operated rail system. BR's reaction was to introduce its winter timetable two weeks early, and curtail a number of lesser used trains. Elsewhere in Wiltshire, three stations between Salisbury and Warminster lost their Sunday trains, while the Western Region Malmesbury branch closed to passengers from the same date.

The passenger service on the Salisbury & Dorset had never been generous, and the loss of one up and two down trains was enough to render the timetable of little use, particularly for return travel via Salisbury. There were now just three daytime trains from Salisbury, at 7.15 and 9.25am, then 5.20pm. The up train withdrawn was the 10.4am Bournemouth West (11.5 Fordingbridge) which had been convenient for people wanting a late breakfast, or to take their children to school before travelling. Also withdrawn was the 12.55pm Salisbury, which connected from the down ACE (11am Waterloo) to provide the fastest and possibly the most conveniently timed service from London to the Fordingbridge area. The third casualty was the final down train (8.24pm Salisbury), which had offered a reasonable connection from the 6pm Waterloo–Plymouth, and the removal of the three trains created a timetable even thinner than it had been during the war.

Following these cuts, a day trip to Salisbury dictated either an eight-hour stay from the 9.10 arrival (7.42am Bournemouth Central) or a short afternoon visit using the

Drummond class S11 4-4-0 No 30403 passes Branksome shed with a Salisbury train in July 1951, while an unidentified Black 5 and 70009 "Alfred the Great" try to stay out of the limelight. The locomotive would not see the year out.
(SC Townroe/Colour-Rail.com/BRS320)

1.3pm Bournemouth West, due in at 2.34; in either case the only return train was at 5.20. Travel from London was severely restricted (unless people were willing to travel the long way round via Bournemouth) because the last departure from Waterloo, with a connection via Salisbury, was at 3pm. BR bravely continued to market cheap tickets to Poole and Bournemouth, although the 9.25 Salisbury was the only service on which they could be used.

The coal shortage had hit BR at the same time as its Regional Branch Lines Committees were casting a hawkish eye at thinly trafficked routes. All the same, the reductions on the Salisbury & Dorset were ill-judged and futile. Large gaps in the timetable made the train service even less competitive with frequent buses. The latest morning trains from Fordingbridge were now at 8.40 northwards and 9.52 southwards. The long walk from town to station had never been a selling point for the line, but became even less appealing when prospective travellers were offered so little choice.

The cuts on the Fordingbridge line produced a daily reduction of 115 train miles, attractive on paper to a Management under pressure to achieve savings in coal consumption. Yet they were a false economy, partly because they were applied only to the winter timetable. Hence there would be no saving in traincrews, who were redeployed on other work or spare turns until the summer timetable commenced. Nor was any reduction achieved in signal operating expenses because Breamore and Fordingbridge signal boxes had to remain open for 17 hours daily, as did the manned level crossings. Crucially, the 3.50am Salisbury–Weymouth, together with freight trains, continued to run in the small hours. No signalmen's hours were reduced by withdrawing the 8.24pm Salisbury, while the 7.50 Bournemouth West continued to run; the up train was due over Alderbury Junction a few minutes before the down train would have reached West Moors. The cuts hit revenue by curtailing journey opportunities, but made little or no impact on the wage bill, which was BR's largest expense. BR was too concerned about mileage-related costs when it could have saved more money by attacking time-related costs. It is difficult to resist the conclusion that the 1951 cuts worsened the line's financial position.

I found no mention of the timetable cuts in the *Salisbury Times* or *Salisbury Journal*, both of whose columns were more concerned about food rationing, the Korean War and Army manoeuvres on Salisbury Plain. The latter activity involved an area with part of the Salisbury & Dorset line as one of its boundaries, but assurances were given that train services would not be affected. Some people may have believed the cuts were just a temporary measure for the duration of the coal shortage, but many more were probably unconcerned.

The withdrawn trains were indeed reinstated for the duration of the summer 1952 timetable, a season which saw remarkable performances by two Drummond 4-4-0s on 23rd August. After working a train from Portsmouth, one of the two surviving L12s, No 30415, powered the 7.15am Salisbury, which was booked to cross at Breamore with the 7.42 Bournemouth Central, headed by T9 No 30703. The L12 returned to Salisbury on the 10.45 Bournemouth West before taking another train to Portsmouth. This loco type had been introduced by Drummond during 1904-05 and, like the T9s, had 6ft 7in driving wheels but a smaller chimney and dome.

Meanwhile the T9 had suffered a spectacular failure just west of Alderbury Junction with a broken coupling rod. The offside rod was involved so there was a risk of it striking line-side equipment or points on the approach to Salisbury, and possibly causing a serious derailment. Fortunately sister engine 30302 was running light from Fordingbridge, and drew the train back into the staff platforms, where the 7.29 Portsmouth & Southsea–Bristol made a special stop. The offending rod, which according to a member of Bournemouth Railway Circle, had been "hitting the splasher with a terrific thud at each revolution", was removed before 30703 and its coaches were moved, first back to Downton and then (reversed) to Salisbury behind 30302 [3, 4]. 30703 never worked again, being condemned after its removal to Eastleigh Works. On 21st September it was towed by L 4-4-0 No 31772 to Ashford, where it was broken up in December.

Hopes for a resumption of the full timetable were dashed when the winter 1952 offered no improvement on that of 1951. BR had shot itself in the foot by making the weekday service less useful and creating a vicious spiral of reduced business justifying fewer trains. If cuts had to be made on the Salisbury & Dorset, the most expendable services might have been the Sunday afternoon round trip, at least during the winter. The down train departed Salisbury at 2.24, nearly two hours after the arrival of a train from Waterloo, and had no onward connection at Wimborne for a similar interval. By contrast, the up train, which conveyed milk, had as late as 1957 enjoyed a good connection out of the 3.10 Bournemouth Central and also into the 3.45pm Yeovil Town–Waterloo at Salisbury, so it may have been useful for people returning to London after a weekend with friends and relations. Whether this was enough business to justify Sunday payments for two signalmen and several crossing keepers is debatable. This pair of Sunday trains continued running all year until September 1959, latterly with a four-hour wait at Wimborne from the down train, and no connection from Bournemouth into the up service. It nevertheless resumed for summer 1960, again with appalling connections at Wimborne but in 1961 and 1962 the only Sunday services over the branch were the dated excursions in July and August, which had been running since at least 1951 *(see Chapter 6)*.

One factor which had worked against the improvement of services on the Salisbury & Dorset was its restricted availability for heavier and more modern locomotives. At the time of the cuts, all ex-SR 4-6-0 loco classes were prohibited from the route, as were "Schools" and D15 4-4-0s. Light Pacifics were allowed, subject to a 30 mph restriction over the entire distance from Alderbury Junction to West Moors, which applied also to N, N1, U and U1 2-6-0s. "Merchant

Probably taken some time in the 1950s, here we see an unidentified T9 class 4-4-0 heading south with a Salisbury Bournemouth West train. (JH Aston)

Navy" 4-6-2s, although permitted over the Corkscrew, were excluded from the Salisbury & Dorset. Q1 0-6-0s were permitted, subject to a 40 mph limit. The cuts of 1951 coincided with the rapid rundown of some of the Drummond loco types which were authorised over the route, such as the L11s, L12s and S11s. The same year saw the last surviving K10 withdrawn and even the T9 class, by now the line's prime passenger motive power, had suffered its first loss. If the ex SECR L class 4-4-0s, which transferred to Eastleigh in 1952, had been used on the line more regularly, it might have proved possible to reinstate the axed trains at an early stage. It was not until 1960 that the "Schools" class was authorised to run via Fordingbridge, without the 30 mph restriction that still applied to Light Pacifics. They would have been very useful motive power, but I am not aware of any occasion on which they were deployed on the line.

Chronic rolling stock shortages seem to have been another factor preventing development of the Fordingbridge line. Two coach formations of elderly stock were standard on its winter services at this time, and even lower levels of passenger comfort were about to appear. Following the withdrawal of passenger services on the Portland branch in March 1952, one of its Isle of Sheppey articulated sets was transferred to Salisbury, where its diagram included workmen's trains to Grateley, running primarily to call at Idmiston Halt, which served Porton Down. These sets, converted from SECR push-pull stock, were chased by closures in their latter years, some having been cascaded to Weymouth to work Portland trains after the closure of the Leysdown branch, on the Isle of Sheppey in Kent, in December 1950. Their migration could be compared to that of four-wheel diesel railbuses on the Western Region, which transferred from one doomed branch to another in the mid to late 1960s.

Salisbury's Sheppey set was sometimes deployed on the Salisbury & Dorset, despite the cramped low seating and minimal luggage space, which Portland branch users had disliked [5]. As late as 1957, this set formed the 12.55 Salisbury on Saturday 27th July [6], no doubt because the Grateley shuttles did not run at weekends, but possibly also because all available better stock was committed to longer distance trains over the line (*see next chapter*). It is difficult to imagine less suitable stock for a route that relied heavily on holiday traffic, and on which typical journeys were of an hour or more.

The line's fortunes were about to revive (though not sufficiently to see it out of danger), mainly through more vigorous marketing and imaginative train planning, as we shall see, but also because the new BR Standard 2-6-0s and 4-6-0s built in the early 1950s were suitable for working heavy trains over the route.

References
1. *The Gate*, January 2003.
2. Wilts & Dorset Motor Services Timetable 203, 17.6.1951.
3. Bournemouth Railway Circle traffic survey, 23.8.1952.
4. *Railway Observer*, October 1952.
5. BL Jackson, *Isle of Portland Railways, Vol 2, The Weymouth & Portland Railway*, Oakwood Press.
6. Photographed at Fordingbridge by JH Aston.

Bulleid Battle of Britain 4-6-2 No 34051, "Winston Churchill" is reduced to waiting patiently at West Moors Junction with a train of cattle vans, while M7 class 0-4-4T No 30056 trundles past with a Brockenhurst to Bournemouth West local service. The date is 14th October 1961. (David Lawrence/Photos of the Fifties)

Chapter 6

A New Lease of Life as a Gateway to the Seaside

Even after the 1951 cuts, BR did not give up on marketing the line. In January 1953, the cheap day return from Salisbury to Poole or Bournemouth (now 5s 6d) was offered using the 9.25 train each weekday. More local journeys from Salisbury now featured in local press adverts, for example, to Downton (2s 0d), Breamore (2s 9d), Fordingbridge (3s 6d) and Verwood (4s 6d), "daily (service permitting) by all trains". The latter destination was promoted for travel to its carnival on Whit Monday. Meanwhile, an underlying trend of growing optimism was affecting the country as it moved away from austerity, and more people were able to afford holiday accommodation (as opposed to staying with relatives) and regular day trips.

The Salisbury & Dorset line offered a relatively fast, though infrequent, means of getting to Bournemouth, where the beaches were within easy walking distance of the West, if not from the Central, station. For reasons of geography it was not well placed to compete with road transport for trips to Southampton, Portsmouth or Winchester. Yet BR was about to identify a summer market which the line could serve admirably, beating bus or coach travel handsomely on speed and convenience. The key to this involved rediscovering the line's original purpose as a route to Weymouth.

The 9.25 Salisbury had been the prime, and in recent winter schedules the only, train offering a day out to Bournemouth from Salisbury and local stations. It was less attractive for travel to Weymouth because the connection at Poole into the 8.38 Eastleigh was very tight, with an hour's wait if it was missed. (Passengers for Swanage had the added disincentive of a second change at Wareham.) Very often these passengers would be crossing to the opposite platform as the 9.25 Salisbury was starting away. David Vidler remembers that the T9 class, the normal motive power of the 9.25, was prone to slipping on sharply curved track, as at the Bournemouth end of the station. He recalls that anyone unlucky enough to be on the footbridge at that point risked getting a shower of hot cindery water as the 4-4-0 struggled furiously out of the station.

Station Masters along the Salisbury & Dorset had no doubt deplored the waste of the line's potential, but the tide turned soon after the arrival of a new Station Master at Salisbury in March 1953. Sydney Tyrrell Stanbridge, previously at Tonbridge, had a vast experience of operating special trains. As Hop Controller at Paddock Wood, he had coordinated the specials conveying hop pickers from London to Kent and East Sussex. He had also been Assistant to the Southern Divisional Superintendent, Southampton during the Dunkirk evacuation. Although I have no conclusive evidence that he was instrumental in creating a direct Salisbury–Weymouth service, he would have been expected to undertake marketing surveys with a view to proposing new services or promotions likely to increase revenue at his station. It certainly is an interesting coincidence that the new train began running four months after the local press report of his appointment [1].

Commencing 27th July and until 31st August 1953, the line enjoyed an additional Monday to Friday train, starting from Salisbury at 9.5am, calling at all stations to Broadstone, then Wool, Wareham and Dorchester South, reaching Weymouth at 11.7. It returned from Weymouth at 6.20pm, making the same stops, and was booked to pass the 8.24 Salisbury west of Alderbury Junction. In both directions, the excursion train ran direct from Broadstone to Hamworthy Junction via the "Old Road". Fares from Salisbury were 11s 6d to Dorchester and 13s 3d to Weymouth, which seem rather high in relation to the distances (55 miles to Dorchester, 60 to Weymouth) when compared with 5s 6d for the day return to Poole (34 miles) or Bournemouth West (38½ miles). No doubt the Bournemouth fare was kept low in line with bus and coach fares, and it was considered that Weymouth would command a higher fare for the convenience of a direct train, which was much faster than by road. The Wareham stop enabled BR to market cheap day fares to Corfe Castle and Swanage at 10s 0d and 11s 0d. The connection into the return train was the 6.36 from Swanage.

The following year, the 9.5am Salisbury commenced a fortnight earlier (on 12th July), when both this and the return working were diagrammed for "West Country" or "Battle of Britain" haulage, although the 76xxx 2-6-0s were also used in later years. The 1954 formation consisted of two three-coach sets sandwiching a third class coach. The 9.37 Salisbury–Bournemouth West (the summer equivalent of the 9.25) remained popular, comprising six coaches throughout the summer 1954 timetable.

To work the train to Weymouth, a Bournemouth crew travelled passenger on the 6.43am Bournemouth West, which reached Salisbury at 8.8. After relieving the Salisbury crew who had brought the loco from the shed, they worked the train to Weymouth, disposed of the engine and went home to Bournemouth "on the cushions". A second Bournemouth crew then travelled passenger to Weymouth, where they prepared the loco, and worked the Salisbury train as far as Broadstone, where they were relieved by a pair of Salisbury men who had travelled on the 5.20pm. Four crews were thus needed to work one pair of trains, which ran for just over two hours each way. The problem was that Salisbury enginemen did not have route knowledge beyond Hamworthy Junction.

A slight improvement to the winter timetable took effect from September 1955, when the 10.4am Bournemouth West and 8.22pm Salisbury were reinstated until 5th November and again from 30th April 1956. As they continued to operate in the summer timetable, they were now running for about half the year, restoring some travel opportunities in the autumn and late spring. On the other hand, the continuing suspension of the last down train during the colder months severely restricted travel to and from London, just when people might want to visit the capital for Christmas shopping or January sales. The lunchtime departure from Salisbury was never resumed in winter timetables. It was a mistake not to restore the full service all year round because this would have made no difference to the opening hours of the branch, which remained unchanged up to closure. Indeed from summer 1960, the last down train was retimed slightly to connect out of a new 7pm Waterloo–Plymouth, giving the Salisbury & Dorset its latest ever connection from the capital.

By the summer of 1956, the line had gained a through train to Swanage, which in that year ran Mondays to Fridays, 23rd July to 31st August. Starting from Salisbury at 8.50, it called at Downton, Breamore, Fordingbridge and Verwood but not Daggons Road. In 1957, it ran for the same six-week period, and was due away from Breamore just before the 9.5 Salisbury–Weymouth was timed to clear Alderbury Junction; it was booked to leave Verwood half a minute after the Weymouth train left Breamore. Usual motive power was a T9 but in the final years (1959 and 1960) tended to be a Standard 4 2-6-0.

The addition of the Swanage train called for some smart timekeeping because there were now three down passenger trains scheduled on the branch between 9 and 10am in high summer, as the regular 9.37 Salisbury was about half an hour behind the Weymouth service. There was no up service on the branch in that hour although the pathing of the 8.50 Salisbury and 7.42 Bournemouth Central was tight at Alderbury Junction, where the up train was due to pass 1½ minutes before the down. A delay to either or both these trains could react on the 8.50 Salisbury, which needed to clear Breamore before the 9.5 Salisbury could run onto the branch. To make matters more complicated, the 7.37 Salisbury–Wimborne freight (10 am from Milford yard) was due over Alderbury Junction at 10.10 as the 9.37 Salisbury was pulling into Daggons Road, although further progress of the freight train was constrained by its long shunting allowances at each station.

There was a similar flighting of the up passenger trains in the evening. In summer 1957, the 6.5pm Swanage, 6.20 Weymouth and 7.43 Bournemouth West, departed West Moors at 7.7, 7.37 and 8.19 respectively. The last of the trio was due to cross the final down train of the day (8.22 Salisbury) at Breamore. The three up trains were pathed further apart than were their outward journeys in the morning, whose timings were influenced by the need to give the local freight half an hour's shunting time at Downton before it had to cross at Breamore with the 10.4am Bournemouth West–Salisbury.

David Wigley recalls seeing the return Swanage train formed by a T9 and five coaches in 1960. This service was still running in 1961, but had gone by 1963. The Weymouth train was still operating in summer 1963, the line's final summer, but remained a Monday to Friday service. A Saturday service would have attracted many additional passengers to the line, but the stock was being used elsewhere.

The Weymouth and Swanage trains enabled people living in the Salisbury and Fordingbridge areas to make the most of Holiday Runabout tickets. Richard Benstead remembers making many journeys from Daggons Road with his mother to resorts on the Dorset coast. The Swanage train did not stop at Daggons Road so the Bensteads travelled up on the 7.42 am Bournemouth Central to catch it at Breamore. He too recalls that the Swanage train was usually headed by a T9.

Inter-Regional Day Excursions

Direct trains from the former Great Western system to Bournemouth via Salisbury were nothing new, having operated at summer weekends on a regular basis since 1932. In the 1950s, these became more numerous, not only as timetabled trains but also as one-off excursions. Although the Somerset & Dorset line was still the main rail artery between Bournemouth, Bath, Bristol and the Midlands, its use for excursions from South Wales would have required two reversals (at Bristol Temple Meads and Bath Green Park) apart from questions of route availability and pathing. As WR crews and locomotives regularly worked to Salisbury, that city was the logical gateway to Bournemouth from South Wales and other locations accessible via Westbury. Despite its handicap of some 18 miles of single track to West Moors, the Fordingbridge route had three crossing places in that distance. Moreover, its regular train services were infrequent and it was 23 miles shorter between Salisbury and Bournemouth West than the alternative via Chandler's Ford and Eastleigh. Both routes between Romsey and Southampton were busy and also had to provide paths for banana trains and other dated WR excursions such as from Bristol or Cheltenham to Portsmouth. The advantage of the Salisbury & Dorset lay in its spare capacity and its bypassing the major traffic centres of Eastleigh and Southampton.

The Western Region excursions to Bournemouth targeted industrial areas that had no direct trains to the resort. Despite starting in the morning, they tended to be half-day trips providing about five hours at the seaside, because in many cases Bournemouth was not reached until mid afternoon (3.12pm in 1954, for example). To a large degree, they were a marketing tactic aimed at people who might well decide to return to the resort for a longer stay, probably as their main annual holiday.

These excursions ran on specific Sundays, largely because many people were working on Saturday mornings. Long trains were provided (10 WR corridor coaches being the 1954 formation) in order to convey enough trippers to offset the cost of Sunday operation. The 1954 starting points were Aberdare (18th July and 5th September), Barry (1st August) and Cardiff General (29th August), with each train due off Salisbury at 1.34pm, then non-stop to West Moors. The WR engine was detached at Salisbury and replaced by a "Battle of Britain" 4-6-2, which worked through to Bournemouth West and then back to Salisbury. The excursion returned from Bournemouth West at 8.45pm, passing Fordingbridge at 9.35 and reaching Salisbury at 10.2, where the Light Pacific returned to shed with the same crew who had taken the outward train forward.

A NEW LEASE OF LIFE AS A GATEWAY TO THE SEASIDE

Contrasting motive power at Daggons Road on 27th July 1957. Heading the 1.20 pm Bournemouth to Salisbury (top) is T9 No 30707, while above we see Standard class 4 2-6-0 No 76017 with the 9.28pm Cardiff to New Milton train. (Both, JH Aston)

By 1956 there were two excursion paths each way for WR Sunday excursions, leaving Salisbury at 11.30am and 1.44pm. The earlier of these two was used on 4th August 1957 by a 9.35am from Wellington (Somerset) and on 25th August of that year by a 7.15 ex-Llanelly. The train from Somerset also served Taunton, a major railway hub, well placed for rail travel to resorts in Devon and the Bristol Channel, but less so for those on the coast of Hampshire and Dorset. In 1957 the afternoon path from Salisbury was the one used on 14th July from Aberdare, 28th July from Treherbert and 11th August from Hirwaun. By 1956 the return excursion paths were at 8.45 and 10pm from Bournemouth West. The latter, passing Fordingbridge at 10.50, gave the Treherbert and Llanelly excursionists a longer day at Bournemouth to make up for the gruelling journeys they had undergone to get there.

During July and August 1956, a 9.30am Salisbury–Weymouth and 6.20pm return were run on Sundays. These do not appear to have been repeated in 1957, although instead the SR ran an Andover Junction–Bournemouth West excursion on four Sundays, leaving Salisbury at 10am and calling at all stations to West Moors. This gave people joining at the branch stations a very full day at Bournemouth, as the return service left the West station at 8.30pm, and from Fordingbridge ran in the path of the dated 8.45 Bournemouth West, although the latter was non-stop between West Moors and Salisbury. Thus for a few high summer Sundays, the Salisbury & Dorset was open from 10am to 10pm (or until after 11pm when the WR excursion left Bournemouth West at 10pm). Despite this enhanced service no trains were booked to cross anywhere between Alderbury Junction and West Moors, in fact the last down train (2.24pm Salisbury–Wimborne stopper) returned as the first up, namely the 4pm Wimborne passenger and milk. This round trip, diagrammed for an M7 0-4-4T, was for most of the year the only Sunday working between Salisbury and West Moors. After arriving back at Salisbury, the M7 performed carriage shunting until 1am Monday.

Saturday Inter-Regional Trains

Many of the people discovering the delights of Bournemouth on a WR excursion decided to return for a longer holiday. The summer timetable catered for the traditional seaside holiday by providing two trains each way on Saturdays between South Wales and the Bournemouth area. All four trains utilised long gaps in the basic all-year-round service on the Salisbury & Dorset, but each was itself timed fairly close to the other South Wales train in the same direction. This enabled the second train to act as a relief to the first when

Fordingbridge in the 'Fifties...
Above: T9 No 30721 prepares to restart the 12.54 Salisbury to Bournemouth West on 27th July 1957. *(JH Aston)*
Opposite page, top: Seen from the road bridge, sister engine No 30702 hauls a Bournemouth-bound train into the station, also in the summer of 1957. *(CL Caddy)*
Opposite page, bottom: Completing a trio of T9s, 30304 prepares to take its train in the opposite direction. *(CL Caddy)*

A NEW LEASE OF LIFE AS A GATEWAY TO THE SEASIDE

loadings were especially heavy. In 1954, the first down train was due away from Salisbury only 17 minutes after the 12.54 stopper to Bournemouth West, so it also provided an overspill for day trippers from Salisbury. As with the WR Sunday excursions, these services were non-stop between Salisbury and West Moors.

The four Saturday South Wales trains all served Bournemouth Central, not West. This was partly because of pressure on carriage siding space at the West station, the booked formation in 1954 being nine or ten WR corridor coaches or an SR eight-coach set plus one or two third class coaches. The return trains from Bournemouth started in the morning so it was not possible to work the stock of incoming trains back to South Wales the same day. Keeping a long rake of main line carriages out of the way until the following Saturday required them to be stabled somewhere with suitable sidings that were not intensively used. Hamworthy or Wimborne were possibilities, but in both cases the stock would have needed to reverse at Bournemouth. The natural choice was Brockenhurst, which not only had plenty of siding accommodation, but could be reached from Bournemouth Central without reversal, thereby minimising the platform dwell time at the latter station. This allowed the extension of one train each way as passenger services to and from New Milton, although Pokesdown became the destination of the Cardiff train in some later years.

North of Salisbury, these trains were worked by Western Region locos and crews. South of Salisbury, each pair of trains was worked out and back by an SR loco with long layovers at Bournemouth or Salisbury sheds. The crewing arrangements were more economic than, for instance, those required for the Salisbury–Weymouth stopper during the week. In 1954, two sets of Bournemouth enginemen worked the Cardiff and Swansea trains to Salisbury and back. The 8.50am New Milton–Swansea was diagrammed for an Eastleigh Standard class 4 (the diagram does not specify whether the locomotive was to be a 4-6-0 or a 2-6-0) as far as Salisbury, where the crew took it to shed and prepared it to work the down train (9.28am Cardiff General–New Milton), due out of Salisbury at 1.11pm. An Eastleigh crew had worked the empty stock from Brockenhurst to New Milton and the loaded train as far as Bournemouth Central, where the first pair of Bournemouth men took over. On their return journey they in turn were relieved by the second Bournemouth crew, who worked the loaded train to New Milton and the stock thence to Brockenhurst.

For the Swansea trains, their booked motive power south of Salisbury was a Q class 0-6-0 from Bournemouth shed, although Peter Cupper recalls that Q1s were often substituted. Two years earlier a Q (30532) had worked the Cardiff train on 23rd August, when the Swansea service had left Salisbury behind U 2-6-0 No 31622 [2]. The Qs (and Q1s) were designed primarily for freight traffic, but could work passenger trains because they were fitted with steam heating pipes. This loco had a longer working day than the 4MT working the Cardiff train because it had to work a stopper from Southampton to Bournemouth West after taking the set off the down Swansea train to Brockenhurst. Three Bournemouth crews were involved with this loco diagram, although one set of men covered the core duty from Central station to Salisbury and back. Richard Benstead, who started at Salisbury loco depot in 1959, recalls that one of his first firing turns over the line in was on a Q heading the Cardiff–Pokesdown train, although this was by now diagrammed for a BR Standard 4.

Resourcing the Train Services in the Mid-1950s

The main passenger flows on the Salisbury & Dorset were highly seasonal and overwhelmingly a leisure market, with the greatest numbers travelling down the line from mid-morning until lunchtime, before returning in the evening. There was a modest flow of people visiting shops or professional services in Salisbury, but little commuter business. Even before the 1951 cuts, schoolchildren were not catered for as there was no departure from Salisbury between lunchtime and 5.20pm. The latter was the only train home for office workers, unless they had cause to linger in the city during the period when the 8.20 ran. With such disincentives to use of the railway, it is hardly surprising that in summer 1954, the 6.43am Bournemouth West, due into Salisbury at 8.8 and the only arrival via Fordingbridge before 9am, was diagrammed for a single coach behind a T9. By September 1959, however, this service had become a three-coach formation in order to provide sufficient accommodation for a morning train from Salisbury to Yeovil.

The only down train for people working normal office hours in Poole and Bournemouth was the 7.15am Salisbury–Bournemouth West. In summer 1954, this was formed of four coaches but catered mainly for the larger population from West Moors downwards. This train also carried pupils from Verwood to grammar schools in Wimborne (boys) and Parkstone (girls). Trains later in the day were longer formations catering for the summer leisure travel which BR had done so much to cultivate. The 9.25am Salisbury consisted of six coaches plus a WR van, the latter originating at Swindon. In the same season, the 5.20pm Salisbury amounted to five coaches Mondays to Thursdays, three on Fridays and eight on Saturdays. Not only did it carry long distance passengers, returning shoppers and a few commuters, but during the week one two-coach portion was used to strengthen the 7.43pm Bournemouth West, which brought people home from the seaside.

On summer Saturdays even some of the regular stopping trains were long formations. In June 1954, three up trains were diagrammed for five coaches, while the 7.43pm Bournemouth West was seven. The 10.27 SO Salisbury and its back working, the 1.20pm Bournemouth West, provided the unusual combination of a six-coach WR set behind the same Eastleigh T9 that had spent the previous night on Bournemouth shed, and worked the lightweight early morning train into Salisbury. Many of these trains had to pull up twice at the relatively short platforms of the branch stations, which did not help timekeeping.

Class T9 No 30288 brings its train over the junction and into West Moors station en route for Bournemouth West around 1958. (CL Caddy)

In 1957, T9 30304 heads a Salisbury train towards the level crossing and into the station. (CL Caddy)

The Monday to Friday service of summer 1954 required four T9 and two 700 diagrams, plus two dated Light Pacific turns, one for the Weymouth excursion and another on Mondays only to work empty stock down to Hamworthy Junction. The day began with the 3.25am Salisbury–Weymouth passenger and newspaper train. A news van brake detached from the 1.15am Waterloo–Plymouth at Salisbury was attached to a two-coach lavatory set, and worked forward by a Salisbury T9 as far as Wimborne. Stops were made at Breamore for token purposes, and at both Fordingbridge and Verwood to set down passengers also.

Meanwhile a Bulleid Pacific had left Bournemouth shed to take over the train from Wimborne to Weymouth, whence it worked the 7.34 express to Waterloo. (In both summer 1959 and winter 1959/60 this was a "Merchant Navy" duty and the first loco of the day off the shed). It was a busy turn for the Salisbury guard, who worked the newspaper train through to Weymouth and then the 7.34 Waterloo train as far as Southampton Central. Meanwhile the T9 hauled the 5.26 Wimborne–Bournemouth Central, and was turned on the shed turntable. Its return working, 7.42am Bournemouth Central–Salisbury, was the only up passenger train over the Salisbury & Dorset on a normal weekday (SX and winter SO), which started from the Central instead of the West station at Bournemouth. Engines that had brought trains into Bournemouth West from Salisbury were generally turned on the Branksome triangle.

On arrival back at Bournemouth West, a loco would take water before taking its train to Salisbury. This was still the usual arrangement in summer 1962. David Evans, who returned to Salisbury as a passed fireman in June of that year, when Andover shed closed, recalls an occasion when the departure of the light engine, a Standard 4MT, was delayed by other movements at Bournemouth West. He and his driver agreed to take on water while they waited for the road. Unfortunately, when the elderly driver pulled the chain to swing the water crane hose round to the tender, the chain came away in his hand, and he fell onto the running rail. David Evans helped his mate, who was in extreme pain, back into the cab and drove the engine to Branksome.

At Branksome they collected the guard, who was also based at Salisbury, and he looked after the injured man, whom he tried to persuade to go to hospital. The driver refused and insisted on driving back to Salisbury. He was able to operate the brake, but had great difficulty in moving the regulator or the reverser. Noticing at Poole that the driver seemed to be in more pain, David Evans again assumed control of the engine, doing both firing and driving although the driver managed to work the injectors. At Fordingbridge, the guard rang to arrange a relief driver to take the engine from Salisbury station to the shed. The train was met by a running foreman, who helped the driver off the footplate. He accepted a lift home from one of the station staff, and subsequently saw a doctor, who diagnosed a cracked rib and signed him off work for six weeks. David Evans believed the driver eventually received compensation from BR, but wondered how he managed to endure that journey. The author knows of other instances from the steam age in which injured railwaymen insisted on completing a difficult task, and believes it must have been their hardiness and extreme pride in the job that saw them through.

Left: On 14th October 1961, having given way to a Brockenhurst to Bournemouth West local service at the junction, Battle of Britain 4-6-2 No 34051, "Winston Churchill" (seen previously on page 44) effortlessly brings its train of cattle vans through West Moors station. (David Lawrence/Photos of the Fifties)

Opposite: Also seen on pages 49 and 51, T9 30304 has reached Downton with its Salisbury train some time in 1957. (CL Caddy)

A NEW LEASE OF LIFE AS A GATEWAY TO THE SEASIDE

Freight services

Despite serving little intermediate population or heavy industry, the Salisbury & Dorset saw a surprising amount of activity in the small hours. Following the 3.25am Salisbury–Weymouth news train was a down freight, which in summer 1951 left Salisbury East Yard at 4.5, and ran to Bournemouth Central, passing West Moors at 5.12. By this time it had no booked intermediate stops before Wimborne (where wagons for the Dorchester line would be detached), although Richard Benstead recalls that urgent wagons might be detached at Fordingbridge with the cooperation of the traincrew and signalman. By summer 1954 the destination had changed to Poole, whence the loco (normally a class 700) ran light to Hamworthy Junction to work two round trips over the Hamworthy branch. This loco returned home to Salisbury with the afternoon freight from Wimborne.

On Mondays in summer 1954 there was a 5.30 am Salisbury–Hamworthy Junction ECS, hauled by a Light Pacific. This had cleared West Moors before either of the two morning peak-hour passenger trains had begun their journeys. The engine returned light from Hamworthy Junction at 7.15, crossing at Verwood with the 7.15 Salisbury–Bournemouth stopper. There was a similar working on summer Saturdays in 1958, except that in the peak period from 19th July to 9th August, the 4-6-2 worked back to Salisbury with an 8.30am Bournemouth Central–Cardiff service.

Besides the T9, BR Standard and Q diagrams already mentioned, summer Saturdays involved a round trip (7.15am Salisbury and 10.45 Bournemouth West) by a Fratton U class 2-6-0, which had stabled overnight at Salisbury after working a stopping train from Yeovil Town.

Freight services over the route at this time were in the hands of Salisbury based 700s. One down and both up trains had traffic stops at stations on the branch, but the down pick-up goods (7.37am Salisbury in 1954) was the only one booked to call at all goods yards, Downton to Verwood inclusive. By 1954, the shunting allowance at Fordingbridge was long enough to allow the loco to run back to Breamore after servicing Burgate siding. At Breamore, the engine would then run round any wagons it had collected from Burgate. Fordingbridge goods yard was the largest on the branch but had no headshunt, thus requiring the engine to run round its train in one of the platforms, a situation feasible only because of the sparse passenger service.

Inwards freight in the 1950s and '60s was mainly general merchandise and household coal, although Fordingbridge received tinplate for the canning of fruit grown in the Avon valley. The station also despatched soft fruit such as strawberries. Verwood received an empty container each week for a local furniture factory. This was transferred from the Conflat wagon to a lorry by the yard crane, and the reverse process took place when the container was laden with furniture. Fordingbridge was a release point for racing pigeons. Tim Hale remembers seeing a pigeon special provided with an ex-LMS Stanier 45-foot full brake van, which had a ducket to enable the guard to look along the train.

Watercress was despatched from the area by passenger train. Verwood was the railhead for growers in the Crane Valley, while Fordingbridge was the loading point for Burgate, Damerham and Rockbourne. Two growers used Daggons Road as their railhead, and Richard Benstead recalls that the 4.40pm Bournemouth West conveyed two utility vans to carry the produce. In the 1950s, he and other local trainspotters would sometimes help the leading porter with the loading, but even with their assistance the train often incurred overtime in the station, especially if the road vans were late.

David Evans remembers the down pick-up freight as one of the turns on which, as a young cleaner in 1953, he trained on firing duties. He recalls that crews changed at West Moors so that the Salisbury pair could work back.

The down local freight had a leisurely schedule of three to four hours between Alderbury Junction and West Moors, although its timings were different on Saturdays in high summer when the South Wales passenger trains were running. Even on the busiest Saturdays there were only eight booked passenger trains each way, so the timetable could accommodate a 25-minute shunting allowance at Daggons Road, which was not a crossing place. Likewise, the Monday to Friday passenger timetable, inflated to eight services in each direction when the dated Swanage and Weymouth trains were running, could allow the down freight to spend half an hour shunting at Downton which, like Daggons Road, was not a block post. This was achieved by pathing this down freight train behind the morning excursion trains from Salisbury to the coastal resorts, and by timing the up freights well ahead of the trains taking the trippers back to Salisbury.

Before the Weymouth excursion train began running, the up afternoon freight (4.30 Wimborne) had been tightly timed between up and down passenger trains. In summer 1951 the, 4.52 Bournemouth West was booked to overtake it at Fordingbridge, where it then crossed the 5.20 Salisbury, due away at 5.50. The 4.52 then departed and the freight remained in the yard until 6pm, when the passenger train had just cleared Breamore.

The up express freight (6.50pm Wimborne) called at Verwood and Fordingbridge *en route* to Salisbury. At this time it was worked by the 700 off the down pick-up freight, which was due into Wimborne in mid-afternoon. The 4.25 Dorchester South–Southampton Bevois Park, which was due in Wimborne at 6.18, often conveyed wagons for the Fordingbridge branch, Salisbury or beyond; these had to be marshalled next to the engine on leaving Hamworthy Junction, which had to advise Wimborne immediately.

References
1. *Salisbury Times*, 27.3.1953.
2. Bournemouth Railway Circle, traffic survey for 23.8.1952.

Opposite: A quiet moment between trains at Downton in 1950. We are looking towards Salisbury.
(South Western Circle/Eyers Collection)

Chapter 7

The Dark Forces Gather

Had BR been allowed to pursue its 1955 Modernisation Plan as it had intended, the route might well have benefited from dieselisation. In September 1957, local passenger services in the Salisbury–Portsmouth corridor had converted to diesel electric multiple unit operation, resulting in more frequent services, economies in vehicle mileage and a nearly 30 per cent rise in passenger numbers. During November, the South Hampshire demu network was extended to include the highly rural Andover–Romsey line, and in May 1958, another rural route, Alton–Winchester, was dieselised. BR had placed orders for centre trailers to create three-car sets to cope with passenger demand. An upbeat article in the December 1957 issue of *Trains Illustrated* implied that, even with recently imposed Government restrictions on expenditure, the expansion of dieselised passenger services in Hampshire was unstoppable:

The summer 1960 timetable is likely to include a widespread network of new dmu operations, taking in Brockenhurst–Ringwood–Bournemouth West, Southampton–Sway–Dorchester–Weymouth, the Swanage branch and introducing workings between Salisbury and Bournemouth West.

It is not clear which trains on the Salisbury & Dorset were to have been dieselised, but it is a reasonable assumption that these would have been balancing moves to return Eastleigh-based sets to either Salisbury or Bournemouth for stabling. Quite possibly the more favourable economics of diesel working would have allowed all-year-round reinstatement of the trains withdrawn in 1951. The article went on to suggest that reopening of the Gosport branch, closed to passengers in 1953, was a distinct possibility because a demu had recently traversed that line; in reality this would have been for driver training purposes.

The same article anticipated an hourly demu service between Portsmouth and Reading would be up and running in June 1958, although as things turned out this was not fully implemented until June 1962. By that time the political climate in Britain had turned very strongly against railways, and the speculation became not about the degree of expansion but the extent of retrenchment. Two of the main factors in this had been the appointment of Ernest Marples as Minister of Transport in 1959 and the Government's decision in 1960 to accept the findings of the Guillebaud Report into railway pay.

Mr Marples, who had a business interest in highway construction, strongly promoted the development of a national motorway network, and lost no time in curtailing

U class 2-6-0 No 31808 approaches Breamore with the 10.45 Bournemouth West to Salisbury service on 27th July 1957. (JH Aston)

spending on railways. By 1960 the Prime Minister, Harold Macmillan, was ominously referring to the need for railways to have a new (in essence a reduced) role in meeting Britain's transport needs, and he urged BR to relinquish long established but no longer profitable activities such as stopping passenger and local freight services. The implication for routes such as Salisbury–West Moors, which carried relatively few passengers outside the summer months was clear, even though no list of threatened lines had been published.

One factor that had undermined the financial health of the railways had been a significant loss of freight traffic following the strike called by the drivers' union ASLEF in May 1955 in a dispute over pay differentials. Few trains ran for 17 days, and this was long enough for people and particularly businesses to discover how easily they could manage without rail transport. Road hauliers were able to exploit the 1953 Transport Act, which had extended the distances over which they were allowed to operate, and in many cases insisted on long term contracts from firms whose rail services had been disrupted. With incredible timing, BR then substantially increased its freight charges! The result was that many traders never returned to the railways, and locally this led to the Saturday closure of goods yards on the Salisbury & Dorset by summer 1958, when the only scheduled freight over the line at weekends was the 4.5am SO from Salisbury, which had no booked traffic stops until Poole.

Whereas the summer 1954 service had needed nine loco diagrams (four T9, two 700, one Q, one U, one Standard class 4 and one Light Pacific) to work the line on Saturdays, this had reduced to seven by summer 1959. In the latter service, the early morning Weymouth news train was booked for a T9 (to Wimborne) for the start and end of the season and a Light Pacific for the high summer. The latter returned to Salisbury with a dated 8.30am Bournemouth Central–Cardiff train. Four of the other six diagrams were now diagrammed for Standard class 4 and two for T9s. The decrease was all down to reduced freight activity, reflected also in the ending of booked class 700 work over the line. In summer 1958, the 4.5am Salisbury–Poole freight had been a 700 turn, but a year later a BR Standard class 4 had displaced it. A number of the 700s had transferred to Guildford, and the class had suffered withdrawals. Salisbury now had just one 700 duty on Saturdays, confined to shunting and local trips within the city.

Eastleigh-based Standard class 4s were now the regular motive power for the South Wales trains. Another Eastleigh Standard 4 powered the express freight to Poole, followed by trips over the Hamworthy branch before returning with the 4.40pm Bournemouth West. On Saturdays in summer 1959, the latter train was double-headed with a Bournemouth T9, which returned home with the 8.22pm Salisbury. The double-heading was because there was no longer an up afternoon freight for the Standard 4 to work back to Salisbury on a Saturday. It also made sense not to have a light engine occupying paths on the branch when it was being used to capacity on summer Saturdays.

The same Bournemouth T9 (duty 410 in summer 1959) had a full day's work, starting with the 7.42am Bournemouth Central–Salisbury, and then taking over the 12.16 Templecombe–Bournemouth West from Salisbury at 1.12pm. The latter train gave stations such as Gillingham, Tisbury and Wilton South a direct service to Bournemouth. It was still running in summer 1962, although the usual motive power from Salisbury was by that time a BR Standard 4 or SR Mogul. Four E1 4-4-0s displaced by Kent Coast electrification (Nos 31019, 31067, 31497 and 31507) made a brief appearance on the line in 1959.

Despite their resourceful deployment of traincrews and rolling stock, the railways remained very labour intensive, especially on steam operated routes, and this had tended to depress wage levels to the extent that BR was having difficulty in recruiting and retaining staff when other industries were offering better pay and conditions. In 1958 a Joint Committee of BR management and trade unions had appointed Mr CW Guillebaud, Reader in Economics at

U class 2-6-0 31802 runs past the yard crane and a new-looking concrete hut at West Moors with a train from Salisbury in April 1960. (PJ Cupper)

THE DARK FORCES GATHER

Cambridge University, to examine pay and conditions between railway work and other comparable employment. His conclusions were that in most cases BR pay was significantly lower than in comparable manual occupations, and he recommended that they be improved. In the meantime, BR awarded an interim pay increase from 30th June 1958, but this had followed a recession in the coal and steel industries that were its bread and butter. Its response to the financial crisis was to slash train services on a number of thinly trafficked routes, including the Midland & South Western Junction (Cheltenham–Andover) and the Didcot, Newbury & Southampton lines, in a desperate attempt to reduce working expenses. Clearly this was not the time for BR to introduce more trains on routes which were not making much money.

By accepting Mr Guillebaud's recommendations, the Government helped to create a situation whereby a reduction in the size and scope of the rail network seemed a natural conclusion. If more routes had been dieselised, the financial benefits of lower running costs and higher revenue might have given BR more leverage with Whitehall, but this would have depended on higher investment, which Mr Marples was not willing to authorise. BR was now caught between its high overheads and increased pressure from the Government to reduce its deficits at a time when private motoring and road haulage were rapidly expanding.

The boom in car ownership roughly coincided with the appointment by Mr Marples in 1961 of Dr Richard Beeching as Chairman of the British Railways Board. His remit was to bring BR as near as possible to profitability, and he was soon making it clear that the Government must either subsidise loss-making rail services or cut them out. The latter course of action was clearly what Mr Marples had in mind because in the same year the Ministry of Transport established its Railways 'B' Division, whose agenda was to process uneconomic lines for closure.

Misplaced Optimism

Dr Beeching's appointment naturally resulted in the advancement of senior managers, many from outside the railway industry, who supported his vision of a profitable core network. The Fordingbridge line must have seemed an obvious candidate for closure to those who saw it only in terms of its meagre winter passenger loadings and its considerable signalling expenses. Yet ironically, the scarcity of trains over the route made it more attractive to the Operating Department for diversions when busier routes were disrupted. These diversions even gave rise to speculation in the railway press that BR might upgrade the line to carry Bournemouth–Bristol traffic then using the Somerset & Dorset, which it was widely rumoured the Western Region wished to close. The Somerset & Dorset was almost isolated from the ex-GW system, as well as having difficult gradients and tunnels. By contrast, the Salisbury & Dorset would fit neatly into a strategy for a Bristol–Bournemouth service via

Standard class 4 2-6-0 eases a lengthy Cardiff to Bournemouth train over the junction and through the station at West Moors on a wet 6th July 1963. (E Wilmshurst)

Top: U class 2-6-0 No 31614 leaves Downton with a Salisbury-bound service in the 1960s. (RK Blencowe)
Bottom: Standard class 4 No 76005 has a somewhat easier load than her sister on the previous page. Seen here around 1963, with a Salisbury train at Daggons Road, we also get a good view of the drive down from the main road on the opposite side of the line to the main station buildings. (CL Caddy)

A delightful view of a double-headed service to Salisbury as it races through Downton in the 1960s. Showing a contrast in tenders, Standard class 4 2-6-0 76018 is matched with a BR2 type, and its unidentified class-mate (leading) has a BR1B type. (Roger Holmes/Photos of the Fifties)

Bath Spa and Salisbury. Unfortunately, BR's strategy envisaged closure of all three routes via Broadstone – Somerset & Dorset, Salisbury & Dorset and Castleman's Corkscrew. Beeching did not have a background in railway operating, and looked upon alternative routes, even between main centres of traffic, as an undesirable extravagance.

Nevertheless, optimism about the line's future had been generated from its use as a diversionary route when the Somerset & Dorset had been obstructed, as in December 1960, by the collapse of an embankment at Midford. It was during this detour that a superb performance by the crew of West Country No 34102 *Lapford* had managed to get the down "Pines Express" to Bournemouth on 6th December after the engine had run out of coal near Breamore.

34102 had worked the up "Pines" via Fordingbridge as far as Birmingham the previous day. On the return journey, the WR pilotman, who accompanied the Branksome crew from Bristol to Salisbury, overruled a request from the Southern men for the loco to take on more coal at Westbury. Peter Smith, who has described the incident in his Somerset & Dorset footplate reminiscences, believed that the Western man had not appreciated the prodigious coal consumption of unrebuilt Bulleid Pacifics, and might not have noticed the almost empty tender as darkness fell. Some time after Downton, the fireman announced to his mate that the tender was empty and the horrified driver later threw out a note to the Wimborne signalman requesting a banking engine to assist the 11-coach train up the Parkstone incline. Thanks to assistance in the rear by Q 0-6-0 No 30548, and excellent work by the train engine's crew, the "Pines" reached Bournemouth West with just enough steam for *Lapford* to run light to Bournemouth shed [1]. Peter Cupper considers that the driver deserved a medal, and that the outcome demonstrated just what a Bulleid Pacific could do in the right hands. In his view the West Country's boiler was one of the finest ever designed.

For the remaining two days of the diversion, engine changes were arranged at Bristol or Gloucester. Normal working resumed via Midford on 9th December.

Another cause for optimism about the future of the Salisbury & Dorset was the continuing intensive use of the line during the summer. For instance on Saturday 12th August 1961, an 8.30am relief from Bournemouth Central to Blaina ran ahead of the usual 9am to Cardiff and the 8.48 New Milton–Swansea. The latter two were reported as well loaded (the Swansea train worked by 75066 amounted to 12 coaches) but the 8-coach 8.30 was not, possibly because it ran too early to attract returning holidaymakers who wanted a decent breakfast. As was often the case with relief trains, it may not have been arranged until the booked trains had become heavily reserved, leaving little time to publicise the additional service.

Bournemouth Railway Circle observed that the incoming South Wales trains were also very heavily loaded on that date. The 11-coach 9.28 Cardiff–Pokesdown reached Salisbury behind 9F 2-10-0 No 92227 and was relieved by 75066. Its departure was regulated for a stopping train to Basingstoke, but the 4-6-0 made up nine minutes to Broadstone on a schedule of one hour. The 9.20 Swansea–Brockenhurst also recovered time beyond Salisbury. Its engine is not recorded, but may well have been a Standard class 4 2-6-0 because these could be accommodated on Brockenhurst's small turntable. The 76xxx 2-6-0 was 11 tons lighter than the 75xxx 4-6-0, despite being nearly 6ft longer, so it may be that the turntable restriction was based on weight.

A year later, on 11th August 1962, 75066 worked the 8.48am New Milton–Swansea (12 coaches) to Salisbury, where it was relieved by 5964 *Wolseley Hall*. The Standard 4-6-0 then took over the 9.32 Cardiff–Pokesdown (10 coaches) from 6846 *Ruckley Grange*. South of Salisbury, the 9.55 Swansea–Brockenhurst (10 coaches) and 9am Bournemouth Central–Cardiff (9 coaches) were powered by 76029. The 8.30am Bournemouth Central (8 coaches) was headed by 76027, but now ran to Cardiff because the Monmouthshire Valleys lines, including that to Blaina, had closed to passengers on 30th April [2].

In winter as in summer the Salisbury & Dorset line demonstrated its value to the community. During bad winters Salisbury shed was able to keep the local railways open with snowploughs. These were powered at first by a class 700, and later by a Q 0-6-0. The severe weather of early 1963 saw many local people rediscover that they had a railway, which also became a lifeline for traincrews living some distance from the depot. Richard Benstead recalls that when roads out of Salisbury were blocked, his only means of getting home to Alderholt after a late shift was to travel in the brake van of the 4.5am Salisbury freight. As officially this did not call at Daggons Road, the driver would slow down for him to jump out but not actually stop the train in case it had trouble restarting. On one occasion Richard jumped on to what he thought was the station platform, only to land in a deep drift. It took him a two-mile walk to shake off the snow. He also remembers working the same train with BR Standard and SR 2-6-0s during blizzards. The stretch between Alderbury and Downton was difficult to work when snow was on the rails because of its gradients. The cab of a U or N could be a very chilling environment if no weather sheets were available.

References
1. PW Smith, *Mendips Engineman*, Oxford Publishing Company.
2. Bournemouth Railway Circle newsletters.

Below: Two views showing the line in Winter. An unidentified class U 2-6-0 is seen arriving and then leaving Breamore in January 1963.
(Roger Holmes/Photos of the Fifties)

Chapter 8

Going Down Fighting

Unfortunately for the line, many of the locals deserted it in favour of their cars when the weather improved. The advantage of rail transport in severe weather was not even mentioned in Dr Beeching's report, *The Reshaping of British Railways*, when it was published on 27th March 1963. Its vision was a profitable core of express services between main centres of population and industry, with no future for stopping passenger trains in rural areas. In this context, it was hardly surprising that Salisbury–Bournemouth and Brockenhurst–Ringwood–Bournemouth featured in a long list of proposed closures.

BR published formal proposals to close these two routes early in the summer, but it was aware of the negative media coverage this would produce in the Salisbury area, especially as most of the smaller stations between Basingstoke and Exeter were listed for closure also. All stations between Salisbury and Warminster (a distance of 19 miles) had closed in 1955, and the closures now proposed would leave no station open on the main line between Salisbury and Andover Junction (17½ miles) or between Salisbury and Gillingham (22 miles). Only 14 miles away from the city along the A30 was Stockbridge, on the Andover–Romsey line, which was facing closure despite enjoying an hourly diesel service linking it with Southampton and Portsmouth. Whatever benefits might be claimed nationally from the Reshaping Plan, the imminent reality for Salisbury and district was the prospect of greatly reduced access to rail transport and fewer journey opportunities from surviving stations. BR realised it had to do something to limit the damage to its image if it was to retain and develop the traffic that it wanted to carry.

So in an attempt to sell its policies to local business and civic leaders, BR convened a meeting at the Red Lion Hotel, Salisbury on 10th July. Guests and railway officials chatted over cocktails before watching a film, *Reshaping the Railways*, in which Dr Beeching discussed his report and its implications. BR's Divisional Manager, Mr FPB Taylor, then gave a presentation in which he claimed that the Salisbury–West Moors line was losing £100 a mile per week. (On the basis of 18½ route miles from Alderbury Junction this would equate to £96,200 annually). Many of the traders in the audience were said to be deeply concerned about the future of rail freight services but Mr Taylor declined to discuss issues that he considered would turn the meeting into a dress rehearsal for the closure hearings to be held by the regional Transport Users' Consultative Committee, the statutory body representing rail users. Accordingly, only half

The 9.23 Salisbury to Bournemouth West runs into West Moors, hauled by U class 2-6-0 No 31798 on 4th April 1964, the last full month of services. (CL Caddy)

a dozen or so questions were asked, and their content was not reported in the *Salisbury Journal*, although the newspaper summarised the attitude of departing guests by quoting a businessman who said, "I enjoyed the drink, but I thought otherwise it was a waste of time." [1]

The Salisbury & Dorset line was almost certainly losing money for most of the year, but it is very doubtful that the quoted weekly deficit of £100 per mile had any basis in fact. It looks too much like the hypothetical example of "a fairly typical branch line….with little or no freight" that Dr Beeching had outlined in a speech to the Institute of Directors on 31st October 1962. He estimated such a line would lose £100 a week per route mile on the basis of "a reasonably frequent service", 5000 passengers per week, average fares at 2.4d (1p) per mile, infrastructure costs at £50 per mile and train movement costs at £100 per mile [2]. Salisbury–West Moors was hardly this "fairly typical" line; its local passenger service was infrequent, but the route was used nearly to capacity in the high summer and still carried a significant amount of freight. Indeed the line's freight traffic might have increased because the Salisbury–Wimborne pick-up goods train was now booked to run Mondays to Fridays again instead of Mondays, Tuesdays and Thursdays only, as in summer 1962. BR may well have instructed its senior managers to avoid getting into details regarding the costs and income of any specific line.

Dr Beeching did at least have the support of Salisbury MP, Major John Morrison. He was quoted as saying that he supported the Reshaping Plan in principle, while admitting that its policies would not be popular or pleasant. He advocated the minimising of the hardship arising from the closures, which in effect amounted to a tweaking of bus services [3]. In contrast, Sir Richard Glyn, MP for North Dorset, which included Alderholt and Verwood, put forward suggestions from constituents for improving the train service with diesel railcars.

Meanwhile, opposition to the Salisbury–West Moors closure began to mobilise. After receiving a dozen letters, mainly from coal merchants and watercress growers concerned at loss of freight services, Fordingbridge Parish Council convened an extraordinary meeting on 24th July to plan its official objection. Councillor AG Brewer told the meeting that BR had done nothing to improve the timetable, and ought to try a diesel railcar service. He added that the local branch of the Royal British Legion had asked him to register a protest on behalf of ex-servicemen, many of whom relied on the railway for their holidays. Mrs H Wilson referred to the difficulty of getting coal to the town during the most recent severe winter, and suggested that closing the line would make winter transport worse. EA Poole considered that Fordingbridge needed a railway because the town had been earmarked for development.

The Parish Council agreed unanimously to lodge an objection with the South Eastern Transport Users' Consultative Committee, and also to support Ringwood & Fordingbridge Rural District Council's objection to the closure of Ringwood station, the latter being much more convenient for travel to Southampton. The Parish Council argued that the existing timetable discouraged workers and businessmen from using trains into Salisbury, where the first two arrivals at 8.8 and 9.10am were too late, while 5.20pm was too early a departure, for most commuters. Buses, it maintained, could not accommodate pushchairs, carrycots and heavy luggage. Users of Holiday Runabout tickets would be deprived of cheap travel, thereby causing hardship to poorer sections of the community. More publicity was needed for these tickets, together with a timetable more suited to community needs and use of diesel railcars. Noting that BR intended to close Alderbury Junction–West Moors to all traffic, the Parish Council considered that remaining freight railheads at Salisbury and Ringwood would not be adequate for Fordingbridge, which could not build up sufficient winter stocks of coal or avoid delays to the supply of goods without its own railway [4].

Salisbury City Council appears at first to have overlooked the implications of the closure. In early August, it was reported as deciding not to object provided the line remained open for freight, as councillors were mainly concerned about the additional lorry traffic on main roads. When the Deputy Town Clerk, Mr FW Colquhound, discovered that total closure was planned, BR reacted angrily to accusations from councillors that it had misled the Council. It claimed to have made its intentions clear in March, although it admitted it had not specifically written to the Council about the withdrawal of freight services. Despite missing the deadline for objections and then criticising the TUCC for not representing the interests of Salisbury as a railway city, the Council was allowed to put its case at the public hearing which was scheduled for 17th September in Bournemouth [5].

Although written off by Dr Beeching and at least one local MP, the Salisbury & Dorset gave an excellent performance in the summer of 1963. Whilst it no longer enjoyed Sunday services or the through train to Swanage, it was still alive and kicking as a route for long distance trains aimed at holidaymakers. Its traditional South Wales trains continued to run on Saturdays in July and August, while the direct Weymouth train (retimed to depart Salisbury at 8.56am) ran Mondays to Fridays in those two months. Ironically the line gained an additional train serving London Midland Region destinations that had hitherto been routed via the Somerset & Dorset, which had ceased to carry long distance services starting or terminating north of Bath or Bristol with effect from 10th September 1962.

As a result, a 7.35am Nottingham Midland–Bournemouth West and 10.30am return were booked to run via Fordingbridge. Both trains ran non-stop between Salisbury and Poole. The down service took up what had been the path of the 9.20 Swansea in previous summers and crossed the 1.18pm Bournemouth West stopper at Fordingbridge to reach the West station at 3.10. The up Nottingham train, very conveniently timed for returning tourists, crossed the 10.30 Salisbury at Verwood, and had the 10.40 Bournemouth West local on its tail, the latter timed to

Top: Standard class 4 4-6-0 No 75003 with the 1.3pm Bournemouth West to Salisbury train stands at Downton on 18th April 1964. (R Brough/RK Blencowe Collection)
Bottom: With the line having only days left, the 4.42pm Bournemouth West to Salisbury service moves onto the Salisbury & Dorset at West Moors, hauled by West Country 4-6-2 No 34092 "City of Wells" on 25th April 1964.
(R Brough/RK Blencowe Collection)

be approaching Fordingbridge as the express passed Alderbury Junction. It was due into Nottingham Midland at 6.42pm. These Bournemouth–Nottingham trains were considerably slower in both directions than those running via Reading, Banbury and the Great Central main line.

On 10th August, the 10.30 Bournemouth West, an 8-coach formation worked by BR Standard 2-6-0 76064, was 33 minutes late into Salisbury despite starting "right time". It had been regulated at Alderbury Junction for the heavily-delayed 9.27 Portsmouth–Cardiff. It would appear that Fordingbridge line trains were still being routinely regulated for main line services at this junction as in LSWR and Southern Railway days, even though the Cardiff train, powered by sister engine 76069, had been steadily losing time and stopped specially at Dean in an effort to raise steam. 76064 detached at Salisbury to take over the down Nottingham express, a 10-coach train that had arrived behind Grange 4-6-0 6814. Despite this setback, the down train was only a minute late into Poole, although four minutes were lost from Branksome following the Bournemouth Belle. There would, however, have been significant delay to the 10.40 Bournemouth West–Salisbury stopper, which would have been held at Breamore until the up Nottingham train had cleared Alderbury Junction.

Just to add to the complexity of operation on that date, an 8-coach 11.50am Bournemouth West–Kidsgrove relief train was routed over the branch behind 76016, which came off at Salisbury to work forward a 7.45 Bradford–Bournemouth West. The Kidsgrove service reached Salisbury at 1pm, three minutes early, and another good performance by 76016 brought the Bradford train to its destination on time [6]. On this particular Saturday, the line was thus accommodating four long-distance expresses in each direction, while its very survival was in doubt, although this was primarily because BR had removed these trains from the Somerset & Dorset to expedite closure of the latter.

Battle is Joined

The South Eastern Transport Users' Consultative Committee had received 122 objections to the closure of the Ringwood and Fordingbridge lines. 58 related specifically to the latter and many objectors were concerned for both lines. Councils objecting to the Fordingbridge closure included Dorset County, Poole Borough, Salisbury City, Wimborne & Cranborne Rural District and seven Parish Councils. Conspicuous by its absence from the list was Bournemouth Borough Council, despite the obvious implications of the closures for its economy. Hampshire County Council's objection related to the Ringwood line only, possibly because Breamore and Fordingbridge, although in Hampshire, had always looked to Salisbury rather than Winchester or Southampton for shopping and professional services. Other objectors included the Viscount Cranborne Estates and the National Union of Agricultural & Allied Workers.

The public hearing to consider the objections took place at St Peter's Hall, Bournemouth on 17th September. Some 60 persons, including BR, TUCC and press representatives attended, which suggests that 45 to 50 of the objectors were present, a respectable proportion considering that this was a Tuesday; naturally many of those objecting as individuals were at work. *The Times* for 18th September nevertheless talked down the attendance in a report headed, "Few champions for dying railway", written by its Bournemouth correspondent, who could not contain his boredom with the whole proceedings. He even drew a comparison with the high attendances at midweek football matches!

BR's case was presented by Mr FPB Taylor, Divisional Manager, SR South Western Division, who told the gathering that the Salisbury–Bournemouth passenger service was earning just £5,000 per year but costing £51,400 in direct working expenses. Whilst these figures looked bad for the line, they equated to a loss of about £47 per mile per week on the basis of 18½ route miles between Alderbury Junction and West Moors; and about £23 per mile per week over the 38½ miles from Salisbury to Bournemouth West. Yet in his presentation to Salisbury business leaders only two months earlier, Mr Taylor had asserted that the Salisbury–West Moors line was losing £100 per mile per week. It was difficult for objectors to challenge these figures as they had no access to BR's calculations. The statistics presented by BR at closure hearings were officially intended for the guidance of TUCCs in compiling their recommendations to the Minister. The financial statements were not subject to independent scrutiny but, by giving the distinct impression that the threatened lines were basket cases, may well have influenced the tone of TUCC reports.

A fallacy of BR's financial case for closing lines was that only revenue from the section of route to be closed was credited to the train service. Most of the passengers using the Fordingbridge line were travelling between Salisbury or beyond and Bournemouth or stations in Dorset, but its income was measured by the usage of the branch stations multiplied by the average fare paid. This was the case with many lines that relied on through traffic and had no large intermediate towns. A high proportion of the line's true income was generated elsewhere on the network but not reflected in its earnings.

Nor did the results of BR's two passenger censuses, which were made available to the TUCC and objectors, give the whole picture. These had recorded the numbers of people joining and alighting each train at all stations between Salisbury and Bournemouth inclusive for a whole week in April and another in July. Both surveys understated the usage of the Fordingbridge line. Firstly, it was not until 29th April that the 10.4am Bournemouth West and the 8.30pm Salisbury had resumed running after a six month interval, so the "April" data was based on a timetable that offered very limited journey opportunities. Secondly, the most heavily loaded trains in July were the inter-regional Saturday services, most of whose passengers were travelling to or from Western Region or (in the case of the Nottingham trains) LMR stations. The censuses did not record people joining north of Salisbury on these southbound trains or alighting on the WR or LMR from trains heading north. Passengers joining at say, Cardiff and alighting at say, New Milton, both outside the census boundaries, were not counted at all.

Decades of sparse all-year services, particularly after the 1951 cuts, had resulted in the line having very few commuters, and indeed most users were seasonal or casual. BR advised that there was only one season ticket holder between Verwood and Poole, adding that no seasons (it failed to mention the Holiday Runabout tickets) were currently sold at Downton, Breamore or Fordingbridge. It noted that no Breamore residents had submitted objections, which is interesting considering that their station was possibly the most conveniently-sited of all those on the branch. The average daily number of users at the five branch stations during the April census was 6 at Downton, 4 at Breamore, 8 at Fordingbridge, 13 at Daggons Road and 21 at Verwood. The low numbers at the three northernmost stations was not surprising as all had good bus services to Salisbury that took only slightly longer than the trains. By contrast, Daggons Road served a remote locality with few buses except to Fordingbridge, while Verwood had no direct buses to Salisbury, and its trains were much faster for travel to Poole or Bournemouth than was the bus.

The most articulate defenders of the line emphasised its importance for holiday and long distance travel. Mr Colquhound, for Salisbury City Council, said closure would threaten Salisbury's prosperity as a centre of tourism and kill the Holiday Runabout ticket, which was used by local people. (The usefulness of the Runabout tickets in enabling less well-off people to make day trips to Bournemouth and Dorset resorts was also stressed by Fordingbridge Parish Council). Contrasting bus and train journey times between Salisbury and Bournemouth, he pointed out that rail travel was quicker and cheaper. (At this time Cheap Day Return tickets from Salisbury were 6s 9d to Poole and 7s 2d to Bournemouth, valid by any train.) The City Council's own census at Salisbury station had recorded 2,025 passengers arriving and 1,873 departing via the Fordingbridge line over the eight days from 27th August. He concluded by saying that rail had the advantages of comfort, safety and adequate luggage space [7]. Dorset County Council described the proposed closures as "utter folly" because they would adversely affect tourists and holiday businesses. Verwood Parish Council deplored the loss of long distance connections via Salisbury, such as to London, the West Country and South Wales.

BR took the view that existing bus services in the area provided an adequate alternative for local people wishing to travel beyond Salisbury by train. This came under fire from objectors, who pointed out the distance between the bus terminus and the rail station, which would cause the most difficulty for people with luggage. Curiously the TUCC did not regard this as a hardship.

None of the objections seem to have carried much weight with the TUCC, which reported to the Minister of Transport in mid-November that the closure of both lines would cause no appreciable hardship, and that existing and additional bus services would meet the needs of almost all rail users. A weakness of the consultative procedure was that it was really only concerned about regular, relatively local travel such as journeys to work and school. It was much easier to assess the requirement for substitute bus services when there was a known quantity of regular users on a particular line. Nor did the exercise have any strategy to develop more business and reduce costs on the threatened railways so that they might remain open.

The TUCC's report was considered by a working party within Railways 'B' Division, which consulted other Government departments, and then met on 16th December to prepare its case to the Minister. One of its conclusions was that "the lines are lightly used". The April census had revealed a daily average of 245 passengers on Salisbury–Bournemouth services, compared with 748 on Brockenhurst–Ringwood–Bournemouth, but in July the figure for the Salisbury line had risen to 899. Yet the minutes of that meeting reveal a disdain for the needs of holiday and summer travellers:

It is noteworthy that the (Fordingbridge) line carries three times as much traffic in summer and that no proposals have been made for extra road services to carry it… If there is a demand for holiday trips between Salisbury and Bournemouth, bus operators would be very ready to step into the breach. The loss of the traffic would not seem to have any serious effect.

The working party was equally dismissive of the suggestion made by some objectors for new or diverted bus services to cater for people facing a long trek between bus and train at Salisbury with their baggage:

The only users would be casual (holiday) travellers, and they could time their journeys to suit bus connections or take a taxi.

The minutes stated that the Board of Trade did not support retention of the line on the grounds of holiday travel demands. In fact the BoT's General Division had written to the Ministry of Transport listing some 20 lines, among them Salisbury–Fordingbridge–Bournemouth, which it said ought to be considered for retention because of holiday and tourist traffic. More surprising was the stance of the Ministry of Housing & Local Government in not opposing the two closures, despite projections of population growth in the Poole–West Moors area, claiming that expected increase of 42,000 people by 1981 would not produce many additional rail passengers.

The meeting noted that the increase in Verwood–Poole journey times if the railway closed would be very large but decided against suggesting any improved alternative because few passengers made the journey and no objection had been made to the TUCC regarding this flow. It would appear that at least one of the censuses had been conducted during school and college holidays, so would not have recorded journeys such as from Verwood to grammar schools in Wimborne and

Parkstone.

The working party made just one proposal for additional buses to replace Salisbury–Bournemouth trains, and this amounted to one service each way for commuters between Daggons Road and Poole. Its timings did not compare favourably with the train, particularly for outward travel, which would involve a 7.20am start from Alderholt instead of the 7.58 train from Daggons Road.

Even this solitary bus posed a problem for the Ministry. It would have to run on an unclassified road from Alderholt to Verwood, which Dorset County Council considered to be unfit for buses unless improvements at Cripplestyle were made at an estimated cost of £2,000. The Council wanted the Ministry to pay for the work, so the working party decided that the bus service could go ahead subject to the judgment of the Western Area Traffic Commissioners. It added that, "while the improvements to this and the Ringwood–Brockenhurst road were desirable, closure should not await their completion".

It is clear from the minutes that closure of the Fordingbridge line was viewed within the Ministry as an opportunity to reduce the cost of larger road schemes. Removal of a hump bridge over the line at Three Legged Cross, near to an awkward four-way junction of the B3072 Verwood–West Moors road, was estimated to save £15,000 on a road improvement if the line did not remain open. This bridge crossed the railway on a steep incline that offered little forward vision for northbound motorists. The MoT's Highways Department had already written to Railways 'B' Division detailing examples of where savings could be made on projected improvements to main roads in the event of a decision to close particular railways. Naturally the letter denied any intention to influence decisions in favour of closure! On the Salisbury–West Moors line it claimed that removal of the bridge over the A36 at Whaddon would reduce the cost of improving that stretch of road from £80,000 to £50,000 [8]. This was a narrow bridge protected by black and white chequer boards on either side of the road. Highway planners also had their eyes on Burgate Arch, where the line went under the A338 north of Fordingbridge.

Not long after the working party submitted its conclusions to Mr Marples, BR produced revised figures concerning the financial health of the Ringwood and Fordingbridge lines. The annual earnings of the Salisbury–Bournemouth service were now shown as £12,000, and its contributory revenue to the rest of the BR system was said to be £7,800. This combined amount almost quadrupled the income figure presented to the TUCC hearing. The figure for direct working expenses had also increased substantially to £83,370, the explanation being that £26,000 worth of costs previously shared between passenger and freight services were now reallocated to the passenger service because BR intended to withdraw freight from the line also. (In which case, why were expenses not revised downwards to reflect fewer staffing hours?) The deficit now claimed was larger, although the ratio of expenses to earnings had improved from 10:1 at the Bournemouth hearing to 7:1 and about 4:1 if contributory revenue was included. BR expected to retain all but £1,000 of the contributory revenue if the line closed, basing this assessment on the belief that most of the line's passengers would continue to use main line services at Salisbury, Bournemouth and Poole.

I find this a very doubtful proposition for several reasons. A rail journey between Salisbury and Bournemouth was longer and more costly via Southampton. The only alternative direct route between Bristol and Bournemouth – the Somerset & Dorset line – was also proposed for closure. The distance between bus and rail stations was a disincentive to using the bus from, say, Fordingbridge to catch trains at Salisbury. Verwood and West Moors were facing the prospect of almost total isolation from Salisbury by public transport. It was far more likely that many people in the catchment area of the line were thinking very seriously about buying their first cars if they did not already have them. In some cases local people gave up using any part of the railway system. Yet as ever, the politicians and civil servants could claim to have made a large financial saving in closing the line.

The Last Rites

According to MoT papers, Ernest Marples approved closure of both Salisbury–West Moors and Brockenhurst–Ringwood–Broadstone on 29th January 1964, although his decision was not made public until 3rd March. The delay was probably to enable arrangements for the additional bus services to be confirmed. As a courtesy, the Minister wrote directly to all MPs in the area and received a prompt reply from John Morrison, who said, "I certainly support you wholeheartedly in this, and I do not think you should have any trouble."

Verwood Parish Council was bitterly disappointed because the closure would mean loss of all public transport in the Salisbury direction. It wrote three letters to the Ministry before receiving a reply that BR had advised that there was virtually no regular travel from Verwood northwards and that the TUCC had received only three objections, including that of the Parish Council, from the village. Wimborne & Cranborne RDC protested about the loss of the long distance trains between Bournemouth, South Wales and Nottingham via the line but the MoT replied that these could be diverted on to other routes.

Reaction in Fordingbridge to the Minister's decision appears to have been of dismay, though not of great surprise. At its meeting the next day, the Parish Council said it would "go down fighting". Chairman, Mr T Player said BR and the Ministry had not wanted to discuss the possibility of making the line pay because the train services had operated for 40 years without regard for the public. The closure decision was very unwelcome for freight users who now faced the prospect of additional costs in road haulage and redeployment of staff. Among them were Messrs JL Gmach, who made fibreglass boats and despatched all their canoes by rail from Fordingbridge. It would now have to take staff off

The Hampshire Venturer

Starting at Portsmouth & Southsea LL, and arriving at Salisbury via Eastleigh, the Locomotive Club of Great Britain's "Hampshire Venturer" Rail Tour on 18th April 1964 then made its way to Poole before returning to Southampton Central. Motive power was provided throughout by Q class 0-6-0 No 30548, except for a shuttle from Eastleigh station to the Works, which was handled by USA Tank No 30073. In addition to the visit to Eastleigh Works, passengers also spent time looking round Salisbury MPD.

*Top: The train is seen entering Fordingbridge station round-about mid-afternoon.
(R Brough/RK Blencowe Collection)*

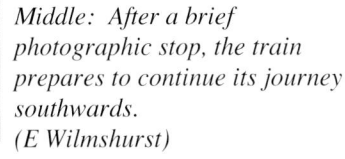

*Middle: After a brief photographic stop, the train prepares to continue its journey southwards.
(E Wilmshurst)*

*Bottom: A final look at the train as it approaches Daggons Road.
(R Brough/RK Blencowe Collection)*

67

production in order to transport its products by road to Salisbury, resulting in higher carriage charges for its customers. Also affected was coal merchant Hood & Son, which had operated from the station yard since the line opened and had recently taken out a 21-year lease to continue its operations there. Jack Hood commented that his firm would incur a great deal of additional expense because all the coal would have to be brought from Salisbury by road [9].

Naturally the closure resulted in career changes for local railwaymen. At the time there were 13 staff at the five branch stations. Fordingbridge Station Master CH Tett, who supervised most of them, transferred to Wool, Dorset. Signalman R Sparey, who was Chairman of the Salisbury branch of the NUR, left the industry after 27 years' service, 26 of them at Fordingbridge. His colleague W Ashton, who had been based at Fordingbridge since joining BR 12 years previously, was offered a position at Salisbury [10].

Closure was fixed for 4th May and, as the line now had no Sunday services, the last trains were scheduled for Saturday 2nd May. Local people began preparations to make it an occasion to remember. 70 members of Fordingbridge Camera Club hired two coaches to Salisbury so that they could return on the final down train, the 8.30pm Salisbury, which had resumed operating that very week as part of the slightly better timetable, which would have extended until late October if the line had remained open. The club also persuaded BR to let them fix floodlights at Fordingbridge station as daylight would be fading by the time of the train's arrival.

Richard Benstead changed links so that he could fire the 5.20 Salisbury on his beloved line during its final week, but realised he would be Spare on the Saturday. Thanks to the kindness of Salisbury shed foreman Stan Tucker, duties were rearranged so that he could travel on the 8.30 as far as Breamore and return thence on the 7.40 ex-Bournemouth.

Trains were strengthened on the Saturday so that local people and visiting enthusiasts could have a final journey over the line. Standard class 4 2-6-0 76005 worked the 10.4am Bournemouth West with five coaches. 76066 headed the 4.42pm from Bournemouth West, which crossed at Breamore with the 5.20pm Salisbury, powered by 34091 *Weymouth*, an appropriate choice in view of the line's long association with the resort. Both trains were loaded to nine coaches. Richard Benstead recalls that the Light Pacific was filthy because BR was no longer recruiting cleaners. He and Stan Tucker managed to clean its nameplate for the occasion. 76066 was to remain in service until the end of steam on the SR in July 1967.

At Salisbury, the 8.30 to Bournemouth, headed by 76066, worked by driver Peter Truckle and fireman Frank Palk, was given "right away" from Platform 2 by Station Master SJ Cooney, and seen off by a large crowd. The *Journal* noted that as the train passed through the city's suburbs, housewives looked up from their washing to wave farewell.

Crowds also gathered at Downton, Breamore and Fordingbridge. Seeing off this train at Fordingbridge was the first official duty for the town's Carnival Queen, Valerie Knibbs. The *Journal* reported that she and local station staff were invited afterwards to a wine and cheese supper at the Fighting Cocks, Godshill [11].

The following day, BR emphatically denied rumours that a "ghost train" had been heard running on it. Yet a few weeks later, Maurice Snellgrove encountered a member of staff on duty at Breamore as a caretaker for signalling equipment, not least the lever frame, which he was told might be vulnerable to theft or vandalism. Very probably this was Jack Mussell, who lived at Breamore and had been a Permanent Way Inspector for the line when it was open. Mr Mussell and a colleague were retained to patrol the route by moped to ensure that no structures or lineside equipment fell into a dangerous condition. Mr Snellgrove has recalled that the inspector had told him the line was being maintained in anticipation of possible reopening to relieve congestion at Eastleigh and Southampton. This might explain why some civil servants involved with the closure were under the impression that the line was still in use for freight. Even Tom Galbraith, Parliamentary Under Secretary to the Minister of Transport, was confused. In a letter on 15th July to Sir Hugh Lucas-Tooth, who had asked whether plans for road widening at Burgate on the A338 could be brought forward now that the line had closed, Mr Galbraith said he understood that BR had no plans at present to close the line to all traffic. In fact freight had ceased along with the passenger service on 4th May.

The 4.5am Salisbury–Bournemouth freight was rerouted via Eastleigh, as were the South Wales–Bournemouth trains on summer Saturdays. One consequence was that the Romsey–Eastleigh line, which enabled these trains to run without reversal at Southampton, would remain technically open for passenger traffic after its regular services were withdrawn in 1969. The 3.17am Salisbury–Weymouth news and passenger train was withdrawn altogether when the Fordingbridge line closed.

Nevertheless the comments made to Maurice Snellgrove by the caretaker at Breamore suggest concern on BR's part about congestion in the Southampton area when the South Wales–Bournemouth trains would begin running via Romsey and Eastleigh. These trains would have to be pathed around the hourly Andover–Portsmouth demu services and the Fawley oil trains. The Andover–Romsey line was awaiting a decision on its future from Mr Marples, amid strong local opposition to its proposed closure. Yet in July, the Minister authorised that closure, against the recommendation of Tom Galbraith and some of his civil servants [12], an outcome which may well have extinguished any hope of the Salisbury & Dorset reopening as a diversionary route to the Bournemouth area via West Moors and Poole. Another possibility is that, with a General Election imminent, the Fordingbridge line was being mothballed in case a new Transport Minister might require its reinstatement as a condition of approval for closure of the Somerset & Dorset.

Unfortunately, the incoming Labour Government continued the policy of closing lines and on 4th November, a

Last Day Scenes

Top: Standard class 4 2-6-0 No 76005 brings the 10.4am Bournemouth West to Salisbury train through West Moors on 2nd May 1964, the last day services on the Salisbury & Dorset line. (R Brough/RK Blencowe Collection)

Middle: The same train is now well on its way along the line, and is seen here at Downton. (CL Caddy)

Bottom: Also active on the day was U class 2-6-0 No 31792, which worked the 9.23am Salisbury to Bournemouth West. It is seen here at Daggons Road. (CL Caddy)

Last Day Scenes

31792 was later captured running "wrong-line" at Verwood.
(R Brough/RK Blencowe Collection)

Later in the day, 31792 returned with a Bournemouth West to Salisbury working, having been turned at Bournemouth.
(C Whetmath)

West Country Pacific No 34091 "Weymouth" eases the 5.20pm Salisbury to Bournemouth West train onto the Salisbury & Dorset at Alderbury Junction.
(EW Fry/RK Blencowe Collection)

Last Day Scenes

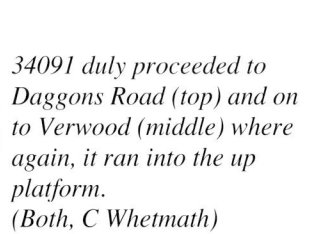

*34091 duly proceeded to Daggons Road (top) and on to Verwood (middle) where again, it ran into the up platform.
(Both, C Whetmath)*

*The last day even witnessed a light engine working. West Country Pacific No 34092 "City of Wells" is seen here drifting through Downton station heading for Salisbury.
(C Whetmath)*

71

few weeks after it took office, the new Minister, Tom Fraser, told Parliament that he had no power to order the restoration of passenger services already withdrawn. This proposition was nonsense but it was to be repeatedly quoted by the Ministry at people who wrote deploring the closure programme and asking for their local railways to be reopened. Among the correspondents was Peter Hingeley of Salisbury, who commented that:

For a large and increasing population of Salisbury and district, (the line) provided a cheap and easy access to South Coast resorts between Bournemouth and Weymouth, and opened up for thousands stretches of Britain's loveliest coastline, which are now virtually inaccessible to those without cars. The bus journey of nearly 100 miles to Weymouth (and back) is now braved only by the toughest of passengers.

Mr Hingeley wrote his letter on 13th April 1966, nearly two years after the line closed and referred to the recent lifting of the track, arguing against the BR Property Board's proposals to sell portions of the formation. Removal of the permanent way had begun in the summer of 1965 from the West Moors end. Richard Benstead recalls one fine day when he worked a demolition train from Salisbury East Yard to Daggons Road behind 76067, which ran tender first. The train was put into the goods loop while the crew and a couple of PW men waited for the contractor's yellow 0-4-0 diesel to arrive from Verwood with wagons laden with short lengths of track. It then became apparent that the 2-6-0's fire had almost gone out, so the men decided to gather up firewood to revive the fire for the return journey. Luckily the station's lamp hut still contained a supply of paraffin.

Another demolition train, which Richard Benstead worked with passed fireman Norman Abbott, ran from Salisbury to Breamore behind 76008 on 25th August 1965. Earlier in the summer a demolition train had been worked from Verwood by Battle of Britain 4-6-2 34066 *Spitfire*, the engine involved in the St Johns, Lewisham collision of December 1957.

As late as 1969, Jack Mussell was still employed to inspect the bridges, crossings and other remaining infrastructure of the dismantled line. This was because of BR's continuing liability for the trackbed which was then still largely in its ownership. He had travelled on the last passenger train, and was unshaken in his conviction that the line had the potential to be a flourishing concern and should never have closed [13].

The line might have stood a better chance of survival if large scale exploitation of gravel or oil deposits had been pursued. Although there is a drift of gravel from near Fordingbridge station across to Woodgreen and Hyde, extraction in Fordingbridge itself would have despoiled valuable farmland. Prospecting for oil was pursued in the New Forest during the 1950s, and in 1958 BP located oil-bearing strata at a depth of 6,000 feet at Ogden's Bottom, about three miles south east of Fordingbridge station. The cost of exploitation was considered prohibitive, and there would in any case have been opposition to the intrusion into an Area of Outstanding Natural Beauty, now a National Park.

For about 20 years after the loss of its direct route to Salisbury, Bournemouth was to enjoy through trains to and from South Wales on summer Saturdays, routed via Eastleigh. These ceased when BR trimmed its InterCity operations, and cut seasonal trains on the premise that rolling stock was either to be used more intensively or scrapped. The philosophy that had condemned the Salisbury & Dorset on the basis of its highly seasonal traffic was still an article of faith in the 1980s. Yet the line had demonstrated year after year the greatest strength of rail transport, namely its ability to move large numbers of people speedily and efficiently, first for Fordingbridge Regatta and later for holidays on the South Coast. If the Salisbury & Dorset Junction line were still with us, it would almost certainly have developed a healthy all-year business from the growth in population and road congestion.

References
1. *Salisbury Journal*, 12.7.1963.
2. *Modern Railways*, December 1962.
3. *Salisbury Journal*, 5.7.1963.
4. ibid, 26.7 and 9.8.1963.
5. ibid, 2.8 and 6.9.1963.
6. Bournemouth Railway Circle traffic survey, 10.8.1963.
7. *Salisbury Journal*, 20.9.1963.
8. Letter from JEM Beale to PD Scott, PRO ref MT 124/777.
9. *Salisbury Journal*, 6.3.1964.
10. ibid, 1.5.1964.
11. ibid, 8.5.1964.
12. Andover–Romsey line closure papers, PRO ref MT 124/778.
13. *Evening Echo, Bournemouth*, 13.6.1969.

Opposite page: It was a while before the demolition trains started to appear. Battle of Britain 4-6-2 34066 "Spitfire" was in evidence at Verwood on 15th May 1965, a full year after closure, and clearly a lot of the infrastructure is still in evidence. Seen in charge of a sole ex-GWR "Toad" brake van in the first two pictures, it was also photographed with train between Verwood and Daggons Road, facing in the opposite direction. (All, Roger Merry-Price)

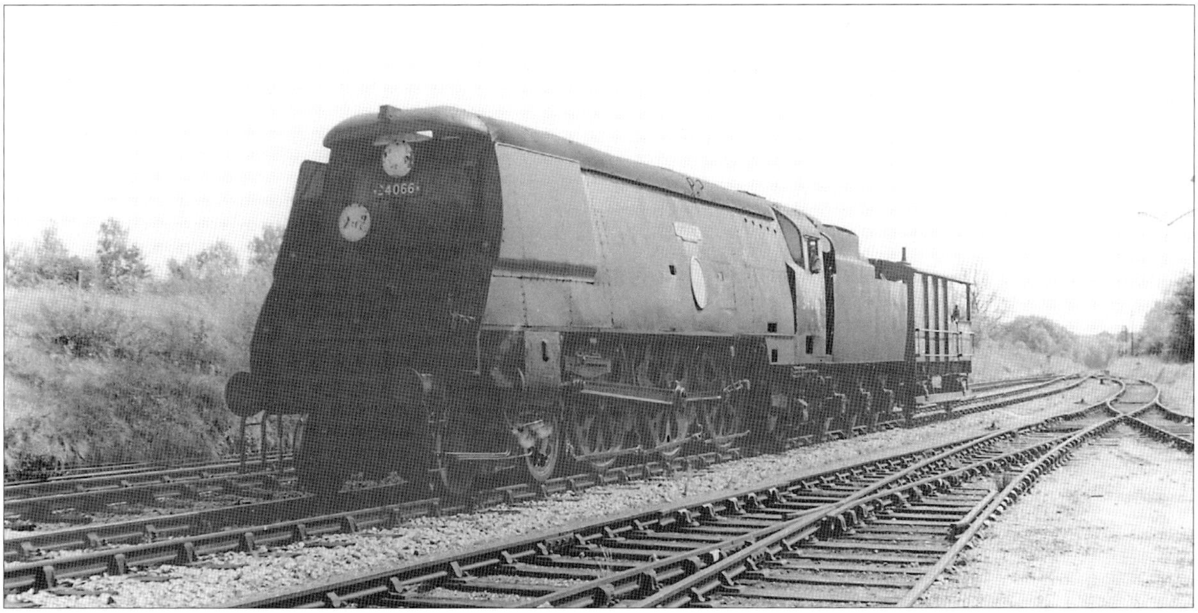

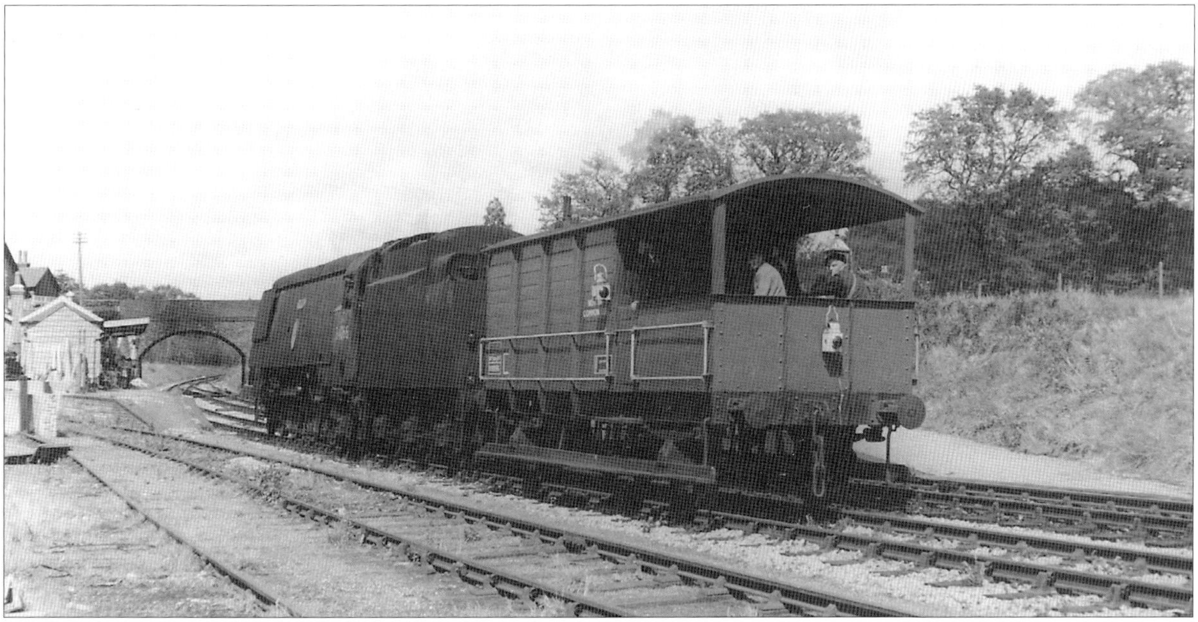

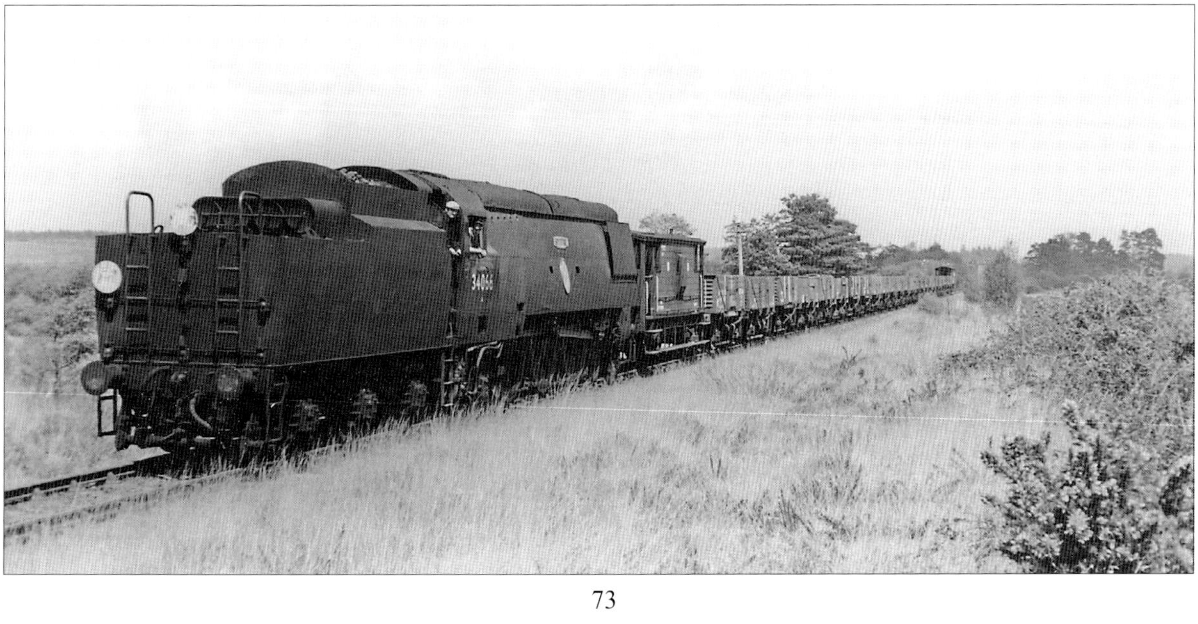

Never to be seen again. U class 2-6-0 No 31792 pulls away from Daggons Road with the 9.23am Salisbury to Bournemouth West on the last day of working over the Salisbury & Dorset Junction Railway, 2nd May 1964. (CL Caddy)

Chapter 9

The Line Described

The line was single throughout from Alderbury Junction to West Moors, with crossing loops at all stations except Daggons Road. On the branch the down direction was towards West Moors, but the reverse definitions applied between Salisbury and Alderbury Junction. Thus a down branch train traversed the up line between leaving Salisbury and joining the branch. In 1885, Electric Train Tablet working was introduced, although from 1931, a miniature train staff was used between Fordingbridge and West Moors instead of the tablet whenever Verwood signal box was switched out. By 1960 the mode of operation had changed to electric token, with a miniature staff used between Fordingbridge and West Moors when Verwood was not in circuit.

The only major engineering work was Downton tunnel but there were many cuttings, low embankments and bridges. Gradients were quite severe in places, particularly between Alderbury Junction and Downton – either side of Fordingbridge and north of Verwood. This influenced the deployment of fairly powerful, but versatile and not too heavily restricted locomotives, particularly on the long-distance trains. Tank locomotives were the exception in SR and BR days, possibly because of the lack of water cranes at branch stations, although there was a regular Salisbury–Wimborne round trip for an M7 0-4-4T on Sundays in the late 1940s and 1950s. Richard Benstead recalls an occasion in the early 1960s when he was working the 5.20pm Salisbury, which was held at Fordingbridge for the delayed 4.40 Bournemouth West to cross it. The booked loco for the up train had either failed or been used elsewhere, and Bournemouth shed had scrambled one of its M7s, normally deployed on push-pull workings to Brockenhurst via Ringwood or on the Swanage branch.

Tank engines were, however, used regularly in LSWR days, notably the Adams Radial 4-4-2Ts in the years leading up to the First World War. This class, with its flexible wheelbase was well suited to the Salisbury & Dorset, which had a number of sharp curves. Also deployed on the line in the 1890s and early 20th century were Adams O2 0-4-4Ts, but tender engines were the normal motive power from the 1920s onwards as passenger trains became longer and heavier with the growth in holiday traffic to Bournemouth.

A distant view of Downton Tunnel, with a Bulleid Light Pacific seemingly reversing towards it. (RK Blencowe)

The schedule for up passenger trains between Downton and Salisbury in BR days was 18 to 21 minutes, which seems generous for a distance of 8¾ miles. This would have included some recovery time, particularly during the summer when long formations needed to pull up twice at the relatively short platforms. There would also have been pathing time at Alderbury and Salisbury Tunnel Junctions, where main line services had priority.

There were some architectural similarities between Breamore and Verwood stations, otherwise each station was very distinctive in style from its neighbours. Breamore, Fordingbridge and Verwood stations were all sited on the West Moors side of overbridges, hence the white painting of an area of brick abutment to create a sighting board for the up starter signal. Downton was the only intermediate station with a footbridge, although West Moors, which opened shortly after the line itself, was given a substantial one. Passengers at Breamore, Fordingbridge and Verwood were expected to use the barrow crossings, Fordingbridge having one at each end of the platforms.

In BR days, none of the goods yards on the branch had headshunts, but leisurely shunting on to the running lines was feasible because of the generally sparse passenger service.

Prior to the introduction of regular interval demu services between Salisbury, Southampton and Portsmouth in 1957, most passenger trains over the Fordingbridge line used the offset bay platform 6 at Salisbury. Thereafter more trains to Bournemouth departed from platform 2. The through platforms were used by the dated Swanage and Weymouth trains of the 1950s, the Templecombe–Bournemouth working of the early 1960s and the direct services between Bristol or South Wales and Bournemouth. Engines working into Salisbury from the Great Western system on the latter services, or on excursions, were relieved by SR locos and crews at Salisbury. I have not discovered any documented or photographic record of a GW loco type on the Salisbury & Dorset line.

Alderbury Junction to Breamore

Alderbury Junction staff platforms, originally provided for the convenience of passengers making connections between the Fordingbridge and Southampton directions, were about half a mile from the village along Junction Road, an unclassified road that continued under the Salisbury–Romsey main line as an unmetalled track. These timber faced platforms were on the Salisbury side of this underbridge, west of the junction. LSWR service timetables of 1875 and 1876 contained a note that the first up train (5.40am Dorchester–Salisbury) would set down passengers wishing to connect into the 7.55 Salisbury–Southampton provided they had notified the guard, but it added that the Southampton

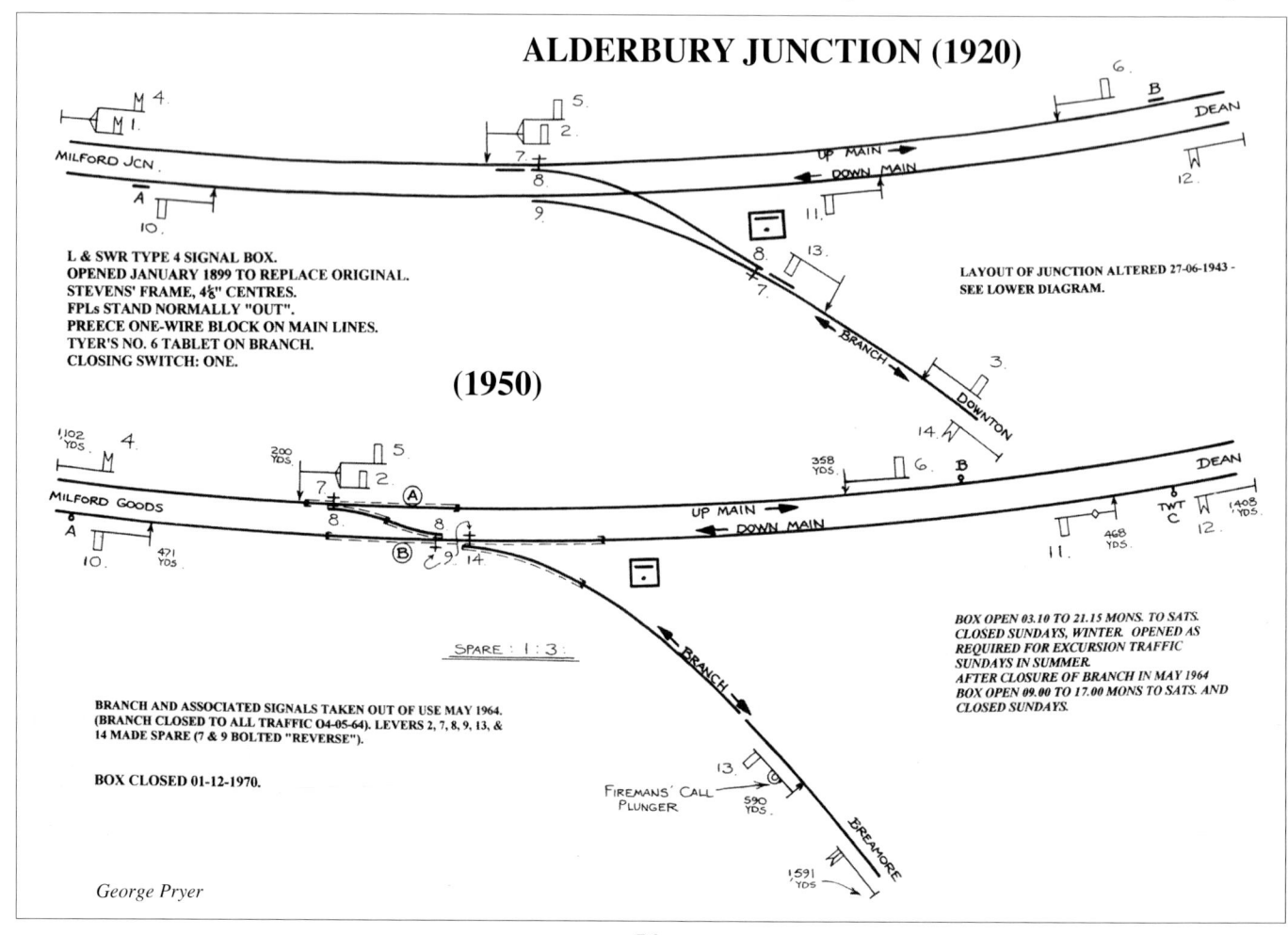

THE LINE DESCRIBED

train was not to be detained if the Salisbury & Dorset train could not be seen or heard approaching. This note had disappeared from service timetables by 1881.

In later years, the platforms were used occasionally to transfer passengers off a failed train from the Fordingbridge direction into a main line service heading for Salisbury, as on 23rd August 1952, when T9 4-4-0 No 30703 bent a coupling rod just west of the junction *(see Chapter 5)*. Their most regular uses, however, were to allow railwaymen's wives to go shopping in Salisbury, and to pick up and set down permanent way staff. Designated passenger trains would stop for these purposes, although of course, were not advertised to do so.

On the Romsey side of the bridge, the landscape changes abruptly from gently undulating arable land to coniferous woodland, the actual junction being close to the western edges of Common Plantation to the north and Whaddon Common to the south. The Romsey line then makes an anti-clockwise curve to alter its course from south-easterly to easterly. The West Moors branch, by contrast, took a clockwise sweep to establish a southerly course which it maintained until a mile or so north of Downton.

In the apex of the junction was Alderbury Junction signal box, built of brick with a gable roof and wooden external staircase. The main windows fronted the main line, but a window in the rear wall gave the signalman a view of trains approaching from the branch. Originally the branch diverged as a double line, which became single at loop points immediately behind the box but by 27th June 1943 [1] the junction was altered to a single trailing lead from the down main line, and a new facing crossover was provided between the up and down main lines immediately east of the junction. In connection with the old layout, there was a splitting distant signal on the up main line, 1102 yards from the box, but the branch arm was fixed because main line trains always had priority. The stop signal for up branch trains, 149 yards from the box, was unusually on the down (right-hand) side of the line and was equipped with a telephone to the box. The fixed distant signal for up branch trains was 957 yards from the box.

Because of the remote location of the box, specified trains were required to call there to supply fuel and stores. In 1920, the 9.30 Salisbury–Wimborne pick-up goods stopped on Saturdays to deliver coal and oil.

Treadles were provided on the main line at each end of the junction. East of the junction, there were treadles on both the up and down main lines close to the down main distant signal. West of the junction, the treadle was on the down main line only, presumably because a down branch train had to cross from the up to the down main lines, and would not be allowed onto the branch if a down main line service was approaching from Dean. Larry Crosier believes the treadles

The approaches to Downton station from the north in September 1962. (South Western Circle/Eyers Collection)

DOWNTON (1920)

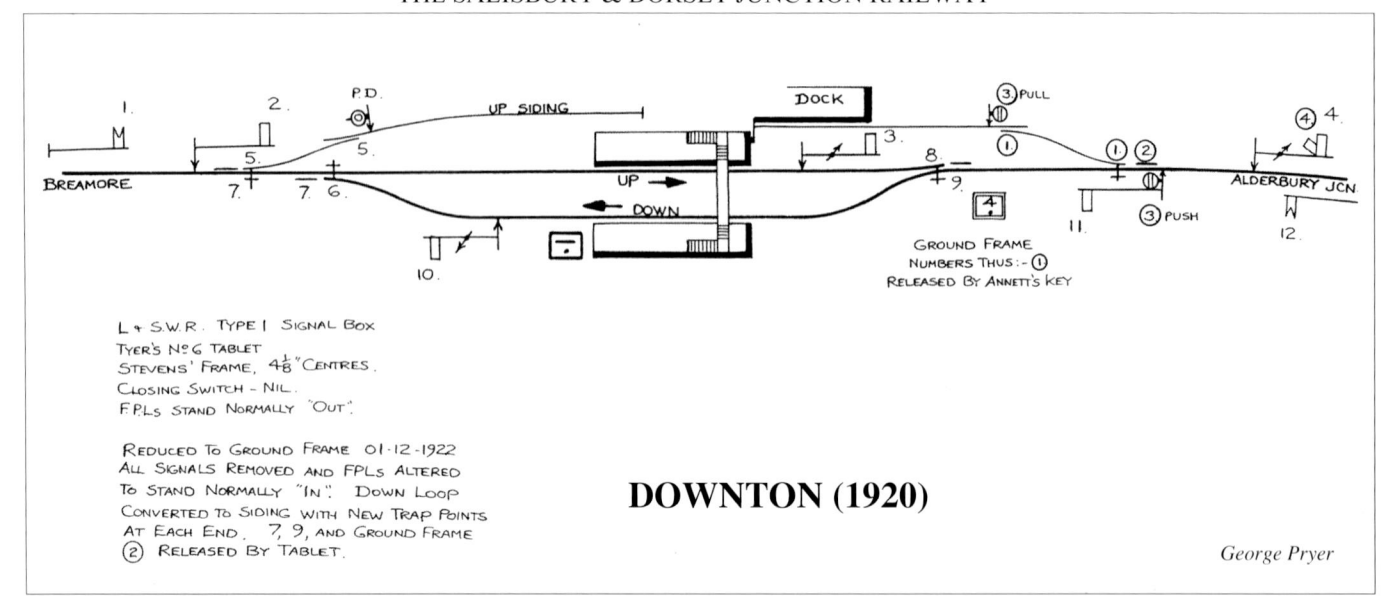

L & S.W.R. Type 1 Signal Box
Tyer's No 6 Tablet
Stevens' Frame, 4⅛" Centres.
Closing Switch - Nil.
F.P.Ls Stand Normally "Out".

Reduced to Ground Frame 01-12-1922
All Signals Removed and FPLs Altered
To Stand Normally "In". Down Loop
Converted to Siding with New Trap Points
At Each End. 7, 9, and Ground Frame
② Released by Tablet.

George Pryer

had been provided by the LSWR under the lock and block system to warn the signalman of a train approaching or clearing the junction. There may have been a treadle on the up main, west of the junction, before the remodelling documented in 1943.

When down branch passenger trains were running late, the signalman was required to advise West Moors of the passing times so that the likely effect on pathing over the Corkscrew, connections at Broadstone or Poole and station working at Bournemouth could be considered. Similarly, the West Moors signalman had to ring Alderbury Junction with timings of late up passenger services which might affect connections at Salisbury.

Initially the branch descended at 1 in 178, and crossed the remains of the Salisbury Canal. Soon afterwards it began a steep climb of 1 in 76 through Whaddon Common and passed over the Whaddon–West Grimstead road. It then crossed the A36 trunk road in Whaddon village. The route became level after Whaddon for around ½ mile, then descended sharply at 1 in 75 for almost that distance. For the next three miles or so the route was through chalk downland, with a series of cuttings and embankments. Overlooking Witherington and Standlynch Downs is Pepperbox Hill, a National Trust beauty spot east of the A36 that gave a distant view of both routes. Etched in Peter Cupper's memory is his view from that hill of a down Bournemouth train headed by a pair of T9s traversing an embankment.

About two miles from the junction, the line entered a shallow cutting and passed under a minor road linking Alderbury with Standlynch Down. To the west of this bridge were the grounds of Trafalgar House (now known as Trafalgar Park) which for generations was the home of Lord Nelson's descendants. Dating from the 1730s, the mansion was originally known as Standlynch House, but was purchased by the Crown in 1814 after the death of its owner, Henry Dawkins, and given to Horatio's brother William, who was created Earl Nelson. The property was renamed Trafalgar *Park* in the 1990s to avoid confusion with a financial institution, but some minutes of the Salisbury & Dorset company had also used the suffix Park rather than House.

About a mile further on, the line began to curve south-westerly on the edge of Barford Down, and soon afterwards passed a small copse on the down side before entering a deep cutting into Downton tunnel, 107 yards long. This was a small bore tunnel, which could be particularly unpleasant for the crews of Light Pacifics, which had a tendency to drift steam back towards the cab. Richard Benstead remembers that another hazard was the risk of a blowback from the boiler if an engine had insufficient power when entering the tunnel. His precaution was to switch on the "blower" to force a jet of steam up through the blast pipe.

The route continued to fall at 1 in 100 for nearly ¾ mile into Downton station, 3m 70ch from Alderbury Junction. The station was to the north east of the village, and was reached by a turning off High Street. The main offices were on the up side and consisted of a single storey building with a sloping roof, with a substantial chimney stack at each end and a wooden canopy. The signal box was at the Breamore end of the down platform. Originally all the sidings were on the up side, a cattle dock (replaced by a pig dock in 1936) being accessed by a lead north of the station, while sidings for coal and general merchandise were connected to the running line south of the station loop. When Downton ceased to be a block post (officially on 1st December 1922) the down platform loop was converted to a siding and catch points provided at either end.

Downton had a steel girder footbridge at the Salisbury end of the station which was the first of its type to be installed on the LSWR. It was approved by the company's Traffic Committee in June 1902 following a complaint from Salisbury Rural District Council about the danger to passengers from having to use the foot crossing over the line. The span and staircases were supported by tong shaped girders that were anchored in concrete. Not all the locals were grateful, for in April 1904, the Vicar of Downton and

Top: Downton on the day of closure, 2nd May 1964. Perhaps the Station Master is walking disconsolately away. (CL Caddy)
Bottom: A view from the opposite direction, possibly on or around the same day. (David Lawrence/Photos of the Fifties)

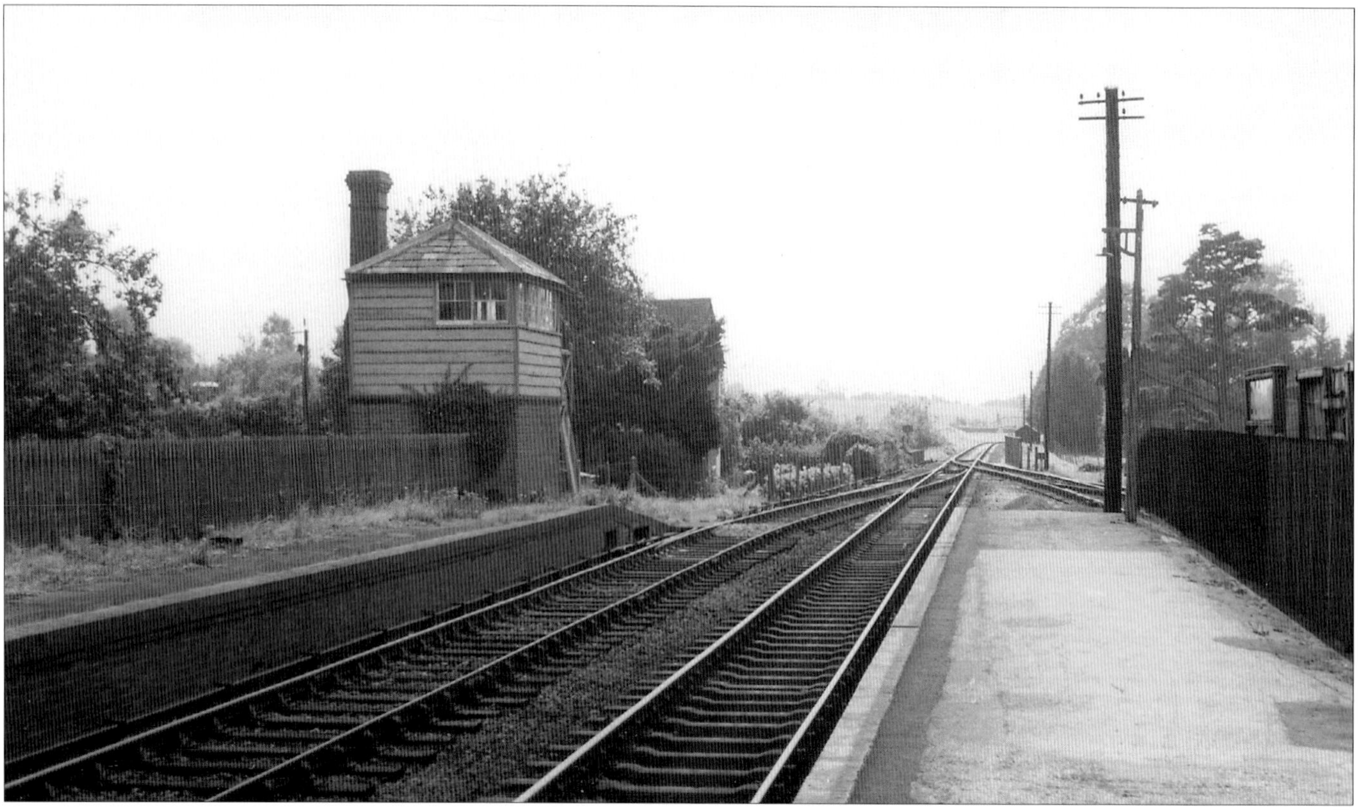

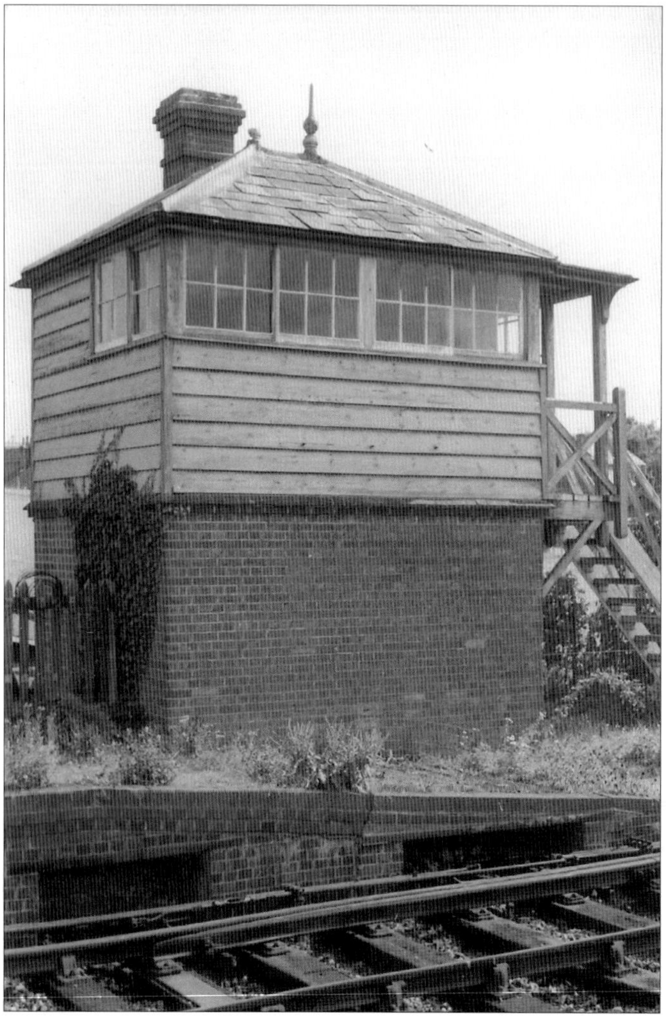

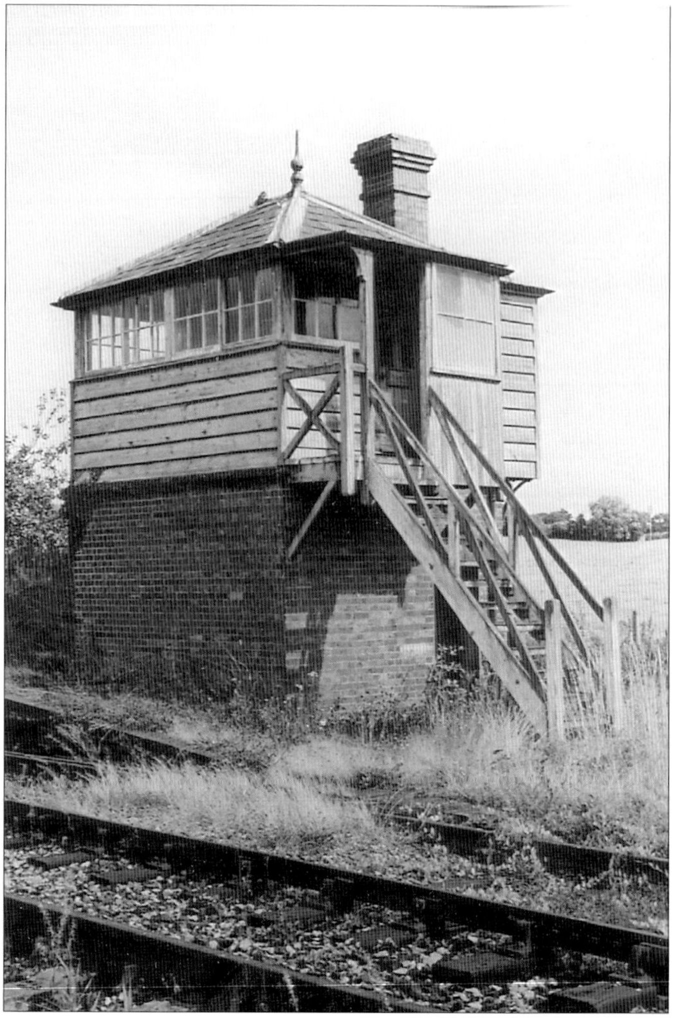

*Opposite page, top: Looking towards Breamore in September 1962 with the Station Master's house behind the trees just beyond the signalbox.
(South Western Circle/Eyers Collection)*

*Opposite page, bottom: Two views of Downton signal box in May 1964 (left) and September 1962 (right).
(South Western Circle/GA Tull & Eyers Collection)*

*Above: In May 1964 the weeds are already taking over, and dereliction is starting to set in.
(South Western Circle/GA Tull)*

*Right: Only the Station Master's house remains today. Bungalows have been built on the platform area, and are served by a road appropriately called "The Sidings". To the south, the bridge over Lode Hill has been removed.
(H Sprenger/Kestrel Collection)*

North Charford crossing ("Crossing No 2") on 1st May 1964. (South Western Circle/Eyers Collection)

Salisbury RDC wrote to the company asking for the crossing to be reinstated. The request was declined [2].

The gradient was level in the station but then fell at 1 in 78 for about a mile as it skirted the eastern perimeter of the village, passing the site of a Roman villa. Continuing the south-westerly direction it had taken since Barford Down, the route crossed the River Avon to enter Hampshire. The A338 Salisbury–Bournemouth road now converged on the up side, and the landscape changed to one of gently undulating downland to the west, and meadow land scored by drainage ditches and rivulets cutting across a meander of the Avon to the east.

The line had been descending since Downton, but at around five miles from Alderbury Junction, the gradient eased to 1 in 895 and the route traversed two manually-operated level crossings, worked by gatekeepers and leading to farms close to the river. These were North Charford, which accessed North Charford Manor, and South Charford leading to the farm of that name. In BR days a local instruction prescribed the method of communication between the Downton porter, the Breamore signalman and drivers. Down freight trains calling at Downton were not permitted to depart that station until the porter had telephoned the Breamore signalman that the train was ready to leave. In the event of telephone failure, the porter had to advise the driver and instruct him to approach the crossings at caution, sound the whistle and be prepared to find the gates open across the line.

Between these two crossings was College Level Crossing (5m 38ch from Alderbury Junction), on approaching which drivers were instructed to open their whistles [3]. This was slightly beyond the site of the 1884 derailment, which occurred on the embankment near the river about 1¼ miles from Downton station and close to the Agricultural College whose staff and students assisted at the scene. In later years, after the College had closed, the crossing was known officially as Harding's Crossing.

At 6m 67ch, Breamore station stood at the south end of the village on the Fordingbridge side of an overbridge carrying an unclassified road from the A338 via Woodgreen to Godshill on the B3078 Romsey–Fordingbridge–Shaftesbury road. Breamore was the nearest point on the railway to the New Forest, which extends westward to Woodgreen, about a mile across another meander of the Avon from the station. Areas of mainly deciduous woodland cover some of the undulating downland about a mile from either side of the railway between North Charford and Fordingbridge. These include Breamore Wood, Radnall Wood, Godshill Enclosure and Castle Hill, the latter two being within what is now the National Park boundary. Breamore's main claim to fame is Breamore House, an Elizabethan manor west of the village off the A338, and maintained by English Heritage. It was used as a military headquarters during the Second World War.

THE LINE DESCRIBED

South Charford level crossing ("Crossing No 3") in May 1964. (South Western Circle/GA Tull)

The station had a passing loop with two platforms, the main building being on the up side, and comprising a single storey, double-gabled structure with a short extension at the south end. The platform canopy was a large flat wooden structure, sloping back towards the building. There were fewer creature comforts on the down platform, which had only a wooden waiting shelter with shorter end walls than on the shelters at Downton and Verwood. It was of very similar design to the waiting shelters at Mottisfont on the A&R. The main building survives today and has been renovated in recent years.

The most unusual feature of the station was its signal box, actually a lever frame inside a fenced compound on the up platform in front of the Fordingbridge end of the station building. Originally, there was a signal box of LSWR pattern at the south end of the down platform *(see page 116)*, but this was closed on 29th July 1930, and replaced by a 13-lever frame, the block instruments thereafter being housed in the station office. This was an economy measure to reduce the staffing to two porter signalmen who worked early and late shifts. A similar arrangement survives at Sheffield Park on the Bluebell Railway.

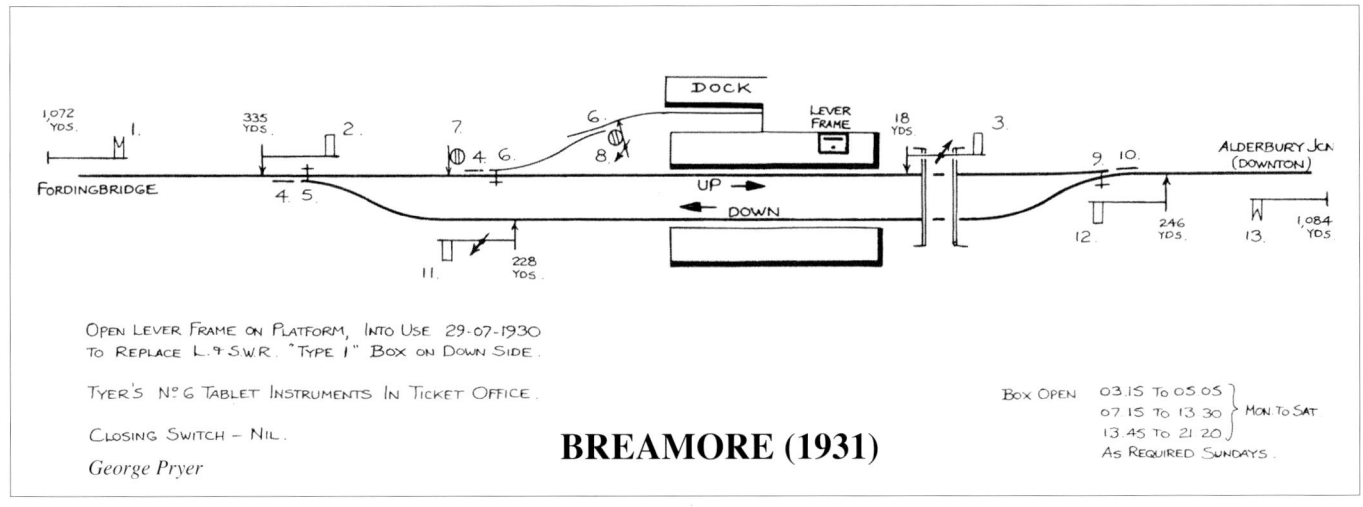

BREAMORE (1931)

Open Lever Frame on Platform, Into Use 29-07-1930 to replace L.&S.W.R. "Type 1" Box on Down Side.

Tyer's No 6 Tablet Instruments in Ticket Office.

Closing Switch – Nil.

Box Open: 03.15 to 05.05, 07.15 to 13.30, 13.45 to 21.20 Mon. to Sat. As required Sundays.

George Pryer

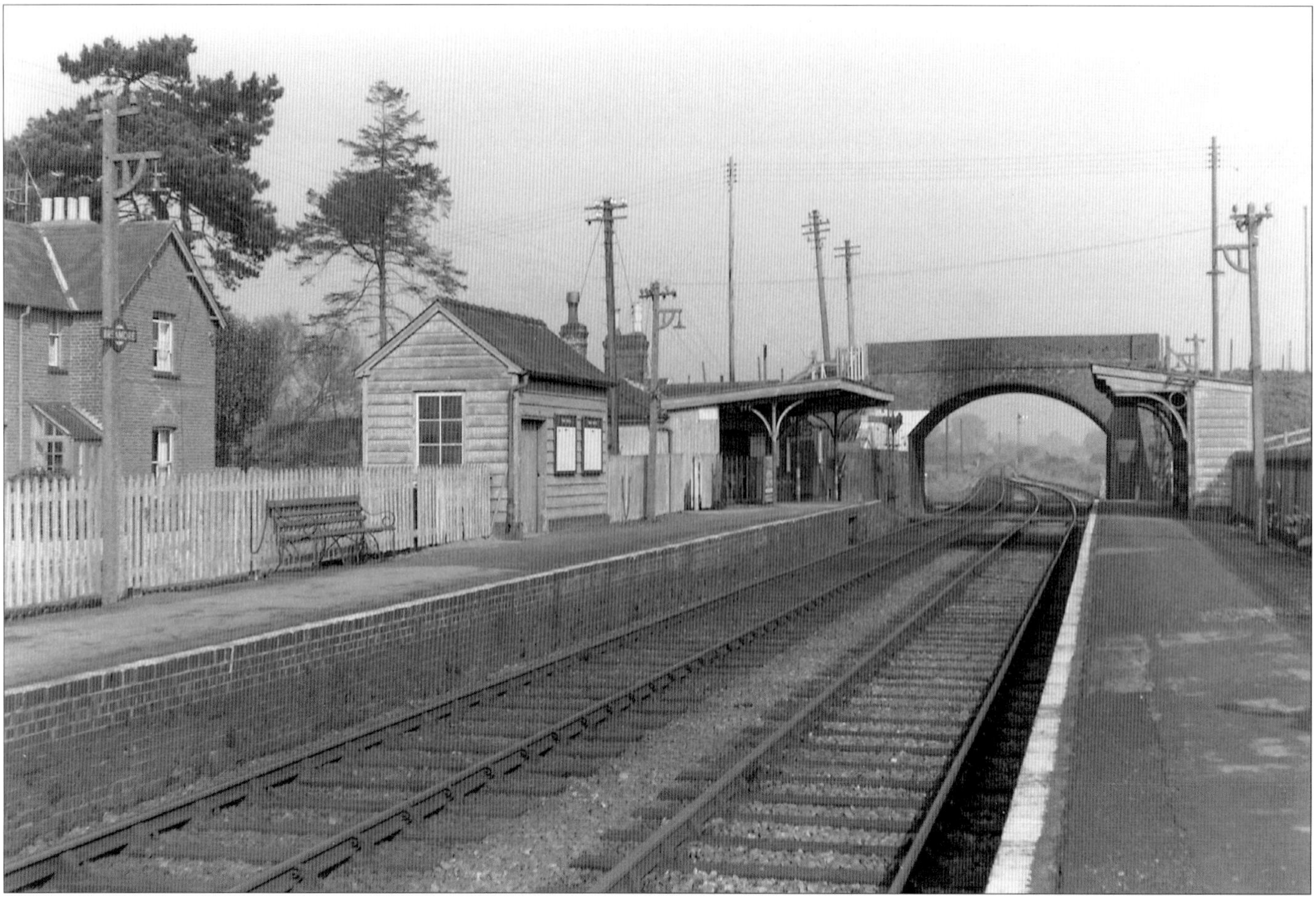

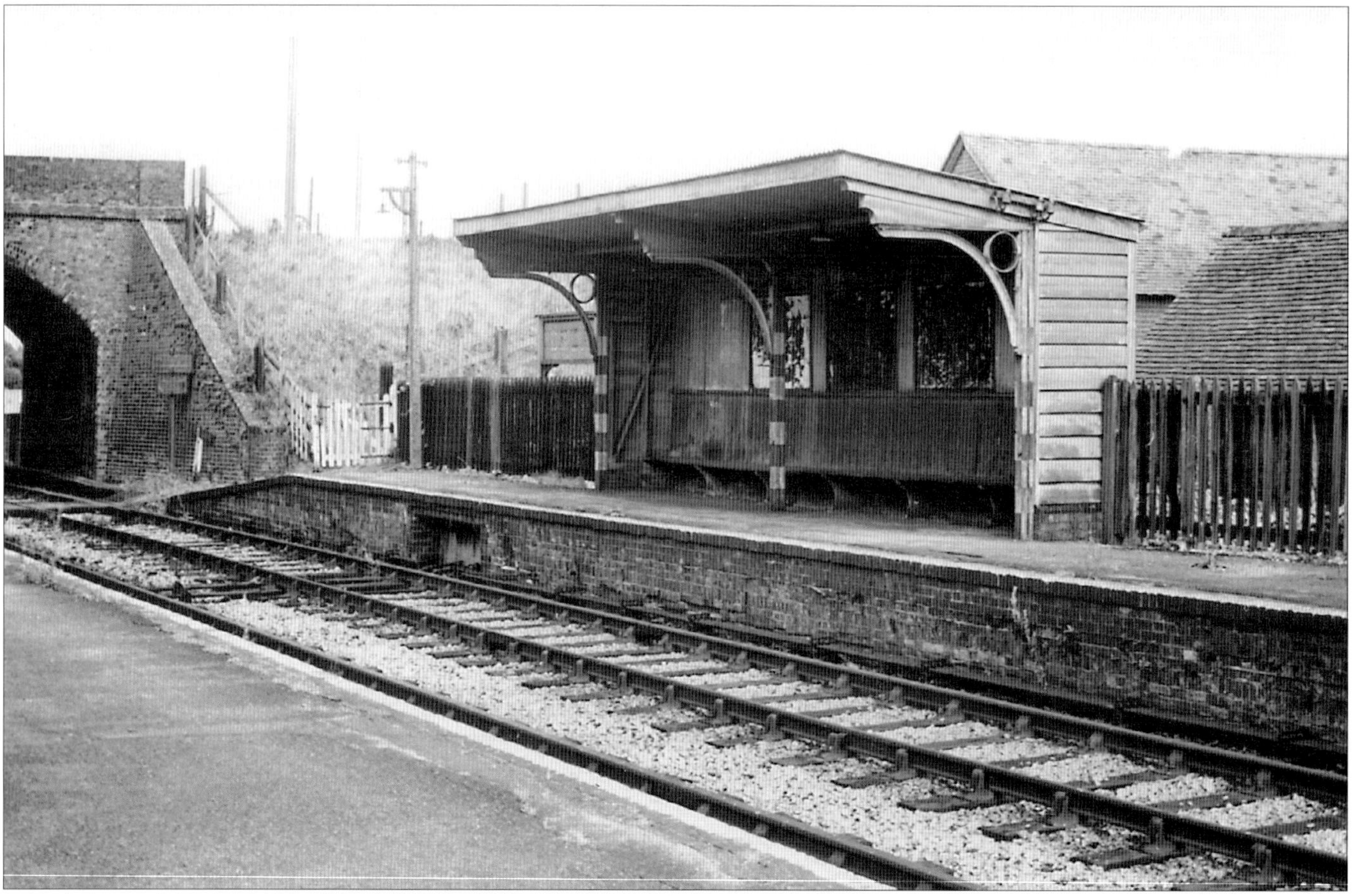

Opposite page, top: Breamore looking north on 14th October 1961. (E Wilmshurst)

Opposite page, bottom: The down platform shelter in May 1964. (South Western Circle/ GA Tull)

Right: The exterior of the station showing the loading dock in September 1955. (South Western Circle/Eyers Collection)

Below: The lever frame (left) mounted on the up platform and (right) the lower quadrant up starting signal in May 1964. (Both, South Western Circle/ GA Tull)

Top: After closure on 6th May 1970. (South Western Circle/Eyers Collection)
Bottom: The station building on 25th September 1971. (South Western Circle/M Snellgrove)

*Top: Even by 9th May 1992, the station building was remarkably well preserved, but was looking for a new use.
Bottom: Seen on 21st June 2009, it has now been nicely restored, even down to the wartime stripes painted on the canopy supports, although somewhat incongruously in green and white. (Both, H Sprenger/Kestrel Collection)*

The goods yard consisted of a single siding with headshunt, accessed from the south end of the up loop, but when the down loop was extended in 1946, the siding was slewed over most of the headshunt and a catch point provided. There was a loading dock alongside the siding, close to the premises of Avon Valley Dairies. The station was said in 1913 to be doing "a very fair traffic in milk" [4].

Breamore to Fordingbridge

On leaving Breamore, the railway remained close to the A338 with water meadows on the down side until Upper Burgate, going under the road just north of Burgate weir, where the river meanders close to the highway. This skew bridge was known as Burgate Arch. Just before Lower Burgate, about a mile from the south end of Breamore station loop, was Burgate Siding (8 miles from Alderbury Junction), which came into use on 14th June 1942 to serve a Ministry of Works & Planning (later Ministry of Food) store. The siding was on the down side of the line, and was operated by a two-lever ground frame released by an Annett's key on the token for the Fordingbridge–Breamore section, which had to be clear as far as Breamore's up home signal. The turnout faced Breamore, but it was the normal practice for the siding to be entered by an up train reversing into it. In the early post-war years, this train was the afternoon Wimborne–Salisbury pick-up, which was allowed about 15 minutes to service the siding. By 1954, a lunchtime trip from Fordingbridge to Breamore and back was made instead, using the loco of the morning local freight from Salisbury, which now had a much longer stay at Fordingbridge. The monthly average of wagons forwarded and received by the siding was said in 1950 to be 27 [5], but by 1957 it no longer appeared in working timetables, which suggests that traffic may have been very intermittent in the final years.

The route began to curve away in a more west-south-westerly direction after Burgate Siding, traversing a minor road at Burgate Green Lane Crossing. It entered a short cutting before being bridged by the Whitsbury road about half a mile from the centre of Fordingbridge. This might have been a more convenient location for the station rather than the one selected at Ashford, a good ¾ mile from the town centre. Two further cuttings were entered before the line reached Fordingbridge station (9m 36ch), situated on the west side of an overbridge carrying the B3078.

It was not well placed for the town, although if the line had survived this would not have mattered so much in a motorised age. At least it was spacious, so that a substantial station building and well laid out goods yard could be provided on the down side. The Railway Hotel was on the east side of the main road above the down side of the line and is now called the Augustus John after the painter born in 1878, and who became the town's most famous resident, living his latter years there until his death in 1961.

The station was by far the largest on the branch, with its main building on the down platform being a two-storey brick structure incorporating the station house, with two large single storey extensions at the Salisbury end. The station garden was situated between these extensions and the road bridge. On the up platform were a brick waiting shelter and a small wooden office.

The goods yard consisted of five sidings, all converging towards a trailing connection into the down platform line. Access to the yard was controlled by lever 6 in the signal box, and this lever interlocked with catch points at the yard throat to prevent a train in the yard from fouling the running lines. The short siding nearest to the down platform ran into a loading dock on which stood a large barrel-vaulted store, while the second siding went through the substantial brick goods shed, which had a large lean-to outbuilding on the side furthest from the station. This goods shed was the largest on the branch, and the only one equipped with a crane (of 30 cwt capacity in 1934), in addition to that of 5 tons capacity in the yard. The outermost siding served an Anglo-American oil depot from the 1920s. Beyond the goods shed near to the road entrance to the yard were cattle cake sheds built of concrete on stilts.

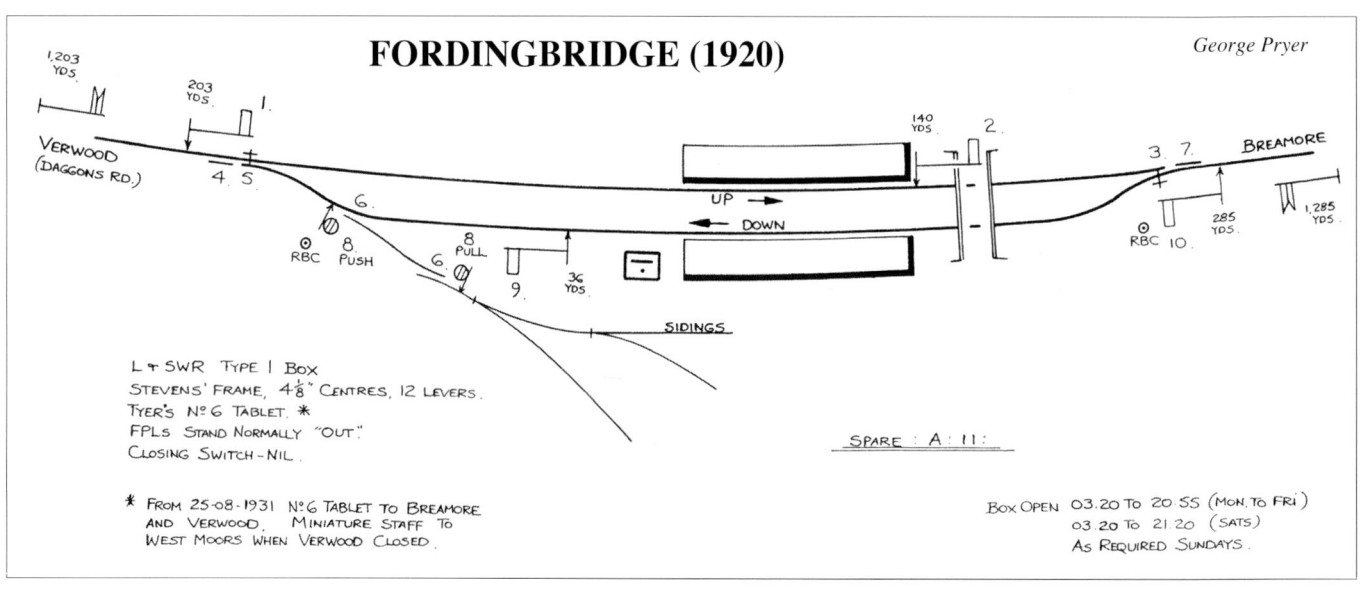

Top: A fine view of Fordingbridge station looking north on 14th October 1961. (E Wilmshurst)
Bottom: The up platform waiting room and bridge on 23rd March 1964. (South Western Circle/Eyers Collection)

Two views of the main building on the down platform on 23rd March 1964. (Both, South Western Circle/Eyers Collection)

Top: Looking the other way, towards West Moors on 2nd May 1964. (C Whetmath)
Bottom: A close-up of the area around the signal box on 23rd March 1964. (South Western Circle/Eyers Collection)

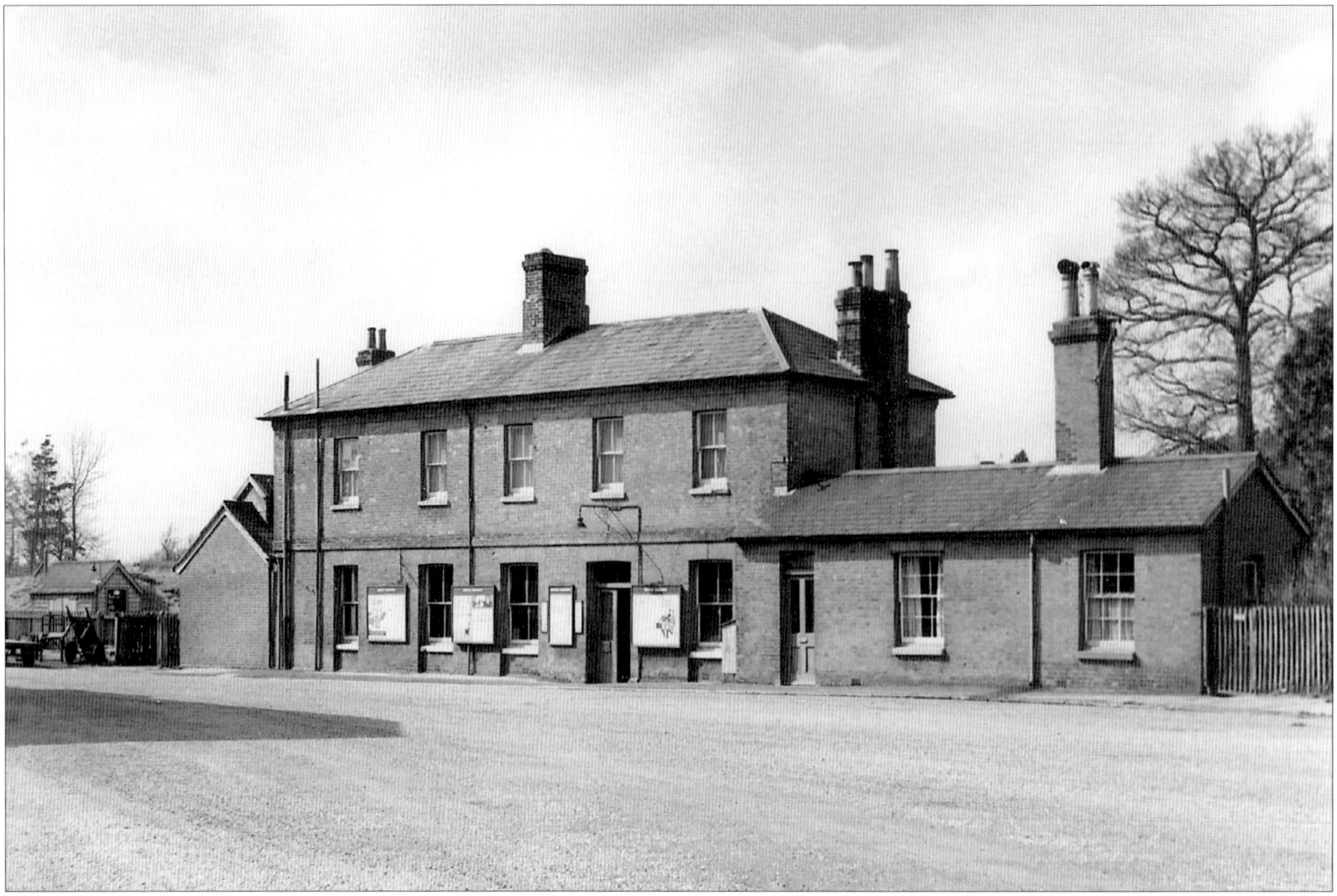

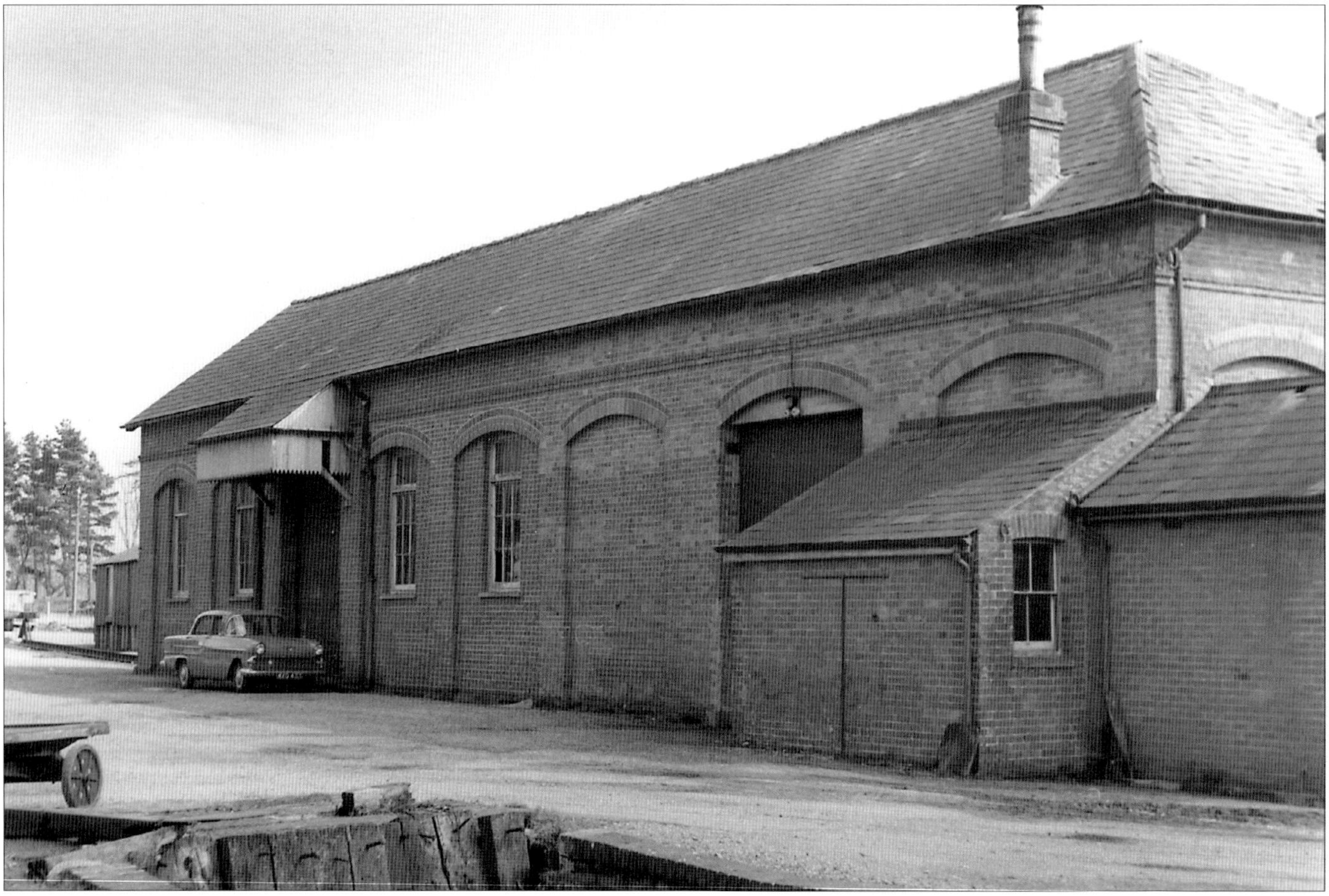

Opposite page: The imposing exterior of Fordingbridge station (top) and the equally impressive goods shed (bottom) whose west side is seen here. Both photographs were taken on 23rd March 1964.
(Both, South Western Circle/Eyers Collection)

Above and right: Detail shots of the goods shed at Fordingbridge, taken some years after closure on 25th September 1971. Above we see the south end of the shed, and right is the associated office in the south-east corner.
(Both, South Western Circle/M Snellgrove)

Bottom: For many years after closure, the only evidence that there had ever been a railway and a station here was the road bridge (which still survives). Seen on 2nd February 1997 are the steps that once took passengers down to the up platform.
(H Sprenger/Kestrel Collection)

The short siding was used on 5th August 1958 to dump a failed T9 loco. Richard Benstead recalls that he and his friend Stan Broomfield were at Daggons Road chatting to Leading Porter Ron Tague. The 'phone rang, and Ron told them that the 10.4am Bournemouth West–Salisbury had failed at Fordingbridge. The two lads sped off on their bicycles to Fordingbridge station, where they discovered that, after receiving the right away, 30301 had stopped with a thumping noise and could not move; it evidently had a damaged coupling rod and valve gear. Jack Mussell, who had to examine the route back to Daggons Road for possible damage, was not amused.

Fortunately, help was at hand in the shape of a class 700, which was in the yard with the down Wimborne goods. The 0-6-0 skidded the defective engine into the siding but, instead of proceeding with its own freight train, took the passenger train tender first to Salisbury, so that the freight crew could get home. Another engine was provided later that day to work the Wimborne goods forward.

The lack of headshunt facilities to keep shunting clear of running lines, particularly at Fordingbridge and Verwood, discouraged improvement of the passenger service, as did the abolition of Downton as a block post. Despite these limitations, the Southern Railway managed to fit in additional long distance trains on Saturdays when freight movements were less numerous. BR accommodated extra trains to Swanage and Weymouth during the week by flighting three services ahead of the down pick-up freight in the morning, returning the trippers in the evening after the up local freight had cleared the branch (*see Chapter 6*).

The signal box was south of the down platform, immediately beyond a lamp hut; the exterior walls of the box were clad with asbestos. Over a brick wall at the far south end of the yard were the vineries and greenhouses established along the Ashford Water, a tributary of the Avon, by Adolph Quertier in the 1890s. These produced flowers, grapes and tomatoes. Large quantities of grapes were being despatched by train by 1913 [4].

Just after leaving the station complex, the line crossed Ashford Water and entered Dorset. It had thus traversed three counties in about four miles since North Charford. Fordingbridge is a frontier town in another sense as the meeting point of several dissimilar landscapes – the chalk downs of South Wiltshire, water meadows of Hampshire, and the clay heathlands of north-east Dorset that gave rise to the brick and tile works of Alderholt, Daggons Road and Verwood. West of Fordingbridge station the locality of Sandleheath had produced bricks for many centuries.

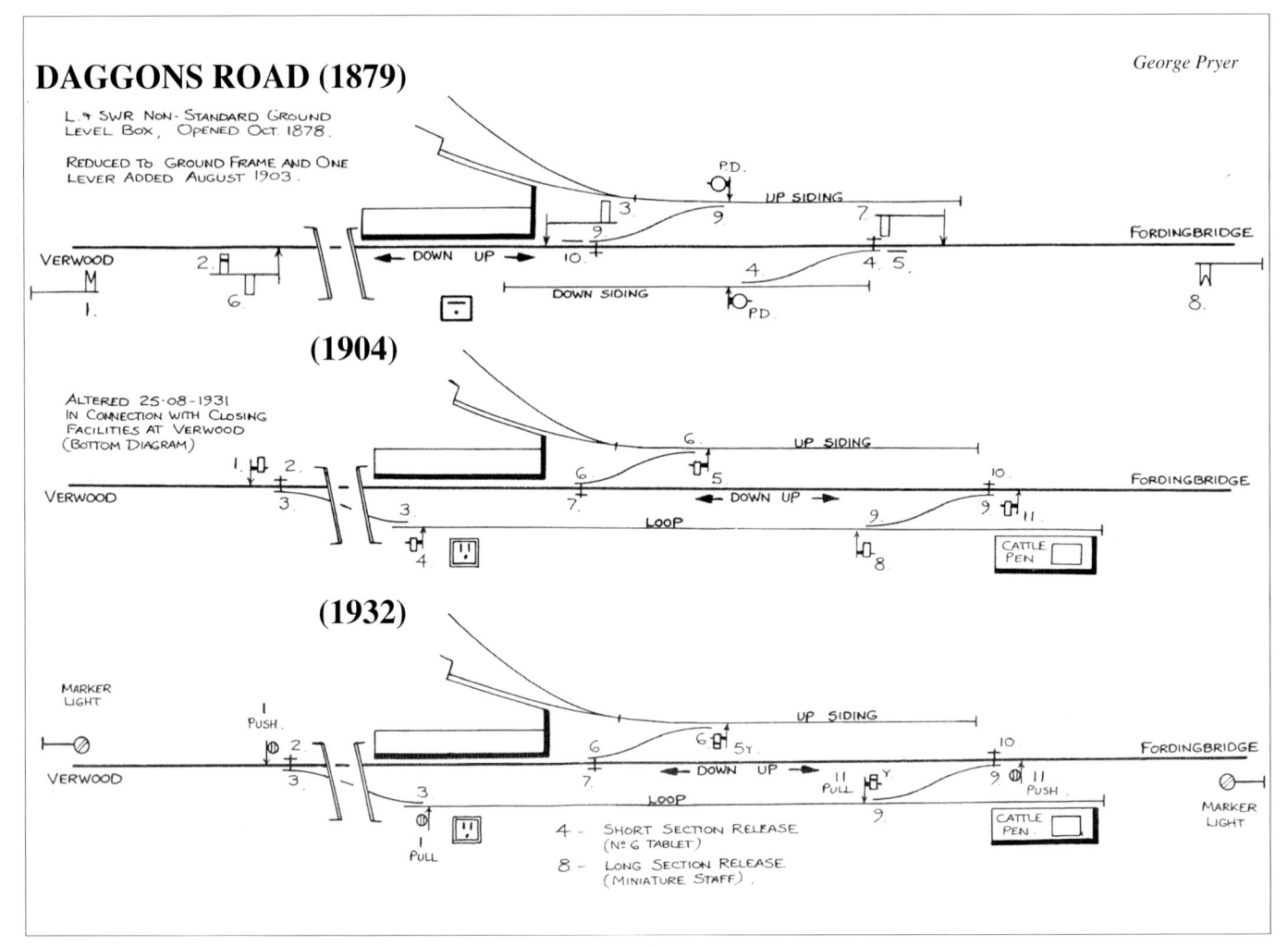

THE LINE DESCRIBED

Fordingbridge to West Moors

The line rose at 1 in 88 for about ½ mile from Ashford Water as it continued south west, passing under a double line of pylons, and then falling for a short distance after the 102 milepost. It entered a short cutting near the hamlet of Bonfire Hill, and then began a gentle rise, crossing a minor road from Sandleheath on a long embankment. The route then entered coniferous woodland west of Alderholt, the largest village in the locality and the name originally given to the station provided at Charing Cross about ½ mile further down the line. At a stroke the LSWR had avoided the trap of confusing passengers with the London terminus of the South Eastern Railway, but created confusion with Aldershot on its own system. Three months after the station opened on 1st January 1876, it was renamed Daggens Road (sic) after a hamlet lying a mile or so to the west. Its final spelling first appeared in the public timetable from 1st October 1903.

Daggons Road station (11m 21ch) was in a shallow cutting on the Fordingbridge side of a bridge carrying a minor road from Alderholt to Cranborne. A platform was provided on the up side only, although the main building was substantial considering this was the most remote station on the line. It was a two-storey, double-gabled brick structure with prominent gas lamps at each end on the platform side. A single-storey extension housed the booking office while a wooden outbuilding provided the ladies' and general waiting rooms. Outside the main station building was another pair of gas lamps mounted on posts made from rail. The main building survives in 2009.

The inner of two up sidings at the north end of the station ran into a loading dock, while the outer siding served the Daggons Road Brickworks company, latterly trading as the West of England Brick & Tile company. The private siding received coal and despatched bricks by rail, and appears on 1921 and 1931 OS maps. In late Victorian times it produced decorative terra cotta work for villas, notably in Bournemouth. Access to the siding was controlled by a ground frame released by the Fordingbridge–Verwood tablet. Wagons ready to leave the siding were brought up to a wheelstop that was released by a key when the Fordingbridge–Verwood section was clear. The siding is listed as out of use in the 1934 WTT Appendix and was removed on 6th December 1953.

The down siding served cattle pens and a Southern Counties Agricultural Traders' store. It had level access for lorries, although it did not receive regular consignments of coal. Tim Hale recalls that coal for the Alderholt area was delivered by Messrs Hood from their depot at Fordingbridge station. The siding originally terminated opposite the booking office, but was extended in May 1904 to form a loop connecting with the running line underneath the road bridge. It was not, however, used to cross trains as the station never became a block post, although Daggens Road *(sic)* appears in the list of signal boxes in the WTT Appendix for 1892 *(see Appendix B)*. Richard Benstead recalls that the points at the north end of the loop were so stiff in the final years that the loop was usually accessed via the south end points. Hence most wagons at Daggons Road were detached or collected by the down pick-up freight, which reversed into the siding.

The ground frame was one of the icons of the line, because of its distinctive appearance with a curiously pointed roof, giving an impression of Oriental design. It stood opposite the main building alongside the down loop, and survived until the line closed. It was released by Intermediate Tablet (later Intermediate Token) Instruments. Lever 4 in the frame was released by the Fordingbridge–Verwood tablet, whilst lever 8 was used when Verwood box was switched out, and the block section was Fordingbridge–West Moors; lever 6 operated the lead to the up sidings. The down loop was operated by push/pull levers, like a two-way switch, which moved a pair of ground position light signals to off. To reverse them, the lever had to be brought to the half way position to release the locking.

As there were no signals on the approaches to Daggons Road, marker lights were provided for the guidance of drivers during the hours of darkness. The up marker light was particularly useful as the view of the station was obscured by the overbridge and road embankment.

Just before reaching Daggons Road station, the line crossed Sandleheath Road. The railway bridge still survives, and is seen here on 21st June 2009. (H Sprenger/Kestrel Collection)

This page: Daggons Road station changed remarkably little over the years as these pictures show. The top view is from the 1930s, the bottom view from the 1950s. (Both Lens of Sutton Collection)
Opposite page, top: A similar view from 14th October 1961. (E Wilmshurst)
Opposite page, bottom: A close-up of the public part of the station building on 2nd May 1965. (CL Caddy)

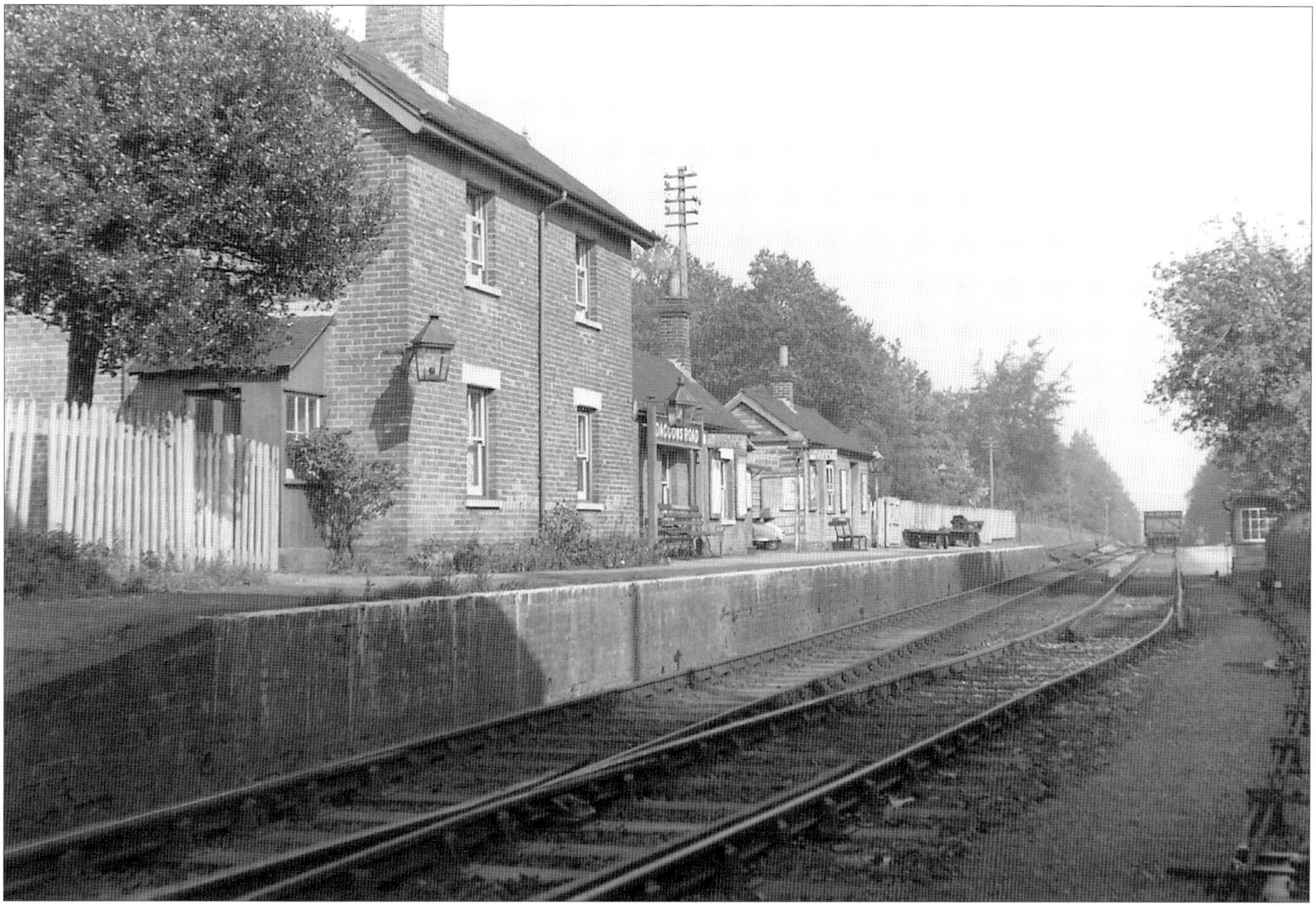
DAGGONS ROAD

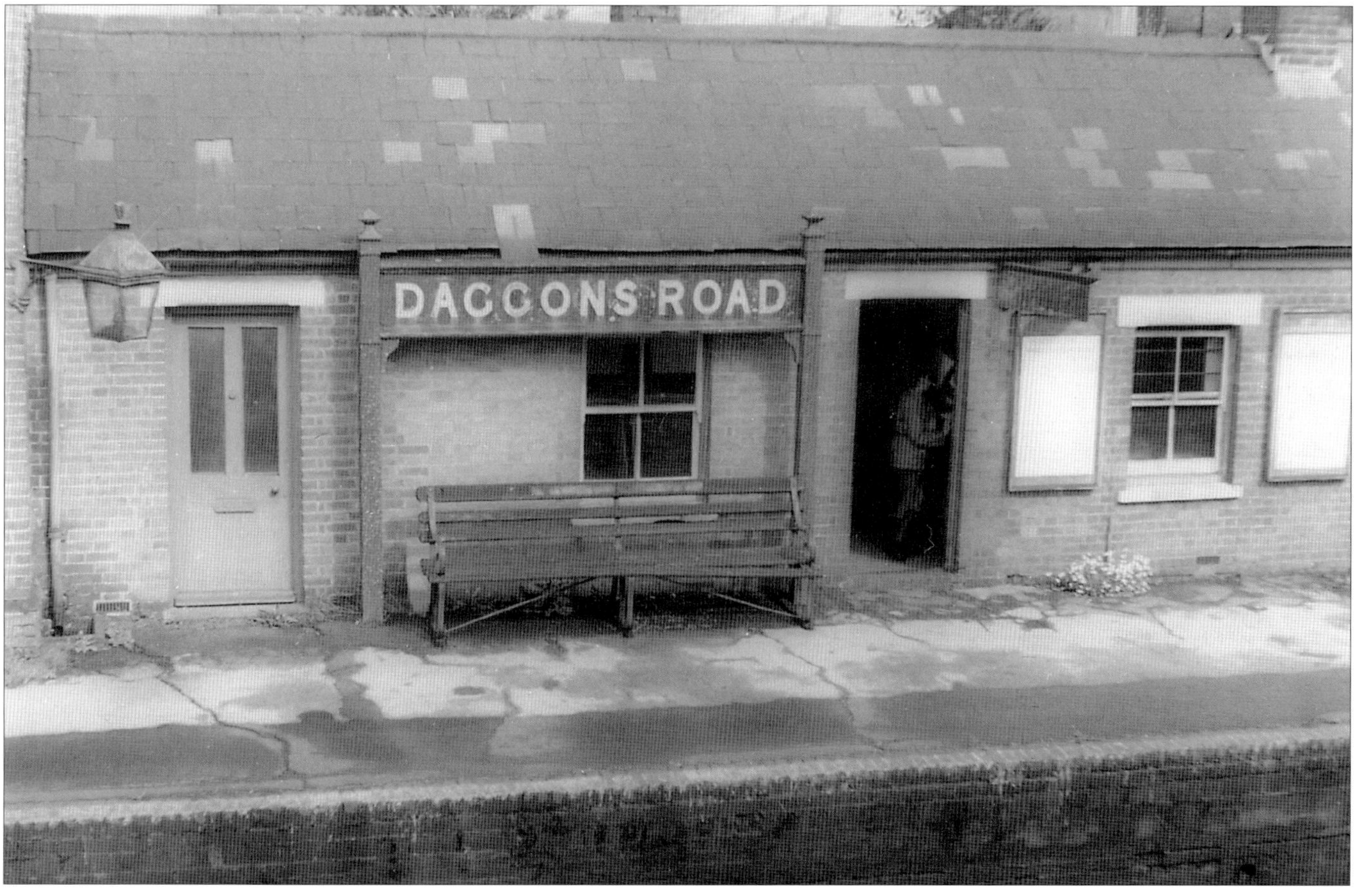
DAGGONS ROAD

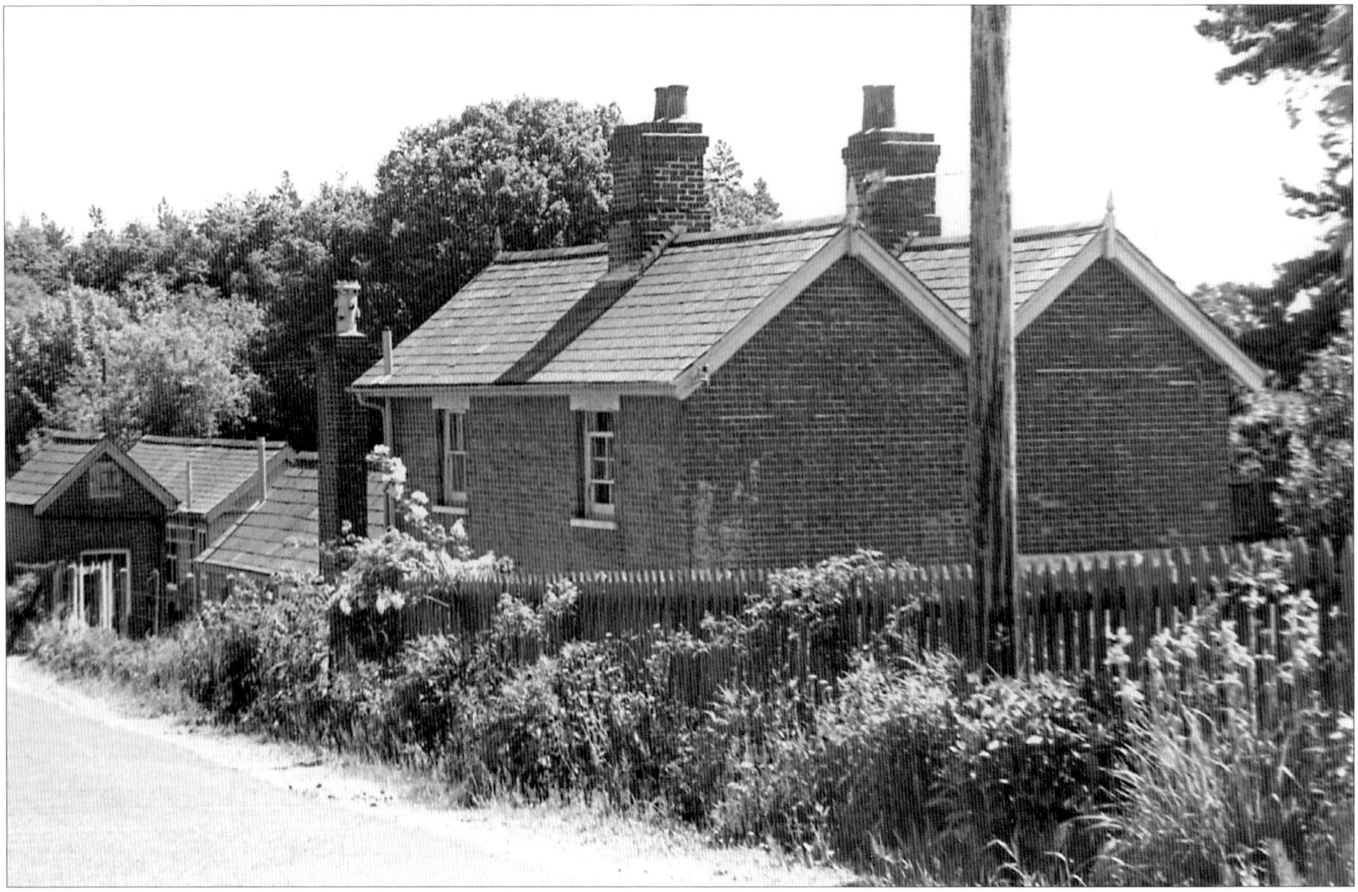

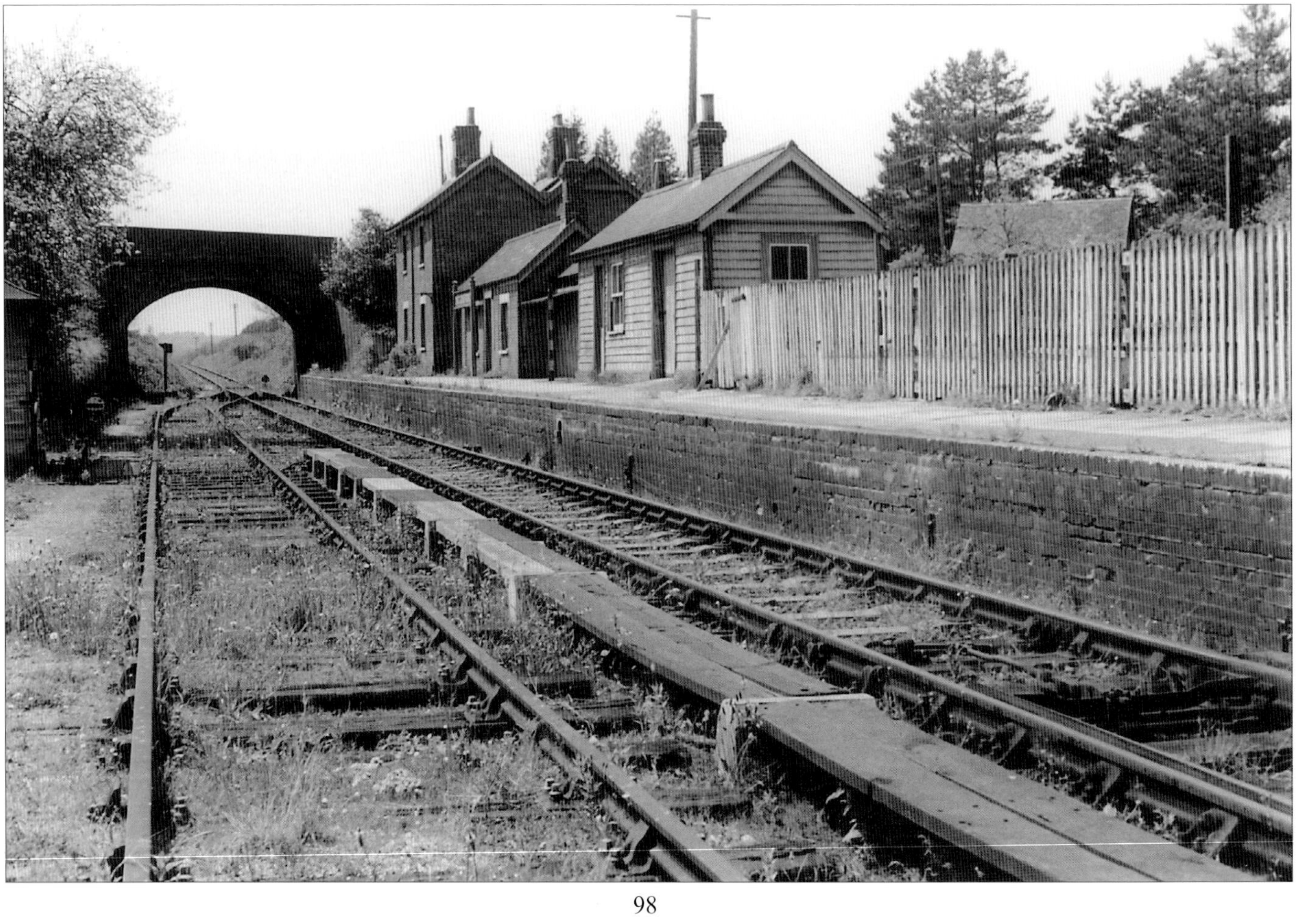

Opposite page, top: There are few photographs of the exterior of Daggons Road. This one is undated, but probably dates from the late 1950s or early 1960s. The shot makes an interesting comparison with the one on the opposite page. (Both, South Western Circle/Colin Hall)

Opposite page, bottom: Looking towards West Moors after closure on 15th May 1965. (Roger Merry-Price)

This page top: The Station Master's house survives, but is now accompanied by some more modern houses that have been built over the platform area to the north-east (6th July 1997).

This page, middle: The station approach, from the main road. Taken on 21st June 2009, the concrete gate posts and fencing suggest how the same view would have looked 50 years ago.

This page, bottom: Also leading down from the road overbridge is the approach road to the area occupied by the down loop and cattle dock, seen on 21st June 2009 (All, H Sprenger/Kestrel Collection)

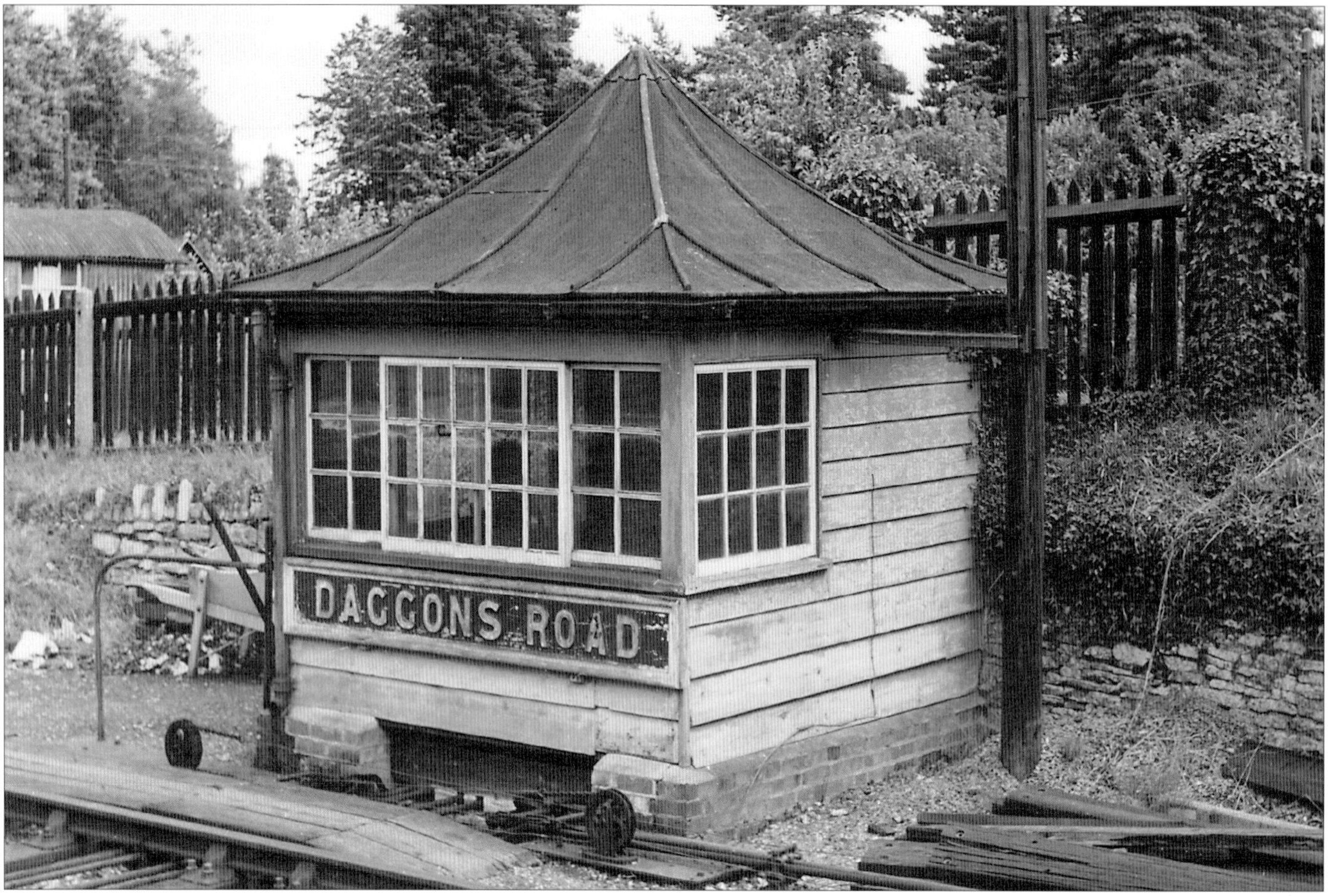
DAGGONS ROAD

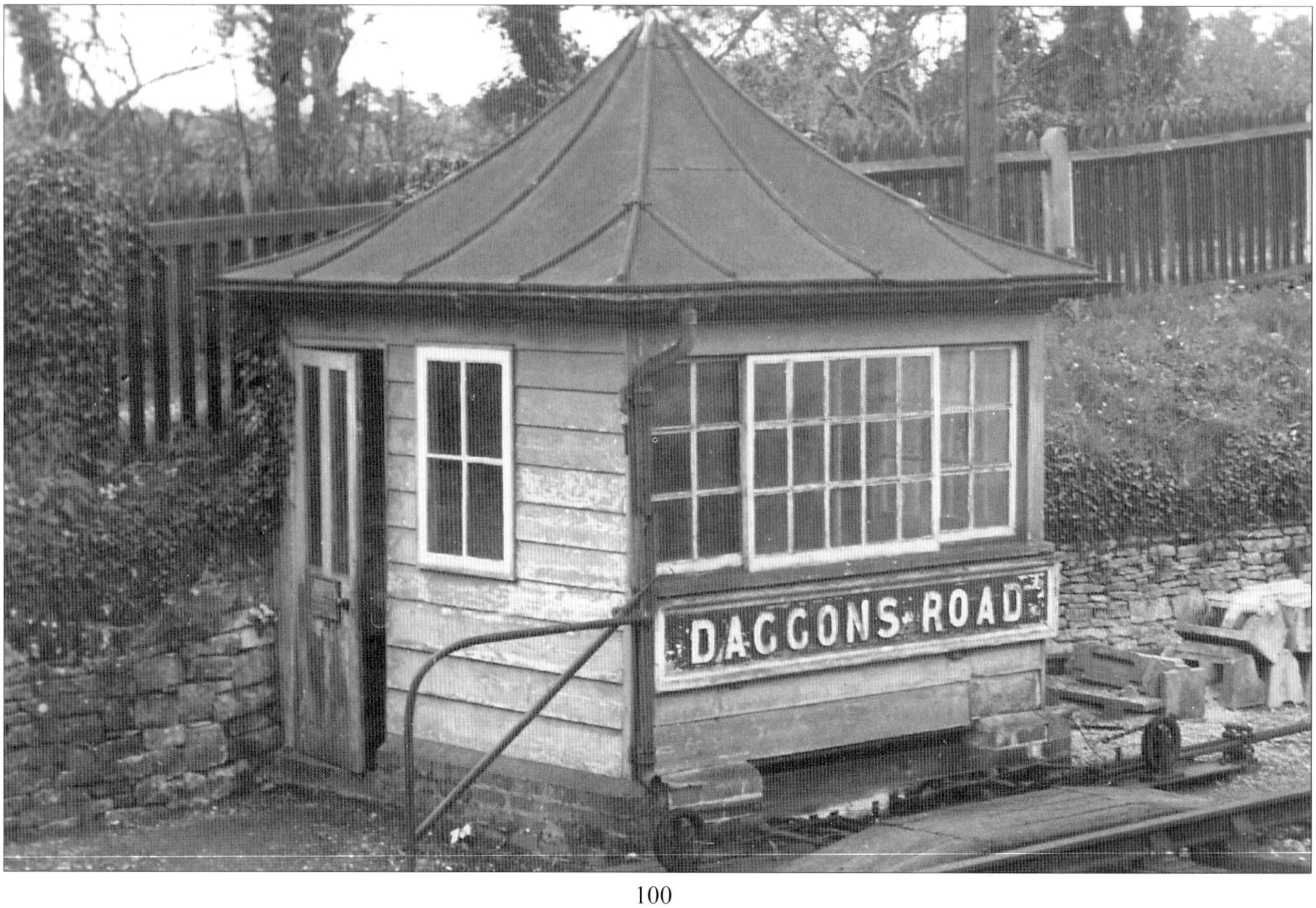
DAGGONS ROAD

THE LINE DESCRIBED

From Daggons Road, the line took a south-westerly course, just north of Cranborne Common and a stretch of coniferous woodland before turning south at Gotham, where it entered a short cutting. After traversing an area of deciduous woodland, it continued in a southerly direction to Verwood.

Verwood station (14m 38ch) was situated on the West Moors side of a bridge carrying the B3081 Ringwood–Shaftesbury road over the line. Southern Railway and early BR timetables showed it as "Verwood for Cranborne", a reference to the township three miles to the north west which had been served by Salisbury–Poole stagecoaches, but bypassed by the railway because of the hilly terrain. The River Crane, which gives Cranborne its name, supported watercress beds that provided a great deal of traffic for the station. When the line opened, Verwood was a hamlet of around 100 people. Its subsequent expansion took place mostly well to the east of the station, although since closure this has now extended up to the station site. The growth of Verwood in recent decades has been assisted by the dearth of good agricultural land in the locality.

Verwood was the second-largest intermediate station, and had most of its buildings on the up platform, including the diminutive signal box squeezed between the main building and a parcels lock-up. Across the station forecourt was the Albion Hotel, which many passengers used as a refreshment room. On the down platform was a flat-roofed wooden shelter of very similar style to that at Breamore, and at the West Moors end of the down platform was a ground frame. The goods yard was on the up side at the West Moors end, and consisted of two long sidings, one of which terminated between a loading dock and the unfenced extremity of the station platform. The yard was accessed by a ground frame at the West Moors end of the station, the frame being released by lever 6 in the signal box. Verwood goods yard was one of only two on the branch to have a crane, the other being at Fordingbridge.

In 1931, the signal box was provided with a closing switch enabling one long section to be operated between Fordingbridge and West Moors at less busy times. Whenever Verwood box was switched out, all trains used the up platform. The down home signal therefore had arms for both normal and wrong line working.

There were at one time four brickworks near to the station, on the down side north of the station, and on the up side south of it. The largest, on the up side, was owned by the Verwood & Gotham Brick & Tile Company, and served by a private siding from 1923. From 1936 the firm traded as the Southern United Brickworks Company. The siding was accessed by a ground frame released by a key held by the Station Master, and was serviced by down freight trains. It was removed around 1945.

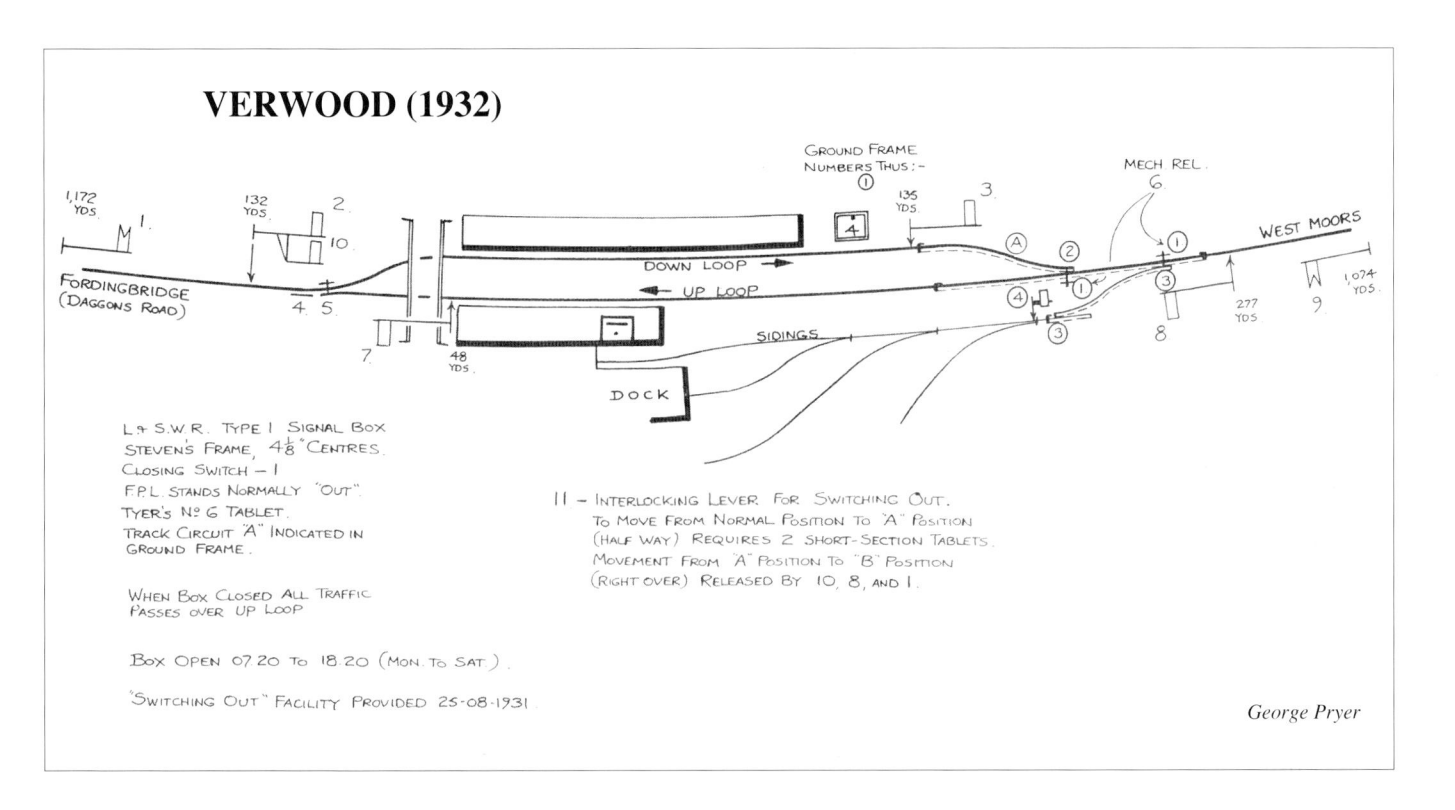

Opposite page: Worthy of a page to itself is the distinctive ground frame at Daggons Road, which was quite unlike anything else on the system. The views date from 27th July 1957 (top) and 1st May 1964 (bottom).
(JH Aston and South Western Circle/Eyers Collection)

Above: A view south, thought to have been taken before World War II. The brickworks is evident on the right-hand side.
(Lens of Sutton Collection)

Left: Looking across to the up platform on 21st October 1961.
(E Wilmshurst)

Opposite, top: The up platform on the same date looking north.
(E Wilmshurst)

Opposite, bottom: A similar view on 2nd May 1964.
(CL Caddy)

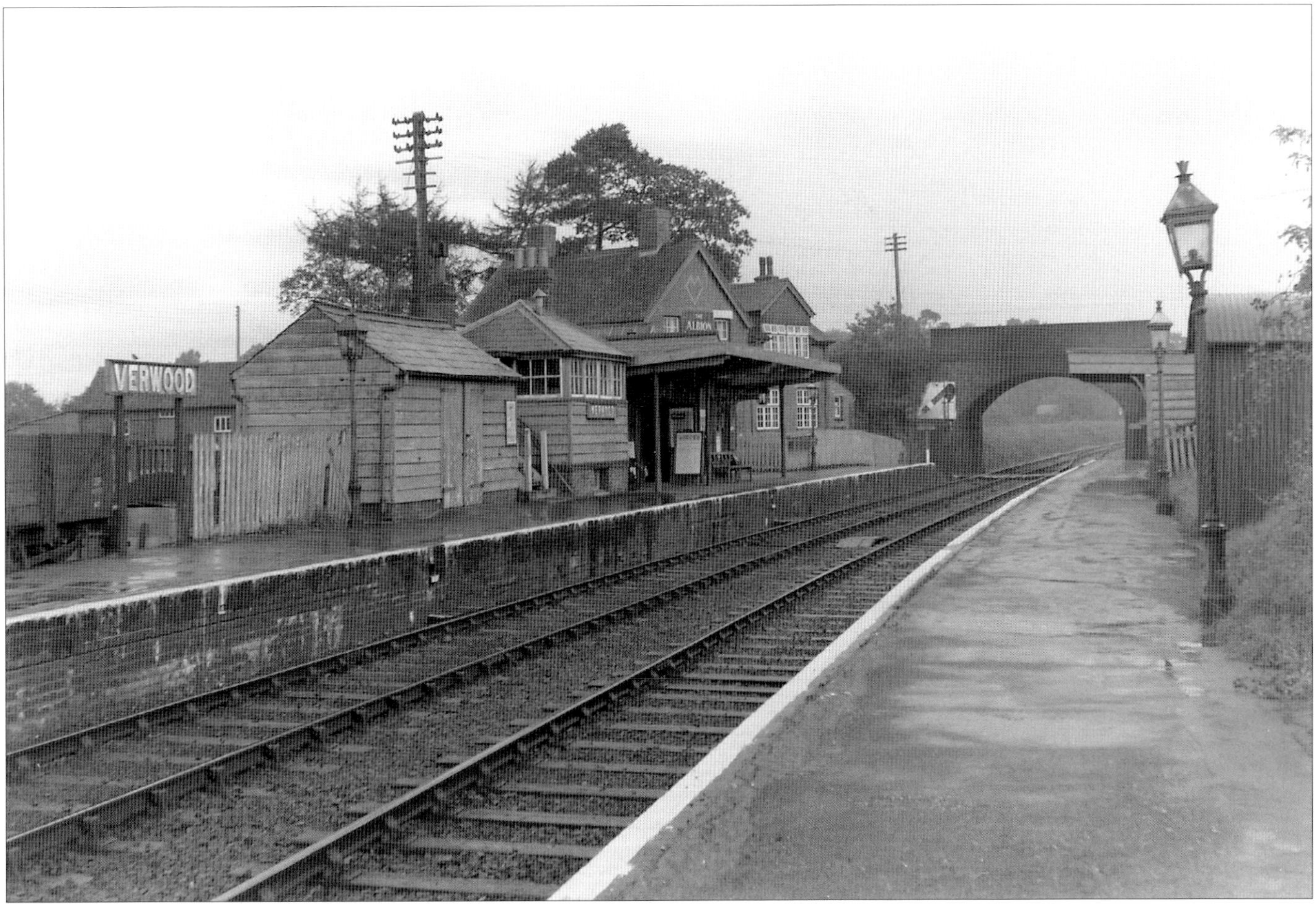
VERWOOD

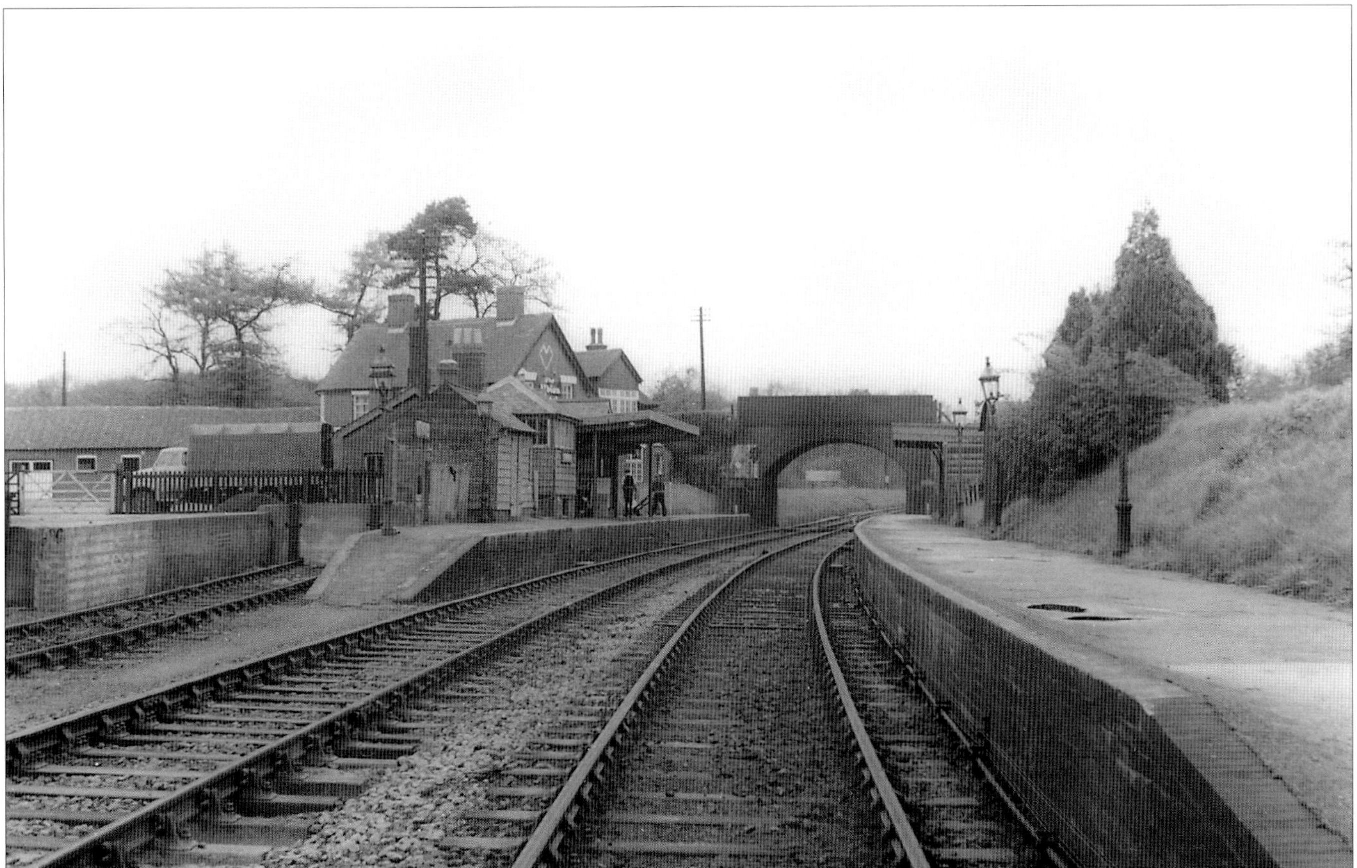

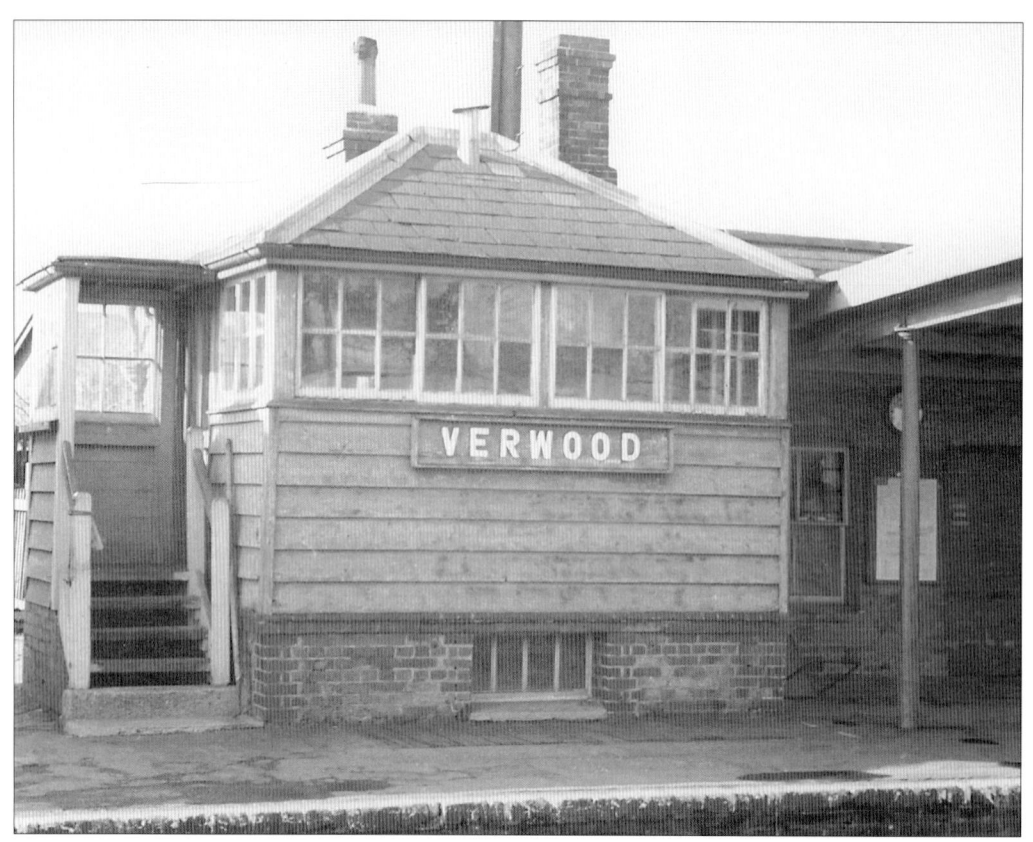

Left: An undated close up of the signal box at Verwood. (South Western Circle/J Cronan)

Below left: Possibly the signalman's moped propped up against the box on 23rd March 1964. (South Western Circle/Eyers Collection)

Below right: In May 1964, the Southern Railway was still in evidence! (CL Caddy)

Opposite, top: The roadside view of the station building was very similar to Breamore (see pages 85 and 86). (South Western Circle/Eyers Collection)

Opposite, bottom: Wally Marr at Verwood. (RK Blencowe)

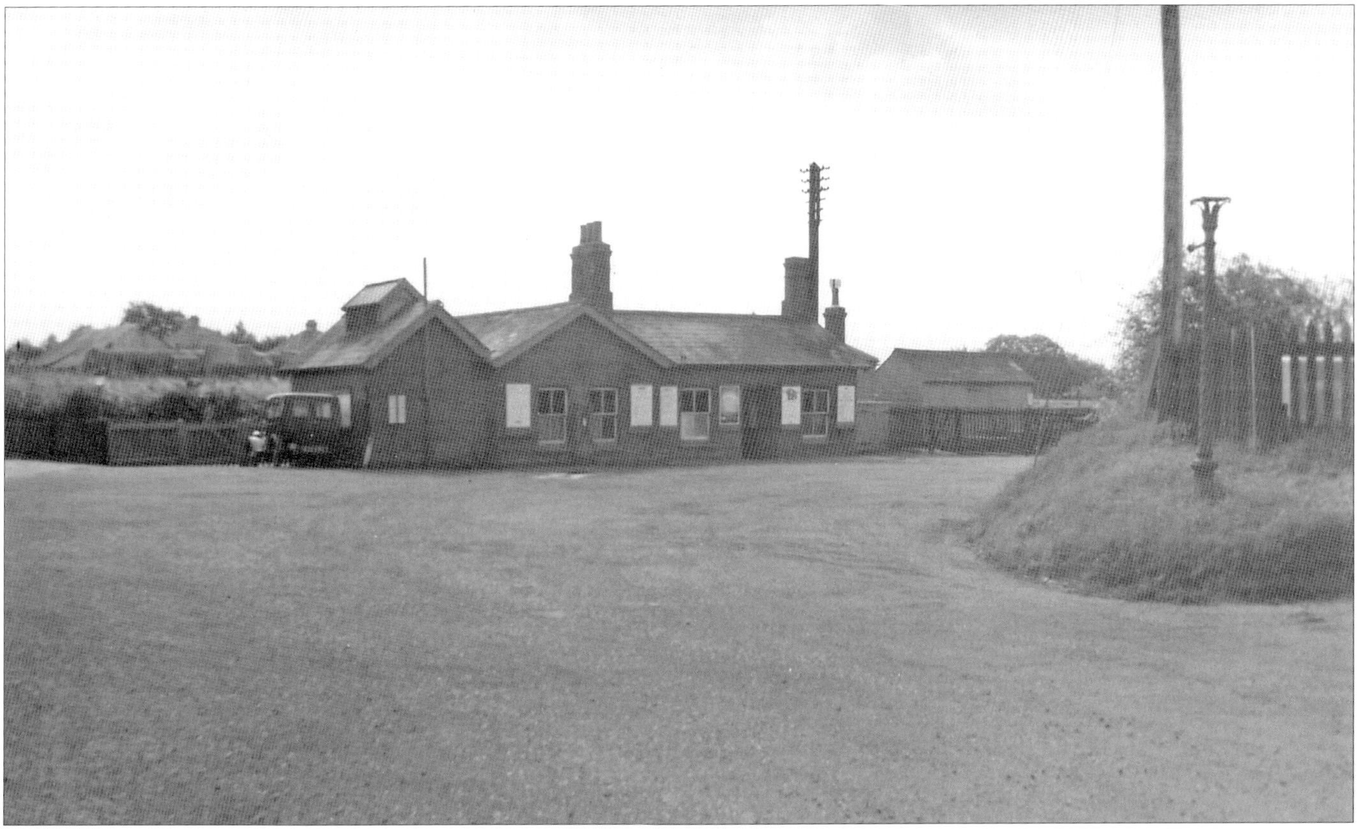

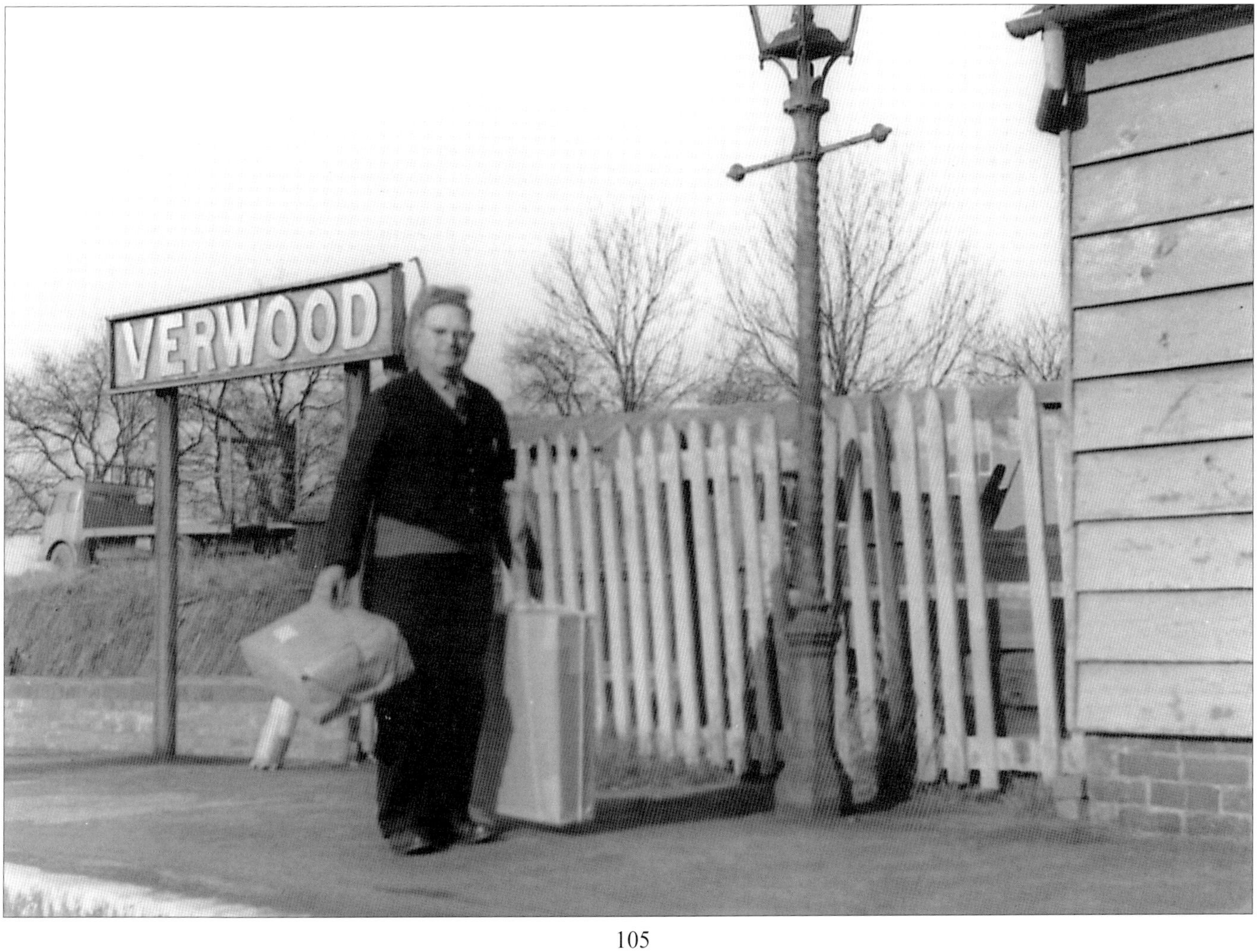
VERWOOD

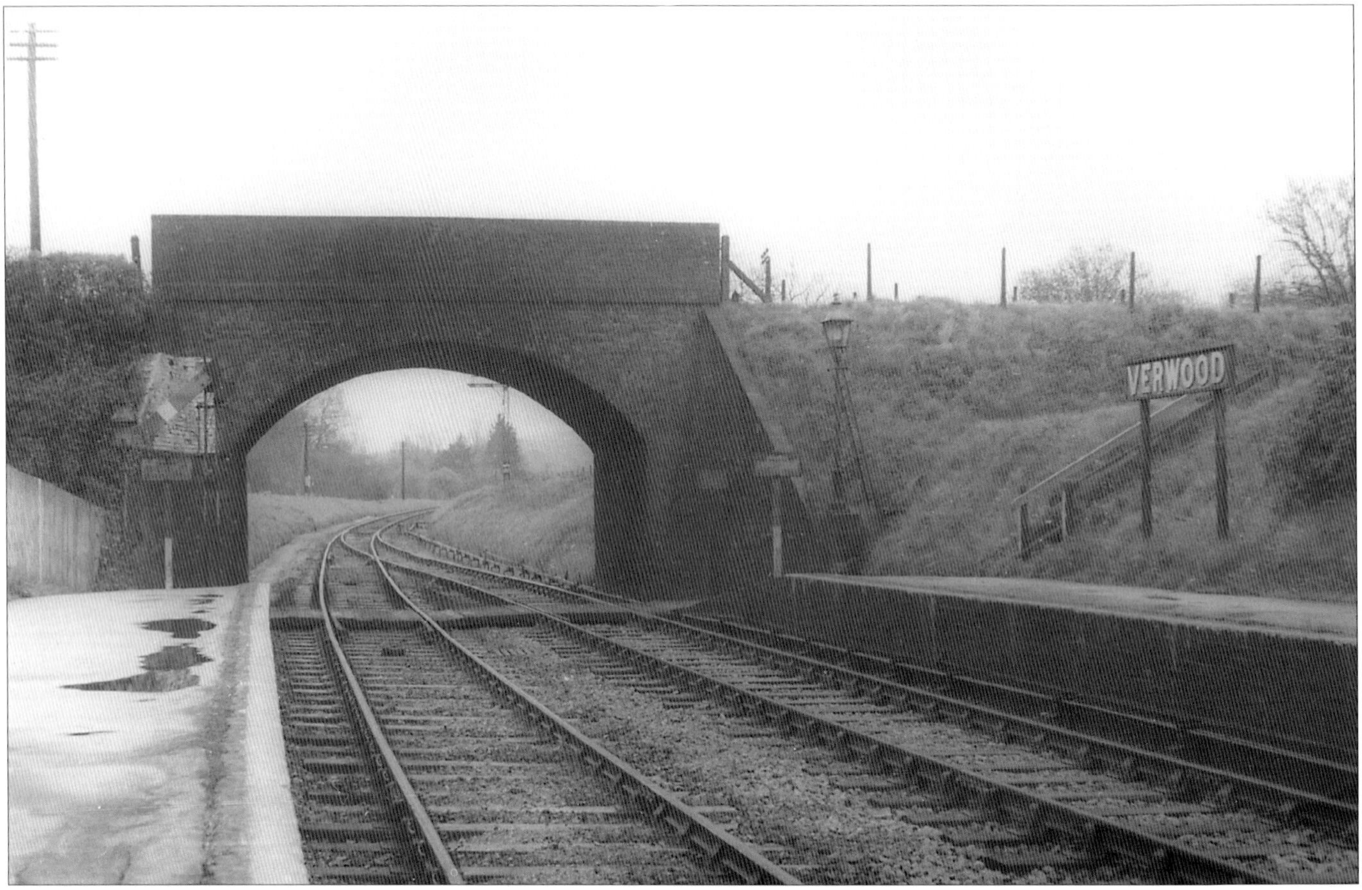
VERWOOD

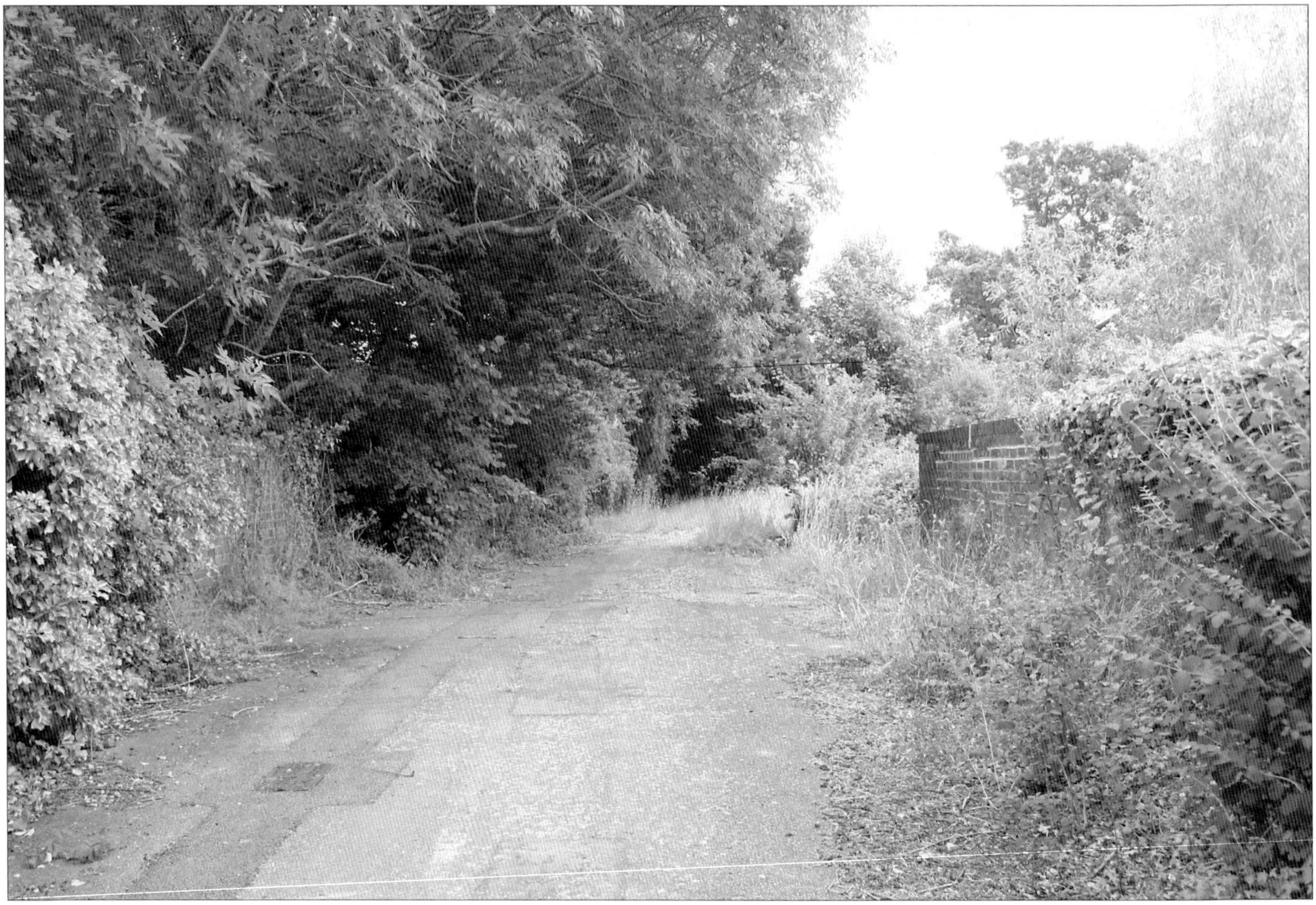

Opposite, top: Seen on 2nd May 1964, like most stations on the line, access to the platforms at Verwood was from a road carried over the line by an overbridge. (CL Caddy)

*Opposite, bottom: The bridge and the Albion Inn are the only reminders of what was at Verwood, and although there is still a tarmac surface across the bridge, no traffic passes this way any more.
(H Sprenger/Kestrel Collection)*

*This page: A new road avoids the bridge (right, seen on 21st June 2009) and cuts straight across the site of the station, which was photographed (below) on 13th December 2009. Compare this shot with the views on page 103. A new use for the bridge is to store the garden furniture during the winter months.
(Both, H Sprenger/Kestrel Collection)*

THE SALISBURY & DORSET JUNCTION RAILWAY

Between Verwood and West Moors were three gated level crossings, Horton, Revell's and Newman's Lane. Revell's Crossing cottage had no mains water, and received churns by train. In summer 1939, the 10.9am Bournemouth West–Salisbury performed this duty on Mondays, Wednesdays and Fridays. By 1957, the designated service was the 1.20pm Bournemouth West.

Newman's Lane crossing (17m 51ch from Alderbury Junction) was controlled from a wooden gatekeeper's hut.

Just after the crossing was Newman's Lane down signal (with stop and distant arms), 1618 yards from West Moors box. The stop arm was the home signal for West Moors, and protected not only the approach to the station, but also shunting movements at West Moors to and from the up goods yard, which was accessible only via the Salisbury line. There was a banner repeater for this signal 692 yards from West Moors box that had replaced a LSW-pattern repeater signal in July 1948.

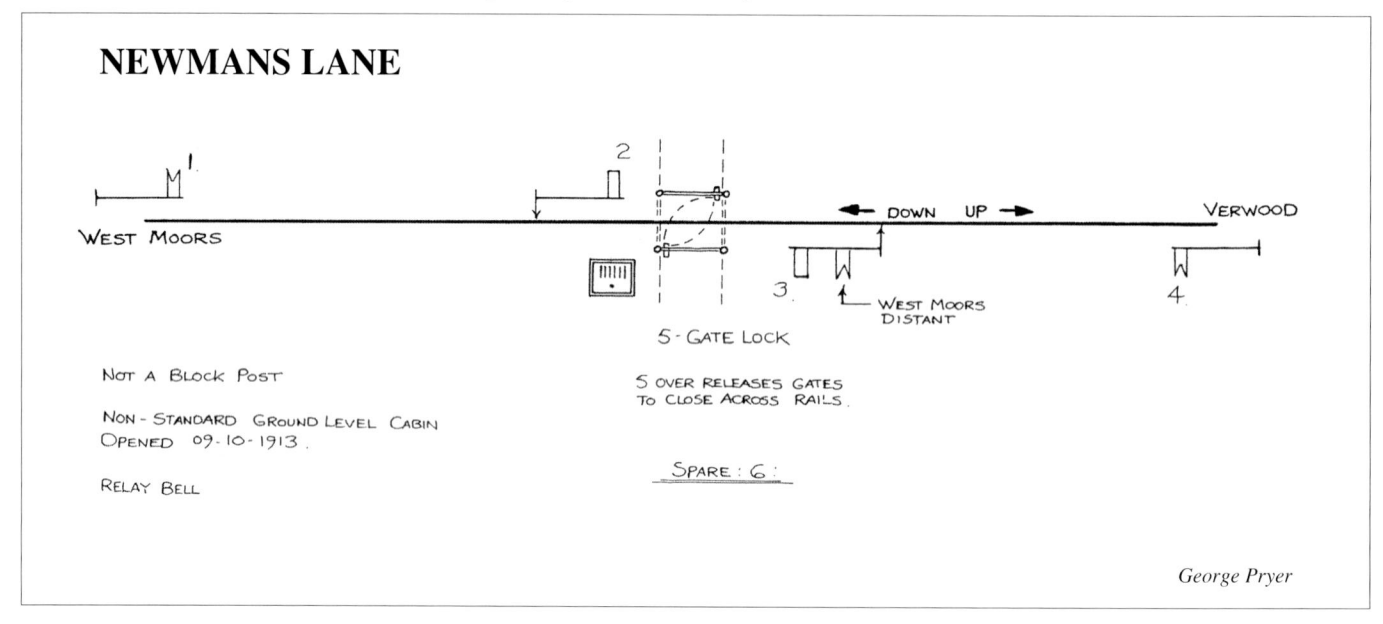

NEWMANS LANE

Diagram showing track layout between West Moors and Verwood, with signals numbered 1–6, including West Moors Distant, 5-Gate Lock.

Not a Block Post

Non-Standard Ground Level Cabin Opened 09-10-1913.

Relay Bell

5 over releases gates to close across rails.

Spare: 6

George Pryer

THE LINE DESCRIBED

Shunting the up yard at West Moors was likely to occupy the West Moors–Verwood section. Down trains were therefore subject to a local instruction which modified Electric Token Block Regulation 5 (section clear but station or junction blocked). This permitted a train to be accepted to the home signal of the box in advance. The Verwood signalman (or his colleague at Fordingbridge if Verwood was switched out) would operate his stop signals before the down train arrived, and would then stand on the platform and exhibit a green flag (or green light by night). The driver had to acknowledge this with a short whistle to confirm that he understood the line to be clear to the home signal only. If he failed to do so, the signalman would not pull off the signal controlling entry to the section ahead until the train had come to a stand. Another use of the "warning arrangement", as ET Regulation 5 was also known, was to protect a train which had failed in the next station.

The branch made a sharp clockwise curve as it neared its junction with the Ringwood line, just east of West Moors station (18m 41ch). The latter route was double track and the station sported two platforms with its main building on the up side. A loading bay at the east end of the up platform was served from the up goods yard. There was another small yard on the down side west of the station. The signal box was located at the west end of the up platform to enable it to operate the level crossing at that end of the station.

Sandwiched between the signal box and main building was a footbridge of unusual design, with a narrow span supported by massive pillars. It was erected by the Concrete Construction Company in 1902 to a striking design, and was only the second concrete footbridge to be installed on the LSWR. The tapering span and the metal handrails along it gave it an appearance not unlike many of the early North Eastern Railway footbridges.

The signal box housed two alternative block instruments for the Salisbury line. One was a Tyers No 6 tablet (latterly electric token) instrument for the Verwood–West Moors section when Verwood box was switched in, the other being operated by the miniature staff used for the Fordingbridge–West Moors long section. Fordingbridge box had corresponding instruments for each system.

Served also by trains on the Ringwood line, West Moors station enjoyed a considerably greater passenger service than did its neighbours on the Salisbury & Dorset. Although the locality was thinly populated when the station opened, there was a rapid growth of population nearby, particularly at Ferndown, from the early 20th century as the area developed as commuter territory for Bournemouth and Poole. Shortly after the First World War, a cooperative pig farm was established here by a group of ex-servicemen, led by the son of the LSWR District Operating Superintendant. The farm built up a reputation for the quality of its produce, much of which was despatched by rail.

Opposite page: Newmans Lane Crossing on 4th April 1964. (CL Caddy)
Above: The site of the crossing as it is today, but facing towards Verwood with the site of the ground frame behind the photographer. The picture was taken on 21st June 2009. (H Sprenger/Kestrel Collection)

THE SALISBURY & DORSET JUNCTION RAILWAY

References

1. This date is from the South Western Circle Portfolio. The official inspection by Col AC Trench did not take place until 8th July 1947, and gave the date of installation as 1942 (PRO ref MT29/95, 11.7.1947).
2. C Chivers, article in *The South Western Circular*, July 2007.
3. LSWR Service Timetables, June 1914, November 1916 and May 1918.
4. JT Burge, *The L&SW Railway in the New Forest District*, article in *Railway and Travel Monthly*, June 1913.
5. MoT Inspection by Brig CA Langley, 11th April 1950, PRO ref MT29/98.

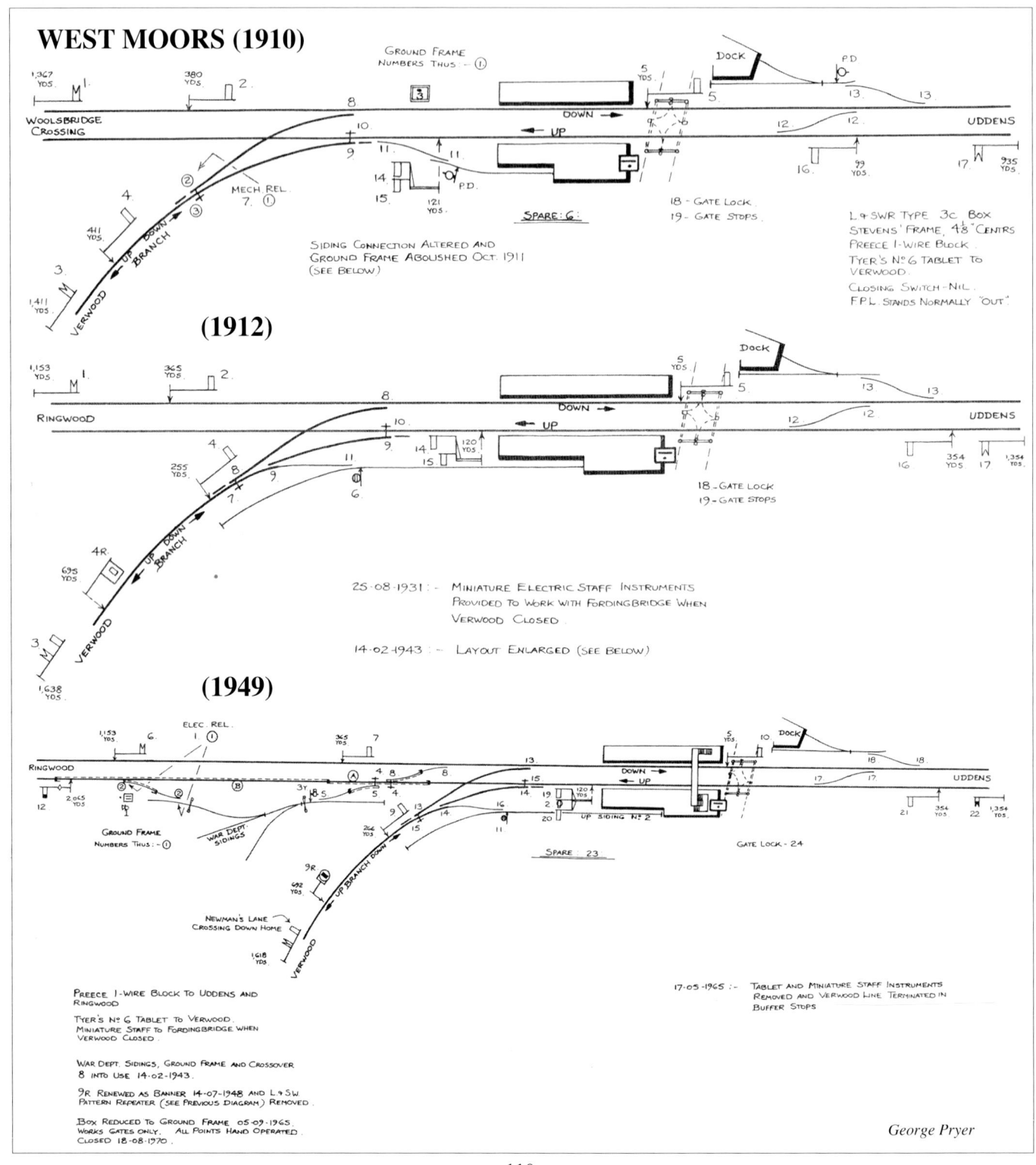

George Pryer

Top: West Moors looking towards the junction for the Salisbury & Dorset line on 14th October 1961. (E Wilmshurst)
Bottom: Looking towards Wimborne, probably taken sometime in the 1960s. (RK Blencowe)

Top: Military trains served a fuel depot at West Moors until 1974, this view being taken on 5th June 1971. (RK Blencowe)
Bottom: Only the crossing keepers cottage remains now, seen here on 21st June 2009. (H Sprenger/Kestrel Collection)

Appendix A

Extract from Southern Railway Census of Staff, 1ˢᵗ November 1926 (PRO Ref RAIL 648/131)

Alderbury Junction
2 Signalmen (managed by Salisbury Station Master)

Downton
2 Booking Clerks
2 Gangers
6 PW Undermen
1 Station Master (Class 4)
2 Porters

Breamore
1 Booking Clerk
1 Ganger
3 PW Undermen
1 Station Master (Class 5)
2 Signalmen
3 Level Crossing Keepers (one each at North Charford, South Charford and Burgate Green Lane)

Fordingbridge
1 Booking Clerk
1 Goods Clerk
1 Ganger
3 PW Undermen
1 Station Master (Class 3)
1 Porter
2 Signalmen
1 Checker

Daggons Road
1 Station Master (Class 5)
2 Porters
1 Office Lad

Verwood (supervised by Daggons Road Station Master)
1 Ganger
3 PW Undermen
3 Porters (one Class 1, two Class 2)
2 Signalmen
1 Level Crossing Keeper (at Horton Common)

The West Moors Station Master supervised Dolman's, Revell's and Newman's Lane Level Crossings. Newman's Lane is listed as having two staff including one coded FF (Female Conciliation grade), which suggests that it was worked by a resident husband and wife. It will be seen from the above lists that 53 staff were based on the branch, excluding Alderbury Junction, but including the four crossing keepers supervised by the SM at West Moors.

Salisbury had a total of 604 staff including 310 at the loco depot and 157 under the Station Master, who was graded Special Class. In addition, there were 55 staff at Milford Goods. Adding the 22 staff at Wilton, 16 at Porton and 23 at Grateley produces a total of 720. The figure of 1,000 railway employees said to be on strike at Salisbury in May of the same year *(see Chapter 4)* must therefore include those at the GWR station and loco depot, together with further outstations, possibly including the whole of the Salisbury & Dorset line, the Bulford branch, the West of England line to Tisbury and the GW line to Codford. The 1,000 or so staff may well have been the combined totals of those in the Salisbury branches of the three rail trades unions, ASLEF, NUR and TSSA.

Appendix B

List of Signal Boxes and Opening Times from the LSWR Appendix to Service Timetables, 1892

Station	Sundays Open at	Weekdays Open at	Weekdays Closed at	Position of signals when box closed
Downton	Train times	6.40am	8.0pm	Off
Breamore	Train times	6.40am	8.20pm	Off
Fordingbridge	Train times	6.30am	8.20pm	Off
Daggens Road	Train times	6.20am	8.20pm	Off
Verwood	Train times	6.30am	8.30pm	Off

Appendix C

Extracts from the Western Appendix to the SR Working Time Tables, March 1934

Signal boxes, crossover roads and catch points

Station and signal boxes.	Distance from next box, above. Mls. yds.	Position of box (in regard to station).	Crossover roads. Position (in regard to signal box), or description.	Yards from box.	Catch points exist in Line.	Yards from box.	Gradient rising 1 in
TUNNEL JUNCTION (SALISBURY) TO WEST MOORS.							
Salisbury Milford Jct.*	*(From Tunnel Jct.)* − 1,607	Down side (Breamore side)	Dean side	178	—	—	—
Alderbury Jct.*	2 1,711	In fork of junction	—	—	—	—	—
(To Dean	*3 1,546)*						
Breamore Station	6 1,414	Up platform	—	—	—	—	—
Fordingbridge Station	2 1,088	Down platform	—	—	—	—	—
Verwood Station*	4 1,737	Up platform	—	—	—	—	—
(To West Moors	*4 113)*						

* Signal box provided with closing switch.

APPENDIX C

Accommodation and equipment at stations

Station	Turntables (Length of Rail) Engine ft. ins.	Turntables Wagon ft. ins.	Cranes Outside T. cwts.	Cranes Outside Ht. of lift ft. ins.	Cranes Inside cwts.	Cranes Inside Ht. of lift ft. ins.	Weighbridges Truck Capacity Tons	Weighbridges Truck Lth. in ft.	Weighbridges Cart Capacity Tons	Highway vehicle docks	Water columns No.	Water columns Where situated
TUNNEL JUNCTION (SALISBURY) TO WEST MOORS.											
Milford (Salisbury)	—	—	10 0	22 0	30	10 0	30	20	20	2	1	At tank
Downton	—	—	—	—	—	—	—	—	10 (D 2½)	1	—	—
Breamore	—	—	—	—	—	—	—	—	—	1	—	—
Fordingbridge	—	—	5 0	15 6	30	10 9	—	—	—	1	—	—
Daggons Road	—	—	—	—	—	—	—	—	—	1	—	—
Verwood	—	—	5 0	23 6	—	—	—	—	15	1	—	—

Intermediate and other sidings

Name of siding.	Position.	(1) Station in charge of working. (2) wagons labelled to †	Gradient at point of connection (1 in)	Catch points provied in sidings at.	Points of siding controlled by or worked from.	If gates provided across siding Key to be obtained from.	If gates provided across siding Key to be returned to.	Worked by.	Remarks.
TUNNEL JUNCTION (SALISBURY) TO WEST MOORS.									
H. J. Suttons	Down side Milford (Salisbury)	Milford (Salisbury)	Level	—	Hand points	—	—	Shunting engine	—
West of England Brick & Tile Co.	Up side Daggons Road	Daggons Rd.	Level	—	Ground frame Train Tablet for Dock siding	—	—	—	Out of use.
Verwood & Gotham Brick Co.	Up side Verwood	Verwood	Level	—	Ground frame	Station Master	—	Down goods services	*

List showing the end at which end vehicles should be marshalled in order to facilitate the work and minimise delay at the detaching station

Station	From down trains	From up trains
Downton	Rear	Rear
Breamore	Rear	Rear
Fordingbridge	Rear	Rear
Daggons Road	Rear	Either
Verwood	Either	Rear
West Moors	Rear	Rear

Dating from before World War I, this is not a top-quality photograph, but is worth including as it shows the original signalbox at Breamore, replaced in 1930 by a ground frame installed on the up platform. (Lens of Sutton Collection)

34091 "Weymouth" at Wimborne on the last day of working on the Salisbury & Dorset, 2nd May 1964. (C Whetmath)

Appendix D

Extract from the BR/SR Western Section Appendix, 1960

Level crossings at which engine whistles are required to be sounded continuously from the whistle board to the crossing

Harding's Crossing	5m 38½ch from Alderbury Junction
Coxmead Crossing	7m 34½ch
Barton's Crossing	18m 5½ch

Note: Staffed crossings on the line were numbered as follows: 2 – North Charford, 3 – South Charford, 4 – Burgate, 5 – Horton, 6 – Revelle's, 7 – Newmans Lane. This raises the question of the identity of crossing No 1. Logic would suggest that it was north of North Charford, but there are few potential candidates, and a definite identification of its location cannot be made.

Appendix E

BR Southern Region Engine Workings, Summer 1954

The following are extracted from *Engine Workings, London West and Southern Districts, June to September 1954*. Some notes concerning dated variations and continuation of services north of Salisbury have been added.

EASTLEIGH DUTY 274 (BR Standard Class 4)

SO 19th June to 18th September

5.7am off Shed, light engine to Brockenhurst, arr 5.50am
5.55–6.35am shunting
8.22am empty stock Brockenhurst–New Milton, arr 8.40am
8.50am passenger New Milton–Salisbury, arr 10.36am (train worked forward to Swansea High Street by WR engine)
To Salisbury Shed and return
1.11pm passenger Salisbury–New Milton (9.28am Cardiff General, worked to Salisbury by WR engine), arr 3.23pm
3.25pm empty stock New Milton–Brockenhurst, arr 3.35pm
4.36pm light engine Brockenhurst–Eastleigh, arr 5.22pm
Return to Shed

EASTLEIGH DUTY 284 (T9 Class)

5am off Bournemouth Shed
5.20am vans Bournemouth Central–Poole, arr 5.49am
6.0am light engine Poole–Bournemouth West, arr 6.14am
6.43am passenger Bournemouth West–Salisbury, arr 8.8am
To Salisbury Shed

SX
8.55am off Shed
9.25am* passenger Salisbury–Bournemouth West, arr 10.57am
12.20pm passenger Bournemouth West–Bournemouth Central, arr 12.28pm
12.39pm light engine to Bournemouth West, arr 12.47pm

* start 9.37am 12th July to 3rd September (dates of 9.5am Salisbury–Weymouth, see Salisbury 442 duty)

117

THE SALISBURY & DORSET JUNCTION RAILWAY

SO
9.55am off Shed
10.27am Salisbury–Bournemouth West passenger, arr 12noon
Light engine to Branksome Shed

Every Weekday (EWD)
1.20pm passenger Bournemouth West–Salisbury, arr 2.51pm
2.57pm empty stock to Salisbury East Sidings
3.10pm light engine East Sidings to Shed, returning to Salisbury, arr 4.25pm
5.7pm passenger Salisbury–Portsmouth & Southsea, arr 7.9pm
Light engine to Fratton Loco Yard and return
8.3pm passenger Portsmouth & Southsea–Eastleigh, arr 8.52pm
Light engine to Eastleigh Loco Yard

FRATTON DUTY 368 (U Class)

SO
6.30am off Salisbury Shed to East Sidings, arr 6.35am
6.55am empty stock East Sidings to Salisbury
7.15am passenger Salisbury–Bournemouth West, arr 8.50am
Light engine via Branksome triangle for turning
10.45am passenger Bournemouth West–Salisbury, arr 12.11pm
Light engine to Salisbury Shed and return, arr Salisbury at 12.55pm
1.23pm passenger Salisbury–Portsmouth & Southsea (10.8am Cardiff General), arr 3.7pm
3.20pm light engine to Fratton Yard
9.0pm light engine from Fratton Loco Yard to Portsmouth & Southsea, arr 9.10pm
9.38pm passenger Portsmouth & Southsea–Southampton Terminus, arr 10.41pm
Carriage shunting 10.45–11pm
11.15pm light engine Southampton Terminus–Eastleigh, arr 11.27pm
Carriage shunting 11.30pm–1am
3.45am freight Eastleigh–Fratton Yard
Light engine to Fratton Loco Yard

BOURNEMOUTH DUTY 414 (Q Class)

SO 26th June to 28th August

6.20am light engine Bournemouth Central–Brockenhurst, arr 6.55am
8.5am empty stock Brockenhurst–Bournemouth Central, arr 8.40am
9.0am passenger Bournemouth Central–Salisbury, arr 10.19am (train worked forward to Cardiff General by WR engine)
To Salisbury Shed and return
2.2pm passenger Salisbury–Bournemouth Central (9.20 Swansea High Street, worked to Salisbury by WR engine), arr 3.30pm
3.40pm empty stock Bournemouth Central–Brockenhurst, arr 4.18pm
6.5pm light engine Brockenhurst–Southampton Terminus Loco, arr 6.37pm
7.40pm light engine Southampton Terminus Loco–Southampton Central, arr 7.45pm
8.10pm passenger Southampton Central (6.45pm Portsmouth & Southsea) – Bournemouth West, arr 9.48pm
10.15pm light engine Bournemouth West–Bournemouth Shed, arr 10.27pm

SALISBURY DUTY 433 (Battle of Britain Class)

MO 2nd August to 13th September

5.0am off Shed
5.30am empty stock Salisbury–Hamworthy Junction, arr 6.35am
7.15am light engine Hamworthy Junction–Salisbury Shed, arr 8.50am

APPENDIX E

SALISBURY DUTY 442 (Battle of Britain Class)

SX 12th July to 3rd September

8.35am off Shed
9.5am passenger Salisbury–Weymouth, arr 11.7am
To Shed and return
6.20pm passenger Weymouth–Salisbury, arr 8.27pm
To Shed

SALISBURY DUTY 443 (T9 Class)

SX

6.30am off Shed to East Sidings
6.55am empty stock East Sidings–Salisbury
7.15am passenger Salisbury–Bournemouth West, arr 8.50am
Light engine via Branksome triangle for turning
10.4am passenger Bournemouth West–Salisbury, arr 11.37am
Light engine to Shed and thence to West Sidings
12.50pm empty stock West Sidings–Salisbury
1.6pm passenger Salisbury–Southampton Terminus via Eastleigh, arr 2.22pm
2.30pm vans (conditional) Southampton Terminus–Southampton Docks
Return light engine to Southampton Terminus Loco Yard
3.30pm light engine Southampton Terminus Loco–Southampton Central
3.46pm freight Southampton Central–Bevois Park, arr 3.55pm
4.1pm light engine Bevois Park–Woolston, arr 4.10pm
4.50–6.10pm freight shunting
6.42pm freight Woolston–Bevois Park, arr 6.52pm
7.38pm light engine Bevois Park–Eastleigh, arr 7.49pm
8.28pm passenger Eastleigh (7.17pm Portsmouth & Southsea) – Salisbury, arr 9.17pm
9.23pm empty stock Salisbury–East Sidings
Carriage shunting 9.30–11.30pm
To Shed at 11.30pm

SALISBURY DUTY 444 (T9 Class)

2.25am off Shed MX, 3.0am MO
(2.30–3.20am MX carriage shunting at Salisbury)
3.25am passenger and news Salisbury–Wimborne, arr 4.23am (train worked forward to Weymouth by Bournemouth engine)
5.17am passenger Wimborne–Bournemouth Central, arr 5.48am
Light engine to Bournemouth Shed and return
7.42am passenger Bournemouth Central–Salisbury, arr 9.10am
9.35–10.30am carriage shunting
Light engine to Shed and return
Carriage shunting 11.30am–12.45pm
12.58pm passenger Salisbury–Bournemouth West, arr 2.31pm SX, 2.22 SO
4.52pm SX/4.47pm SO passenger Bournemouth West–Salisbury, arr 6.22pm
6.27pm empty stock Salisbury–East Sidings
6.35pm light engine to Shed
7.25 pm FO off Shed
7.30–8.0pm carriage shunting at Salisbury

THE SALISBURY & DORSET JUNCTION RAILWAY

SALISBURY DUTY 445 (T9 Class)

7.10am off Shed to East Sidings
7.30am empty stock East Sidings–Salisbury
7.47am passenger Salisbury–Portsmouth & Southsea, arr 9.36am
(SO 9.50am empty stock Portsmouth & Southsea–Fratton Yard, arr 10.0am)
12.25pm light engine Fratton Shed–Portsmouth & Southsea, arr 12.35pm
1.3pm passenger Portsmouth & Southsea–Salisbury via Eastleigh, arr 2.35pm
2.42pm empty stock Salisbury–West Sidings
2.47pm light engine to Shed and return
5.20pm passenger Salisbury–Bournemouth West, arr 6.54pm
Light engine via Branksome Triangle for turning
7.43pm passenger Bournemouth West–Salisbury, arr 9.10pm
9.17pm empty stock Salisbury–East Sidings
9.26pm to Shed

SALISBURY DUTY 451 (700 Class)

4.45am MO off Shed to Salisbury West Yard, arr 4.50 am
5.5am freight Salisbury West Yard–Milford Goods, arr 5.34am
5.40–7.55am freight shunting
8.0am freight Milford Goods (7.37 Salisbury West Yard) – Wimborne, arr 3.15 pm

7.20am MX off Shed to Salisbury West Yard, arr 7.25am
7.37am freight Salisbury West Yard–Wimborne, arr 3.15pm

3.25pm EWD light engine Wimborne–Poole, arr 3.37pm
3.39pm light engine Poole–Hamworthy Junction, arr 3.44pm

4.25pm SX freight Hamworthy Junction (12.10pm Dorchester South) – Wimborne, arr 4.43pm
6.50pm freight Wimborne–Salisbury, arr 9.20pm
Freight (times not specified) to Salisbury West and Salisbury ex GW Yards
Return to Shed

4.25pm SO light engine (or conditional freight) Hamworthy Junction–Wimborne, arr 4.43pm
5.22pm passenger Wimborne (4.47pm Bournemouth West) – Salisbury, arr 6.20pm (double-headed with T9 (Salisbury Duty 444)
Return to Shed

SALISBURY DUTY 452 (700 Class)

3.35am MO off Shed to Salisbury East Yard, arr 3.40am
2.50am MX off Shed to Salisbury West Yard for Freight Trip to East Yard

4.5am EWD freight Salisbury East Yard–Poole, arr 6.8am
6.30am light engine Poole (via Broadstone) – Hamworthy Junction, arr 6.46am
7.0–7.30am freight shunting
7.40am freight Hamworthy Junction–Hamworthy Goods, arr 7.49am
8.0–8.45am freight shunting
8.45am light engine Hamworthy Goods–Hamworthy Junction, arr 8.54am
9.10–10.40am freight shunting (less 15min for carriage shunting)
11.30am freight SX/light engine SO Hamworthy Junction–Hamworthy Goods, arr 11.39am
12.20pm freight Hamworthy Goods–Hamworthy Junction, arr 12.29pm
12.30–1.20pm freight shunting
1.35pm freight SX/light engine SO Hamworthy Junction–Poole, arr 1.44pm
1.53pm light engine Poole–Wimborne, arr 2.8pm
2.15–3.35pm freight shunting

APPENDIX E

3.35pm SX freight Wimborne–Salisbury East Yard, arr 8.37pm
Light engine to West Yard
9.30pm–1.0am freight shunting
1.0am to Shed

3.35pm SO freight Wimborne–Salisbury ex-GW Yard, arr 8.10pm
Light Engine to West Yard
9.0pm–2.0am (Sun) freight shunting
2.30–4.0am (Sun) carriage shunting
4.0am (Sun) to Shed

SALISBURY DUTY 452 (Battle of Britain Class).
Sundays 18th July, 1st, 29th August and 5th September

1.25pm off Shed
1.44pm passenger Salisbury–Bournemouth West (WR excursion worked to Salisbury by WR engine), arr 3.12pm
Light engine to Branksome Shed and return
8.45pm passenger Bournemouth West–Salisbury, arr 10.2pm (WR excursion worked forward by WR engine)

SALISBURY DUTY 454 (M7 Class)
Sundays

1.55pm off Shed
2.24pm passenger Salisbury–Wimborne, arr 3.24pm
4.0pm passenger and milk Wimborne–Salisbury, arr 4.59pm
5.45pm–1.0am (Mon) carriage shunting less 30min meals and engine release
1.0am (Mon) to Shed

Appendix F

Calling Points of Long Distance Expresses Routed via Fordingbridge, Summer Saturdays, 1960

9.28am Cardiff General–Pokesdown, 25th June–10th September

Newport, Severn Tunnel Junction, Bristol Stapleton Road, Bath Spa, Trowbridge, Westbury, Warminster, Salisbury (dep 12.57pm), Poole, Bournemouth Central, Pokesdown

9.20am Swansea High Street–Brockenhurst, 18th June–3rd September

Neath General, Port Talbot, Bridgend, Cardiff General, Newport, Severn Tunnel Junction, Bristol Stapleton Road, Bath Spa, Bradford-on-Avon, Trowbridge, Westbury, Salisbury (dep 2.2pm), Poole, Bournemouth Central, Boscombe, Pokesdown, Christchurch, New Milton, Brockenhurst

8.30am Bournemouth Central–Cardiff General, 16th July–6th August

Poole, Salisbury, Westbury, Bath Spa, Newport, Cardiff General

9am Bournemouth Central–Cardiff General

Poole, Salisbury, Warminster, Westbury, Trowbridge, Bath Spa, Newport, Cardiff General

8.48am New Milton–Swansea High Street

Christchurch, Pokesdown, Boscombe, Bournemouth Central, Parkstone, Poole, Wimborne, Salisbury, Warminster, Westbury, Trowbridge, Bradford-on-Avon, Bath Spa, Newport, Cardiff General, Llantrisant, Bridgend, Pyle, Port Talbot, Neath General, Swansea High Street

A timeless scene near Breamore in January 1963.
(Roger Holmes/Photos of the Fifties)